RESEARCH
— and —
WRITING
— in the —
DISCIPLINES

Donald Zimmerman
Colorado State University

Dawn Rodrigues
Colorado State University

Harcourt Brace Jovanovich College Publishers

Fort Worth   Philadelphia   San Diego   New York   Orlando   Austin   San Antonio
Toronto   Montreal   London   Sydney   Tokyo

Acquisitions Editors: Marlane Miriello, Karen Allanson
Manuscript Editors: Albert Richards, Sarah Smith
Production Editor: Judi McClellan
Designer: Cathy Reynolds
Art Editor: Rebecca Lytle
Production Managers: Diane Southworth, Lesley Lenox

ISBN: 0-15-576608-2

Library of Congress Catalog Card Number: 91-73795

Printed in the United States of America

PREFACE

Research and Writing in the Disciplines is designed to help students who have completed freshman composition to write research papers for advanced courses in different disciplines. Our approach is based on the principle that, with guidance, writers can adapt their general knowledge about writing to the specific demands of diverse writing assignments.

Our handbook is aimed at students in advanced courses, writers who have vastly different needs than they did when they were in freshman English class. The most compelling of those specialized needs, according to our national survey of writing assignments given in courses across the curriculum, is for a different kind of research handbook, one that provides guidance for research and writing in specific disciplines. We learned that not only do instructors in different disciplines require different kinds of research reports, but few of these reports resemble the research paper often taught in freshman English classes. Moreover, we found that the research paper is one of the most common assignments in college.

Research and Writing in the Disciplines stresses the link between research and writing and encourages students to take notes and draft sections of their papers *while* they conduct their research. Further, it stresses the value of writing in exploring a topic, summarizing research notes, synthesizing data, and clarifying ideas.

Research and Writing in the Disciplines provides direction for information-gathering while encouraging students to allow their writing to evolve organically. **Part One** explores general writing principles that must be understood before a student can write successful research reports in different disciplines. **Part Two** presents a sequenced approach to the research-writing process and includes general chapters on information-gathering, drafting, revising, and editing as well as specialized chapters on research methodologies that writers can select according to their individual needs. **Part Three** explains how to write four commonly assigned research reports along with student examples of those reports. The student models include (1) the literature review research report, a genre assigned across dozens of disciplines; (2) the original research report, common to the biological and social sciences; (3) the thesis statement and position research report, common to the humanities; and (4) the problem-solving or design research report, often required in fields such as engineering, architecture, and interior design.

Throughout, we incorporate additional advice and guidance about research writing not found in freshman research-writing texts. Specifically, we

- stress the importance of clearly identifying the problem-statement for research papers in the disciplines;
- provide fundamental guidance on how to prepare and format tables and figures;
- include advice about layout, design, and the visual presentation of information;
- explain how to avoid plagiarism and how to conform to copyright law; and
- explore the effective use of computers and writing software throughout the research and writing processes.

The basic organization of *Research and Writing in the Disciplines* allows instructors to assign the book sequentially or as needed throughout the term. The chapters are organized and formatted so that students can quickly find answers to their questions as their research reports evolve.

Instructors who teach advanced composition classes and instructors in writing-intensive courses across the disciplines will find that *Research and Writing in the Disciplines* provides students with help for most of the research reports they assign. *Research and Writing in the Disciplines* can be used either as a primary textbook or as a handbook to accompany other texts.

Acknowledgments

Many people played important roles in the development of *Research and Writing in the Disciplines*. We would like to thank the Harcourt Brace Jovanovich staff: acquisitions editor Marlane Miriello recognized the need for the text and provided the support necessary to develop it, and acquisitions editor Karen Allanson gave numerous suggestions as we revised and polished the concept. House manuscript editor Sarah Smith guided the manuscript through the production process, while manuscript editor Albert Richards provided many useful suggestions that enhanced the manuscript. We also wish to thank designer Cathy Reynolds, who developed the clean, open design for the book; production editor Judi McClellan, who directed the project through the various stages of proof; art editor Rebecca Lytle, who managed the illustration program; and production managers Diane Southworth and Lesley Lenox, who monitored the project's schedule.

We received useful suggestions and critiques from the following educators who reviewed earlier versions of the manuscript: Christopher M. Anson, University of Minnesota; Mary Bly, University of California, Davis; Robert B. DiGiovanni, University of Michigan; Margaret Eldred, University of California, Davis; Stephen Englehart, California State Polytechnic, Pomona; Jeff Hammond, George Mason University; Kathryn Harris, Arizona State University; and Elbert S. Jones, Maryland University.

We would also like to thank our families: Don's wife Marietta and his children Rachel and Jeramy for their tolerance during the production of the manuscript; and Dawn's husband Ray and her son Brad for putting up with her seemingly endless need to revise. And finally, we appreciate and thank our parents, Don and Dixie Zimmerman and Peter and Dorothy Droskinis, who encouraged our pursuit of college degrees and supported our efforts through the years.

Donald E. Zimmerman
Dawn Rodrigues

Contents

A LOOK AT WRITING ACROSS THE DISCIPLINES

CHAPTER **1**

About Writing and Writing Processes

I n this chapter we

present some general principles about writing,

explain why writing is important to professionals,

look at writing as a social process and as a cognitive activity,

suggest ways writers can develop their writing ability by examining their own writing processes,

explain why it is difficult to describe the features of good writing,

explain how to identify the characteristics of good writing in different writing situations, and

present ways of adapting writing strategies to new situations.

WRITING: SOME GENERAL PRINCIPLES

What is writing? On the most basic level, writing is a system of communication. Anyone who knows how to speak can learn how to write by learning the sound-symbol correspondence of a given language. But writing is much more than letters put together in meaningful patterns. Writing is a way of thinking, a way of learning, a way of sharing ideas with others. Writing often plays an integral role in an individual's personal as well as professional life.

Professionals in all disciplines do an enormous amount of writing on the job, even though their college curriculum may have included little or no course work in professional writing. Engineers write proposals for bids, chemists write articles describing their research, lawyers write legal briefs, and sociologists write case studies. Many of these professionals do not necessarily *like* to write, but most of them have learned over the years to do an acceptable job. By confronting similar writing tasks repeatedly, they have gradually learned how to write well. If they had had appropriate instruction, the time it took them to learn to write well might have been reduced.

WHY IS WRITING IMPORTANT TO PROFESSIONALS?

Writing is important to success in almost any career. Sixty-five percent of workers surveyed in a study by Lee Odell reported that "as their responsibilities increased, so did the amount of time they spent writing" (Odell 1985). It is, therefore, almost certain that — no matter what profession you are in or plan to enter — developing your writing ability will help you advance in your career.

To help you understand the importance of writing to your professional growth, we'd like to expose some common myths about on-the-job writing:

Myth #1. *College writing assignments are unrelated to the kind of writing professionals do on the job.*   College writing assignments — even freshman English essays — help writers understand some common features of good writing. Report-writing tasks help students prepare for the writing situations they will face throughout their careers. College writing assignments help writers learn general principles of effective writing: effective writing is clear, well-organized, and tailored to audience and purpose.

Myth #2. *Most professional writing consists only of routine tasks such as memos, letters, and standard reports.*   By surveying Miami University of Ohio alumni, Paul V. Anderson learned that 1,052 of 2,335 college graduates did indeed write memoranda, letters, step-by-step instructions, general instructions, and reports (Anderson 1985). However, ninety-two percent write not only at the request of others, but also on their own initiative.

Myth #3. *No one reads professional reports and memos; thus the way they are written is unimportant.*   Contrary to common belief, writers write more often to individuals within their own organizations than they write to outsiders. These inside individuals both read and respond to the memos and reports.

Myth #4. *Professionals are too busy to do their own writing.* Midlevel executives do most of their own writing. It is true, however, that most chief executive officers do rely on others — speech writers, administrative assistants, colleagues — to draft many of their speeches and reports.

Myth #5. *By the time professionals are in a position where they must write frequently, they'll know how to do it.* If you don't work consciously on improving your writing skills, these skills are unlikely to develop. People who want to become better writers follow many routes: some consciously develop their powers of observation; others try to "read like writers," noticing ways the authors of the books and articles they read have crafted their texts; still others take courses or read books on writing.

Clearly, good writing skills are an asset to professionals. If, as a professional or a pre-professional, you understand the important role writing plays in your chosen field, you are more likely to take it seriously.

LOOKING AT WRITING AS A SOCIAL PROCESS AND A COGNITIVE ACTIVITY

In college, students often think that writing is nothing more than a rule-governed, mechanical system. They think that by learning to organize paragraphs, craft sentences, and select appropriate words they can master the processes involved in writing. But when they become professionals, they soon discover that writing is much more complicated — and messy — than it had seemed in college.

On the job, writers use writing to solve problems, to work together on tasks, to challenge one another's ideas, and to interact with clients. In every organization, people talk with one another to prepare for writing tasks. Writing is, therefore, a social activity. Writers develop and shape their ideas and views through social interaction: most diary entries are written as a result of an individual's reaction to social events. Similarly, the most renowned history texts are conditioned by a writer's milieu. Historians' perspectives are not individual, objective views of reality; they are subjective pictures, reports of events colored by the historian's own views and by the intellectual climate of a given era.

Writing is also a complex, cognitive process. Researchers have learned much by observing the external dimensions of writing — the rituals writers observe, the tools they use, and the length of time they devote to different activities. They have even begun to learn what goes on inside a writer's mind: By asking writers to think aloud as they write — by talking into a tape recorder — researchers Linda Flower and John Hayes at Carnegie Mellon University have determined the differences between

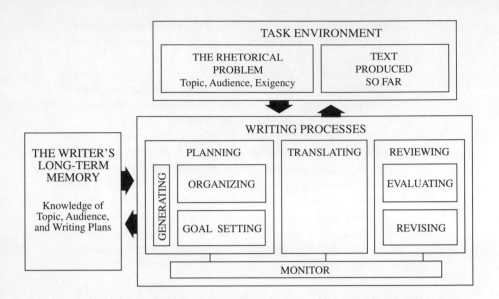

F I G U R E 1-1   The Flower and Hayes Problem-Solving Model
of Writing

expert and novice writers (Flower and Hayes 1982). They have constructed a model
of the writing process, a model that explains what expert writers do (Figure 1-1).

HOW CAN YOU DEVELOP YOUR WRITING ABILITY?

Examining Your Writing Processes

What kind of writer are you? Take time to look at your own writing processes.
After each writing session, reflect on the behaviors and strategies you used. Did you
reread your draft, making changes as you composed? Or did you push forward without stopping? Getting to know yourself as a writer is a crucial step in learning how to
expand your writing horizons.

As they write, most experienced writers reread the words and phrases that have
accumulated on the page or computer screen, and they revise their text to conform to
their changing perceptions of their goals. Less efficient writers, however, rarely
bother to reread or revise; they just keep pushing forward until the task is finished.
Then they submit their work and often wonder why it is not praised by their supervisor or their instructor.

There is no one best way to write, but some ways are more efficient and more
effective than others. If you find that you are less productive than you want to be,

consciously try to monitor your writing behaviors. Try to determine when you are most effective: Do you work best when you begin a project long before a deadline? Is drafting by hand and then entering a completed draft on a computer more effective for you? Do you prefer to compose directly on the computer?

Talk to colleagues or classmates to learn what you can about their composing behaviors. Talk to other students in your field. Ask them how much writing they do on the job, and ask them for advice on developing your writing ability. When you hear others describe strategies that might work for you, try them out. Gradually, you'll settle into a way of writing that feels right for you, a way that, for the most part, leads you to good results. By consciously trying to improve your writing abilities, you will be taking an important step. Your writing skills will improve only if you want them to improve.

Assessing Your Writing Processes

The following suggestions, based on the processes followed by effective writers, can help you assess your own writing processes:

1. *Good writers develop efficient composing processes.* These composing processes suit writers' own way of thinking and working. For letters, memos, and familiar writing tasks, experienced writers typically plan in their heads and then compose their products as they write. For longer tasks, experienced writers often generate lists of ideas, engage in brainstorming sessions, develop tree diagrams, and use rough working outlines or other techniques to aid their planning. Sometimes, writers let ideas incubate while they mow the grass, clean house, or do other routine chores.

2. *Good writers constantly modify their writing processes.* As they understand their individual strengths and weaknesses as writers and as they listen to other writers' advice, good writers consciously try to change their own writing behavior. Professionals have developed an ample repertoire of writing strategies. In studying the writing of scientific, engineering, and technical majors at Iowa State University, Roundy and Mair (1982, 48) discovered "that their respondents adjust[ed] their composing processes to the task at hand." Some writers composed with pencil and paper; others dictated; and still others used the word processor. They found that the majority of those who use dictation equipment had been on the job more than six years; of those who use the word processor, 72% noted that it improves their speed and 46% felt that it improves organization. Clearly, writers adapt their way of writing to the technology available to them.

3. *Good writers learn how to analyze new writing situations and how to adapt their writing processes to those situations.* As they approach new writing situations, good writers either consciously or even

unconsciously analyze the situation and adapt to it. They think about
their audience, about the content of the writing they are planning, and
about how best to present the information to achieve their purpose.

WHAT IS GOOD WRITING?

Although we can define what writing is, and although we have some notion of
how experienced writers go about the process of writing, we cannot easily identify
the *ingredients* of good writing. Why not? The problem in defining good writing is
that different groups of readers value different kinds of writing.

*Good writing is writing that is appropriate to the specific writing situation for
which it was produced.* The formal characteristics of an effective chemistry lab report
are different from the features of a well-written case study in sociology. An environmental impact statement follows different conventions than a biology research report
for a private foundation does. Similarly, a memo written by one executive in an
organization to another executive would adhere to different standards than a memo to
subordinates in the same organization would.

In college courses across the disciplines as well as in many professions, writers
are commonly asked to prepare reports. Writing a report sounds easy enough, so
many writers assume that a style handbook is all they need. The problem, however, is
that the requirements and specific criteria by which a report is judged in one discipline may differ from the criteria for a report in another area. For example, students
in courses ranging from radiation biology to sociology to history are asked to write
research reports. But writing in each of these fields is not judged by the same criteria.
While a history research report can be organized chronologically, an economics report would more likely present key trends. A biology report might include specific
details and moment-by-moment observations of processes, while a mathematics report would include only the findings of the research.

One of the problems you face as you begin writing for a new discipline or for a
new organization is that you probably do not understand the conventions that govern
writing in that field. Nor is it always easy to learn those conventions. Lee Odell's
research (Odell 1985) has made it clear that only an *insider* in an organization or a
discipline can confidently determine whether a given piece or portion of a piece of
writing is good or not. During his research in an accounting firm, Odell tried to
determine what the organization considered important features of effective communication. He interviewed writers after they had completed a task, asking them to
explain their choice of words and suggesting that they delete specific portions of their
texts. He learned that experienced writers had a clear sense of their purpose and their
audience in each situation; further, he found that they justified their stylistic choices
in terms of how well their texts fit the company's image. Rarely was he able to
convince them to change their texts. The employees knew what constituted good
writing for their specific purposes and in their contexts.

Even though specific characteristics of good writing in one setting almost always differ from the features valued by writers in another setting, some features of good writing are common to all disciplines and organizations: *Good writing is writing that is appropriate for the audience and purpose of a specific writing situation.* The content, organization, sentence structure, and word choice of an effective piece of writing should be appropriate for the writer's audience and purpose, as shown in the list that follows.

Characteristics of Good Writing

General Features of Good Writing

appropriate for purpose
appropriate for audience
appropriate content
appropriate style
appropriate tone

Specific Features of Good Writing

effective organization
effective sentence structure
effective word choice
effective visual display of information

HOW CAN YOU IDENTIFY THE CHARACTERISTICS OF GOOD WRITING?

We are all familiar with conventions of dress, of eating, and of behavior. We know, for example, that dressing in blue jeans and a T-shirt would be inappropriate for most wedding receptions, and a meal of hot dogs and potato chips would not be an appropriate formal dinner.

Similarly, each time writers confront new writing tasks, they need to tune in to the conventions expected of them. Each writing situation is unique. The way a writer approaches each task, the writer's choice of words, the arrangement of sentences and paragraphs — all these are different, too.

Although each writing situation is different, all writing tasks have similar relationships between subject, writer, reader, and form or genre (Figure 1-2). The **subject** is the topic or area of the field that a writer is exploring. Writers treat their subjects quite differently if they know their **audience** or their readers. For instance, a young adult novelist would approach a subject differently than would a novelist who writes for a general audience. Similarly, writers approach their topic differently when they have different purposes and different audiences. If their **purpose** is **to inform** teenagers about the need for new officials in local government, they would write differ-

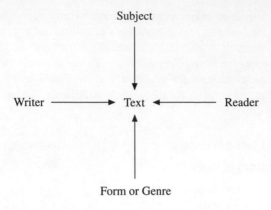

FIGURE 1-2   A Model of the Writing Situation

ently about the problem of ousting incumbents than if their purpose happened to be **to persuade** teenagers to vote so that they can help oust the incumbents. As Figure 1-2 indicates, the **text** that a writer produces is influenced by the **writer's assessment of the reader**, including the reader's **familiarity with the genre** or form the writer is using and the **reader's knowledge of the writer's topic**.

When you know *why* you are writing and when you direct your text to a distinct audience, you will have a much better sense of what to say and how to say it. College writing assignments may not all have an obvious purpose and audience. However, even if your instructor does not tell you the purpose or the audience for an assignment, you can create your own purpose and your own audience — you can imagine a real writing situation in which your report might be valued.

Real-world writing is done in response to a need or request, or as a way of accomplishing a task. Unlike many college students facing writing situations, on-the-job writers not only have knowledge of their audience; they often know the reader or readers personally.

A Look at an On-the-Job Writing Situation

Let's look at an on-the-job writing situation. Assume that you are the affirmative action officer for your campus. Assume, also, that you have been charged with writing a report to a federal agency about affirmative action practices on campus. You have had experience with this agency, and you even know the official in charge of the agency. You could assess your writing situation as shown in Figure 1-3.

With a clear sense of purpose, a knowledge of your audience, and a familiarity with the genre or form that is expected of you, you can write your report with confidence. Without knowing these key components of a writing situation, you would be unable to proceed effectively with your task.

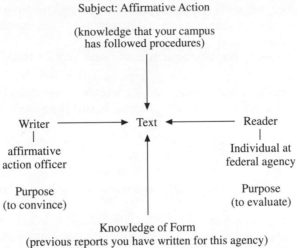

Subject: Affirmative Action

(knowledge that your campus
has followed procedures)

Writer ⟶ Text ⟵ Reader

affirmative
action officer

Individual at
federal agency

Purpose
(to convince)

Purpose
(to evaluate)

Knowledge of Form
(previous reports you have written for this agency)

F I G U R E 1-3   A Model of an On-the-Job Writing Situation

HOW DO YOU ADAPT YOUR WRITING TO NEW SITUATIONS?

What do you do you when get a writing assignment? How do you begin a new writing task? If you assess each writing assignment on its own merit, you have already developed one of the most important skills a writer needs — adaptability. On the other hand, if you always look for easy answers to your writing problems, you may some day realize that your writing is less effective than it could be.

With practice and effort, you can learn how to produce effective documents. By learning as much as possible about your composing processes, you can learn how to use strategies and processes appropriate for new situations. By being flexible and adaptive, you can produce effective writing in any situation.

To learn the conventions of a new field, be inventive and versatile; otherwise, you will be able to tackle only specific tasks or assignments for which you have been given precise models. On the job, as well as in courses across disciplines, you need to know how to assess new tasks. You need to determine how to begin, how to proceed, and how to decide what the finished product should look like. Each new on-the-job writing task is never exactly the same as a previous one, so you must learn how to size up new communication situations.

By learning how to be flexible and adaptable, you can develop strategies that will help you determine criteria for good writing in a given field. By learning how to assess the constraints of each writing situation, you will know how far you can depart from the prescribed formats as you invent your own new pattern of organization. Let the following questions guide you as you assess new writing situations.

Questions for Assessing the Characteristics of Good Writing in Different Disciplines

1. What are the overall formats and organizational strategies? Do the writers use heads? Subheads? Are the headings and subheadings questions? Topics?
2. What about word choice? Do most writers in the discipline choose technical terms? Casual language? Formal?
3. What about sentence structure? Do the writers use parallelism frequently? Do they use complex sentences with several subordinate clauses?
4. What image of himself or herself do the writers seem to be projecting? That of an impartial bystander to events? A committed participant?
5. What kind of ''evidence'' backs up the writers' main points? Stories and anecdotes? Statistical charts? Quotations from authorities? Other evidence?
6. Practice writing a few paragraphs in the accepted style. Does your writing sound like the writing of someone in your discipline or organization?

Remember that specific guidance on how to proceed on a specialized writing task is not always readily available. If you can't locate a formal handbook or guidebook, read widely in a given field to discover the conventions and to isolate the common structural elements of the writing, using the suggestions in this chapter.

CONCLUSION

After having taught composition, technical and scientific, and journalistic writing to students from dozens of fields for more than fifteen years, we know that you can develop a conscious knowledge of your writing processes and a knowledge of the writing produced in your field. Further, we know that by learning similarities between the writing in different disciplines, you will begin to connect what you know about writing conventions in one field with those in new fields.

Our aim in this book is to help you use your prior knowledge of writing — knowledge that you have developed from Freshman English and from other classes — as a basis for understanding new writing tasks. You will learn how to use your knowledge of writing and writing processes as tools to determine how to approach new situations. We will also present you with new ideas about writing and new writing models to help you expand your knowledge of writing.

In addition, we will help you develop your problem-solving abilities by providing you with practical ways of improving your writing and by providing guidelines for approaching new writing tasks. Although it takes time to develop adequate knowledge of new writing situations, you can shorten your learning time through conscious effort.

Chapter Two explores the different kinds of research papers required by different disciplines and different organizations. The points presented will help you develop an understanding of different kinds of research reports you may be asked to write in school and later on the job.

Throughout this book, we will suggest strategies to help you understand your writing processes and the conventions governing your writing assignments. As you read on, remember that your writing processes develop over time, so don't expect dramatic changes overnight. Our goal is to help you learn how to adapt your knowledge of writing to new writing situations. We will give you the tools and strategies for confronting many different writing assignments, but our main focus will be on helping you learn how to write research reports.

CHAPTER 2

A Look at Research Reports in Different Disciplines

In this chapter we

present a definition of the research report,

explain the role of conventions in different disciplines,

explain the concept of "discourse communities,"

present some key distinctions between the conventions of different academic discourse communities,

explain the role of paradigmatic thinking,

present similarities in the organization of research reports, and

present some strategies for writing research reports.

Research reports are one of the most commonly assigned writing tasks — in college as well as on the job. Furthermore, writing research reports is one of the most difficult tasks writers face. Even though most writers have written term papers in Freshman English, they are not prepared for the kinds of research reports assigned in other disciplines. Writers are frequently puzzled when they learn that the criteria for a successful research report vary from one academic discipline to the next and from one business or organization to another. The Freshman English term paper doesn't fully prepare students to write disciplinary and professional research reports.

This chapter explains what research reports are, how they differ from Freshman English essays and term papers, and how they differ from one discipline to the next. The chapter then suggests how you can tap your general knowledge about writing as you learn the demands of specific research reports.

WHAT IS A RESEARCH REPORT?

A research report is a special kind of text in which a writer or a team of writers presents the results of an investigation. Research reports begin with a question or problem, then attempt to resolve that question or solve that problem, and finally offer a concluding argument.

The Freshman English term paper, unlike the professional research report, rarely involves original investigation into a topic. Most instructors are satisfied with a report that presents a writer's assessment of a general topic. The question or problem answered by a freshman term paper is typically a subjective one: Was Hemingway antisemitic? Can Shakespeare's plagiarism of sources be accounted for? Are environmentalists' demands to restrict the amount of logging by the timber industry justifiable?

Most instructors are satisfied if freshmen writers present their opinions on any topic and then support those opinions with quotations from authoritative works. Reports in upper division English classes and other disciplines often require more research.

Professional research reports often focus on solving a problem or answering a specific question. Researchers studying plagiarism in Shakespeare would, for instance, have to conduct original research as they systematically analyzed the text in question and traced the relationship between each passage of the original with the sources from which Shakespeare allegedly borrowed. Moreover, rather than presenting a text that a previous scholar had already analyzed, a researcher would have to tackle a text that no one else had yet investigated.

Similarly, researchers asking "Does clear-cutting in the Roosevelt National Forest increase soil erosion and increase the sediment load in the Poudre River?" would use the scientific method to investigate the question and to present their results. The researchers might, for instance, present one table indicating the erosion rate on a given tract of land both ten years ago and today and another table showing the sediment load in the Poudre River both ten years ago and today. To gather data, the researchers would examine soil maps and conduct on-site tests of the soil erosion that has occurred as a result of logging.

Researchers undertaking literature review and synthesis research papers (See Chapter 14) face a rigorous task, because they must familiarize themselves with the historical literature on a given topic, review the current literature on a topic, analyze the most recent literature, and then select, organize, and present the information in a logical presentation.

DO DIFFERENT DISCIPLINES HAVE DIFFERENT CONVENTIONS?

Professional research reports are distinctly different from freshman term papers. Unfortunately, each profession and each college discipline has its own conventions for conducting and reporting research. The challenge you face when entering a new field is to learn, as quickly as possible, the writing style and practices valued by experts in these disciplines. Specifically, you need to learn as much as you can about the established ways of conducting research, the requirements for research writing, and the preferred styles respected by others in the field.

By learning how to tune into the customs of different disciplines, you can adapt your general knowledge about writing to the requirements of specific fields. You may never have written a report that included charts and graphs, but observing and analyzing the reports in journals in a given field can give you an understanding of the customs of the new field.

Not only academic disciplines have their own conventions; non-academic organizations and professional societies also develop distinct identities and conventions for reporting research. Each organization develops its own internal logic — its own system of operation and its own customs, which are reflected in the use of language in that organization. Thus new employees of a company must develop a sensitivity to the culture of their work place before they can write effective letters, reports, or memos that reflect the company image.

The distinct disciplinary and organizational groups that emerge in both academic and non-academic settings are often referred to as discourse communities, because the discourse or language practices of each discipline are different from those of other disciplines.

WHAT IS A DISCOURSE COMMUNITY?

The concept of a discourse community comes from the linguistic concept of the "speech community," a group of speakers whose language is significantly different from the language used by other groups. As a result, the writing in each discipline is characterized by its own special kinds of texts — lab reports in fields such as chemistry; design reports in industrial science and architecture; case studies in sociology. These special kinds of texts are the genres of the disciplines, just as poetry and drama are genres of literature. The beliefs, values, and attitudes in each discipline help shape the ways writers use language within each distinct field.

Discourse communities are unofficial affiliations. You don't join a discourse community; rather, you gradually develop the attitudes and customs that are characteristic of the people you spend time with. Most people are part of several discourse communities at different times — some reflecting their place of employment, others reflecting their birthplace, their professional interests, or their hobbies.

Lester Faigley has explained that writers in each discipline or discourse community learn "what is worth communicating, how it can be communicated, what other members of the community are likely to know and believe to be true about certain subjects," and how members of the community can be persuaded to agree with one another (Faigley 1985, 238).

HOW DO THE RESEARCH REPORTS VARY IN ACADEMIC DISCOURSE COMMUNITIES?

Although some composition specialists refer to the "academic discourse community" as the primary discourse community students need to enter, it is difficult to describe the general characteristics of this amorphous group of scholarly individuals. But it *is* possible to describe the characteristics of discourse or language used by scholars in the colleges that make up a university: The humanities, the social sciences, the natural sciences, and the professional schools such as engineering. Each group can be further subdivided. For example, the humanities can be divided into English, history, art, music, theatre, and philosophy. The social sciences usually include anthropology, economics, sociology, psychology, journalism, and related fields.

Research Reports in the Humanities

Knowledge in the humanities is based on reflection, observation, analysis, and intuition. Professionals in these fields usually shun or avoid experimental design, believing that important truths in life can be discovered through contemplation and argumentation.

What most students think of as a college term paper is really the humanities' version of a research report. The term paper is characterized by what some call library research. In other words, most of these researchers develop their insights and ideas by reading and reviewing (searching and re-searching) books, journals, and other documents. Library research papers are organized just like essays: they have an introduction, a body, and a conclusion, but these divisions are not necessarily labeled with headings and subheadings.

Organization of Humanities Research Reports

Introduction

makes the purpose clear
reviews pertinent literature
presents the thesis statement

Body

presents evidence to support the research question (quotes from primary sources such as literary texts; facts drawn from secondary sources such as biographies of authors)

Conclusion

    summarizes research
    points to implications of research

The Modern Language Association publishes two style guides for writing research papers, theses, and dissertations: *The MLA Handbook*, Third Edition (Gibaldi and Achtert, 1988) and *The MLA Style Manual* (Achtert and Gibaldi, 1985). Both provide detailed guidelines on mechanics, manuscript preparation, documentation, and other details.

Research Reports in the Social Sciences

    Social scientists value controlled investigation or inquiry, even though they do not believe that they can discover enduring truths. Social scientists strive to clarify social issues. To do so, they use a variety of research techniques, including interviews, focus groups, participant observation, surveys, laboratory experiments, and field experiments. Social scientists follow style guides such as the *Publication Manual of The American Psychological Association* (American Psychological Association, 1983) or the *Chicago Manual of Style* (University of Chicago Press, 1982).

    Formats for social science papers are fairly specific. In addition to following standard headings, writers may include additional subheadings for the subdivisions of each major section, as shown in the following list.

Basic Organization of Social Science Research Reports

Abstract

    summarizes the key points of the paper

Introduction

    makes the purpose clear
    reviews pertinent literature rather extensively (sometimes in a separate section called "Review of Literature")
    presents the research question or problem

Methods

    explains research procedures and research tools used (such as surveys, statistical tests, etc.)

Results and Discussion

    presents charts, data, etc. as evidence to support research question
    explains the results of the research

Conclusion

> summarizes research
> points to implications of research

Research Reports in the Natural Sciences

Researchers in the natural sciences seek hard facts to provide answers to the questions they pose. Their primary methods for conducting research are direct and indirect observation both in the laboratory and in the field. The basic format of natural science research papers is often similar to that used in the social sciences but contains fewer subheadings. Scientists' research questions, phrased in objective and formal language, usually have a prominent position in the introduction of their reports.

The Organization of Natural Science Research Reports

Abstract

> summarizes the key points of the paper

Introduction

> describes the problem
> reviews related research
> introduces hypotheses, research questions, or objectives
> clarifies assumptions

Methods

> identifies research population
> notes the sample size
> explains the research instruments used
> details the procedure(s) followed

Results and Conclusion

> explains results and conclusion(s)

Discussion

> elaborates on results

Summary

> presents a summary of the report

Research Reports in Engineering

Within each profession, general discourse communities can be further subdivided. Engineering can be broken down into special kinds of engineering—agricultural, aeronautical, mechanical, civil, electrical, and chemical. The conventions of any of these specific fields or their subdivisions can be identified by reading their journals.

On-the-job research writing is quite different from writing based on college research. Consultants at a company studied by researchers Broadhead and Freed explain that staff members' writing processes became fairly standardized, for they always developed the same overall line of thought in their papers, as shown in the following list. Also, they did not have to search for effective organization, because the company had developed a standard approach for their proposals (Broadhead and Freed 1986).

Organization of Research Reports in the Firm

Problem

> Introduction
> Background
> Objectives
> Scope
> Study Strategy

Method

> Approach
> Deliverables

Implementation

> Staffing and Qualifications
> Timing
> Cost
> Conclusion

Engineering research reports, along with many in computer science, architecture, and mathematics, do not have as rigid a basic format as articles in the social and natural resources do. Thus, the determination of content, audience, and purpose influences the basic heads and subheads within the report.

THE ROLE OF PARADIGMATIC THINKING IN GENERATING CONTENT AND ORGANIZING RESEARCH REPORTS

Each discourse community uses certain kinds of questions—sometimes called *paradigmatic questions*. These paradigmatic questions can be predicted by anyone familiar with the *paradigm* of the field.

The paradigm of a field is the particular way most members in a discipline approach issues and topics in that field. Disciplinary paradigms represent each field's idiosyncrasies — its use of terms and terminology, its ways of thinking, its ways of approaching problems, its ways of investigating problems, its ways of reasoning, and its ways of deriving conclusions.

Professionals in different discourse communities approach the same topic in different ways because of their differing paradigms. For example, if the topic were "suicide," a psychologist might study the emotional state of a person who attempted suicide, because psychologists focus on individuals. A sociologist, however, would probably examine societal influences on the episode and ask how the actions of the potential suicide victim were caused by external factors.

A direct connection exists between the questions a researcher poses and the kinds of answers or evidence that the researcher collects. For example, if you were asked to write a paper on suicide for a psychology class, you might start with the following questions:

What causes an individual to commit suicide?

How can a psychologist influence a person's decision to live?

To answer these questions, you might interview psychologists, review case studies of suicidal individuals, or even conduct case studies to determine any trends. But if you were assigned the same topic in a sociology class, you would probably ask different questions:

Have changing patterns of family life contributed to an increase of adolescent suicides?

How can social service agencies help adolescents avoid suicidal tendencies?

What kinds of social communities have the lowest rate of suicides?

To answer these questions, you could use surveys or ethnographic research, or you could conduct a secondary analysis of suicide and collect demographic information from different communities. The questions you ask thus lead you to specific research methodologies in the specific discipline.

What all this means is that learning how to write a professional research report involves much more than mastering the overall format and stylistic conventions of a given field. It also involves developing an understanding of the kinds of questions asked and the nature of evidence valued in each discourse community. By identifying the paradigmatic questions of a field, you learn how to explore your topic by posing paradigmatic questions.

THE PROCESSES OF WRITING RESEARCH REPORTS

You can use your knowledge of organization — from Freshman English class or from having written papers in other courses — to help you learn about the specific organization of research reports in different disciplines. By looking for similarities between what you know and what you want to learn, you can shorten the time it takes to learn the customs of a new field.

Although specific differences do exist among the different kinds of research reports, similarities emerge when you look closely at the conventions of each field. First, authors of research reports present the results of their inquiry in a conventional format; all reports have the same overall organization:

Introduction
Body
Conclusion

In the first few paragraphs of a research paper, the writer tells what the paper is about and indicates what questions the study attempts to answer. The **introduction** provides sufficient background information to orient the reader to the topic. The **body** of the paper illustrates or explains how the writer arrived at that point. The **conclusion** of a research report summarizes the main points of the study and points to the implications of the research.

The Introduction

In the introduction you present your topic in the context of other research in your field and review relevant literature on the topic. At some point in the introduction, you may announce the plan for your paper with a tag line such as "In this study I will attempt to answer these questions." You then state your specific research question or questions. These questions become the thesis of your paper. In the social sciences and natural sciences, however, researchers often begin with research hypotheses rather than thesis questions. (See the organizational lists on pages 17 and 20.) These hypotheses are sometimes called objectives or purpose statements.

The Body

The body of a research report usually explains the procedures followed, presents the results (data or information), and discusses the findings. The procedures part of the body section details how the data or information was collected, but the formats vary widely. In the humanities, the body section presents the evidence of the writer's investigation in essay fashion — in standard paragraph form. In a scientific report, specific sections focus on different aspects of the study. Specifically, the results section usually centers around figures, charts, and graphs that present the data; the discussion section in the scientific report usually gives meaning to the results, ties the results to earlier studies, and may include recommendations for future studies.

The Conclusion

The customs for concluding — wrapping up a research report — vary widely among the disciplines. A philosophy or literature paper might not have a separate section titled "conclusion," whereas most natural or social science research reports would end with a conclusion or summary section. Nonetheless, the final sections of papers in these different fields have common features: the conclusion summarizes the research and suggests the implications of the research. The following list provides the general organization of research reports.

General Organization of Research Reports

Introduction

> makes the purpose clear
> reviews pertinent literature
> presents the research question

Body

> presents evidence to support research question
> explains results of research

Conclusion

> summarizes research
> points to implications of research

HOW CAN YOU MAKE WRITING RESEARCH REPORTS EASIER?

Even though the report you produce in one discipline will be different from that produced in another subject, the following suggestions can help you as you write most research reports.

Getting Started

Begin with a research problem, a general question or doubt about how something functions, or a hypothesis about what has happened or what happens under certain conditions. Develop a specific research question (hypothesis, objective, or purpose statement) and then collect evidence to explore your question. Use appropriate data collection methods for the particular discourse community and the nature of your research question. Consider these suggestions as you start a research project:

Use problem-solving thinking processes to explore your topic.

Ask paradigmatic questions (e.g. if you are writing a history paper, ask, "How did x begin? What is the origin of x?" If you are writing a political science paper, ask, "How did the system institutionalize x?" For an economics paper ask, "How does x affect the wealth of some people?" For an anthropology paper, ask, "How x functions in another culture?")

Clarify your purpose and your audience.

Look at some models of research reports in your field.

Determining What Conventions Are Valued by Your Discipline

Although nothing substitutes for immersion in a new field, you can use shortcuts to learn about the practices of a new field. Try these strategies:

1. Determine what research methodologies are favored by your field.
2. Find out what kinds of writing are done in the field (e.g. short reports, lab reports, applied research).
3. Determine what patterns of organization are used in that writing (what kinds of headings and subheadings, what patterns of arguing — comparison-contrast, cause-effect).
4. Examine the style and word choice of sample documents.
5. Examine the tone of the article or report.
6. Try to find out what kind of evidence is valued by specialists (experimental data, observational data, quotations from authorities).
7. Isolate model documents that you can follow for style, organization, diction, tone, and ways of handling evidence as well as conducting and reporting research.
8. Before beginning to conduct your research or write your report, be sure that you understand the implied writing situation of that project (see Chapter 1).

Developing Effective Note-Taking Strategies

Do take notes as you review literature on your budding research question, but do not list the details of everything related to your topic. Give yourself a chance to become literate in the field you have selected. After you have acquired a good overview of the field, you are ready to ask research questions and to take notes. Consider three strategies for taking notes:

1. *The Note-Card Technique.*   This method, a long-respected technique of humanities scholars, involves developing bibliography cards and note cards (see Chapter 6). If you put only one idea on each card,

Author		Garr, Edward E.; Toll, Mark; Amers, John; Prince, Beth
Role		
Year		1957
Article/essay ttl		Ritual hygiene: a Mélaño example
Book ttl		
Descriptor		
Collection ttl		
Editor		
Translator		
Place		
Publisher		
Pages		223-224
Journal		Quarterly Review
Volume no.		9
Issue/edition no.		
Day/month		
Series ttl		
Length/comment		
Abstract		
Keywords		
Access phrase		

F I G U R E 2-1   A ᵂᴾCitation Bibliographic Record for an Article

you can then organize the cards around the key ideas as you plan your report.

2. *Photocopying articles and then extracting notes.*   With the advent of the photocopy machine, many scientists, engineers, and technical specialists photocopy key articles, and then add the key bibliographic information (Publication title, volume, date, pages, etc.) in the margins of the articles. They then extract one or two key ideas that they plan to use in writing their reports. Finally, they then file the articles and notes in file folders and organize them by the major sections of their reports.

3. *Using special-purpose computer programs.*   Some computer programs provide a powerful way of entering information, searching for that information, and organizing it. These computer-based programs provide an effective method for managing and collecting data. With programs such as Citation (Figure 2-1), writers can enter the appropriate bibliographic information *and* they can indicate several key words for each card. When they are ready to reorganize their records, any of the key words can be used as the organizing word.

Collecting and Sorting Information

By organizing your information as you work, you can save time and make writing your research reports easier. Consider three strategies for organizing your information:

1. *Note cards*. Some writers use index cards to record bibliographic information. They also code each card by topic.
2. *Letter-sized file folders*. Some writers organize their file folders by subject. Some may keep separate folders for each point in their papers. Then as they collect more information about that point, they add it to the file.
3. *Computer files*. Recently, writers have discovered that computer files can be used as simplified data storage systems. For more advanced writers, sophisticated data base programs such as Citation (see above) make valuable research companions.

CONCLUSION

This chapter has stressed the importance of convention. By examining the discourse community in which you are working, you can tune into the values of that discipline, acquire the necessary background knowledge about its customs and conventions, and follow them as you research your topic and write your research report.

Remember that *conventions can be challenged* by experienced writers and researchers. But before you challenge any conventions, be sure that you have a solid understanding of the current knowledge and conventions of your discipline. Don't depart from the customs of a new field until you do.

This chapter has also emphasized the differences and similarities between the conventions in different discourse communities. By being aware of both the similarities and differences as you work on research reports in college and on the job, you can more easily adapt to your assigned tasks and produce better research reports. Remember that a textbook, such as this one, can give you a good foundation that you will be able to modify as you work on different research tasks.

The next part, Part Two, takes you through a research-writing process that you can adapt to most writing tasks. As you read on, remember that you will need to adapt our general advice to the conventions of the discourse community in which you are working.

THE PROCESS AT WORK

CHAPTER 3

The Components
of the Process:
An Overall View

I n this chapter we

present a process for writing research papers and
identify and explain each component of that process.

When you embark on a research project, you're setting forth on a journey
you've never taken before, one that has a general destination, but no signs for the
different turns along the way and no finite set of problems and challenges. What do
you do?

As we have noted earlier, the conventions and the research methods expected in
most professional research reports are different from those you learned in Freshman
English; therefore, you must learn how to explore new terrain. Each writing situation
requires you to address complex problems using the conventions and customs of each
discipline, practices that may be totally new to you. After you get a sense of the
conventions of the new discipline, as suggested in Chapter 2, you need to consider
the writing processes and activities — the procedures — that you will follow. Part Two
presents procedural guidelines you can use as you approach any research-writing task.

THE RESEARCH-WRITING PROCESS

Even though each writing situation is unique, the procedures for research writing are quite similar in all disciplines: all writers have to develop their ideas, plan their research strategies, conduct the research, draft and revise the report, and finally, edit the rough draft and prepare a finished manuscript. This chapter provides a general description to guide you with your research. Figure 3-1 presents the components of the process in an order most writers are likely to follow; Chapters 4 through 11 discuss the details of the components. Remember, however, since each writing task is unique, you may rearrange the activities to suit your individual project.

No matter what kind of research report you are writing, you cannot just plunge in and start writing. You must first develop a sense of the general topic you've been assigned to write about or the topic that you have selected. Some textbooks call this phase of the writing process the prewriting phase. The term prewriting implies that much gathering, reflecting, and collecting of information and ideas takes place before a writer begins to structure and draft a piece of writing. Some prewriting consists of informal writing — writing that is intended to help a writer discover and clarify ideas, rather than writing that will become part of the research report itself. Other prewriting activities, such as mapping and clustering (described in Chapter 4), are more structured.

You will also need to do considerable reading before designing your own research. By reading what others have written about your topic, you will get a sense of the conversations that different authors have had with one another and with the discourse community. You develop a sense of the group wisdom about a given topic, whether it is a scientific concept like cold fusion or a literary topic such as the role of metaphor. By reading widely in your field, you not only develop background knowledge of your topic, but also you learn about the writing style valued in your field: the way others in your field sound, the way they organize their presentations, and thus how they expect you to sound.

As you read, analyze your sources. Don't just assume that the author of one of your sources has the same ideological background that you do. Think about when the source was written and determine how its historical context influences you. Read critically and reflectively. Think about how the source connects to the topic you are exploring, and try to recognize any biases the author may have.

Get a sense not only of the ideas you want to research, but also of the language practices the experts use. Let that knowledge help you evaluate articles and decide how much you need to write down about each source on your notecards. If you have access to one of the new computer programs such as Citation (see Chapter 2), which allows you to enter bibliographic data and notes in the same file, use it to complement or substitute for note cards. Computer programs can enhance your ability to collect and sort data. If you don't have a bibliography program on your computer, consider creating a template file with your word processor, such as the one in Figure 3-2.

Before moving to the next component of the writing process — defining the problem and planning the research — be sure you have settled on a general area of investigation after your preliminary reading and note-taking.

Developing Ideas: Prewriting (Chapter 4)	**Conducting the Research** (Chapter 9)
Generate Initial Ideas Gather Initial Information Interpret Information Select Topic	Interviewing
	Conducting the Research (Chapter 10)
Defining the Problem and Planning the Research (Chapter 5)	Observing
Defining the Problem Developing Research Questions Developing a Research Plan Writing a Proposal (optional)	**Drafting** (Chapter 11)
	Organizing Information Generating Illustrations Drafting Report Narrative and Illustrations Redrafting Writing an Informal Progress Report (optional)
Conducting the Research (Chapter 6)	
Using the Library Taking Notes Considering Ethical / Legal Issues	**Revising and Editing** (Chapter 12)
	Revising Content of Narrative Revising Organization of Narrative Revising for Style Revising for Grammar, Punctuation and Usage Revising Visuals
Conducting the Research (Chapter 7)	
Gathering Information through Writing Letters	**Finishing Up** (Chapter 13)
Conducting the Research (Chapter 8)	Formatting Using Style Manuals Footnoting Bibliography Printing
Conducting Surveys	

FIGURE 3-1　　Components of the Research-Writing Process

Title: *Proposals That Work (Second Edition)*

Author: *L. F. Locke, W. W. Spirduso, S. J. Silverman*

Publisher: *Newbury Park, Cal.: Sage*

Publication Date: *1987*

Comments: *An excellent book that gives lots of useful details on writing proposals.*

F I G U R E 3-2   Sample Notecard

DEFINING THE PROBLEM AND PLANNING THE RESEARCH

At this point take a lesson from experienced writers: Allow yourself plenty of time for defining your problem before you begin composing your draft. By carefully defining your problem early in your research process, you avoid wasting valuable time later.

It is impossible to conduct research without clearly defined **research questions**. Research questions drive the research. For example, if you are trying to determine what kind of solar system should be installed for a particular client in an office building, you might ask:

1. What are the clients' needs?
2. What solar systems will meet those needs?
   a. How much fluctuation in temperature is there in different kinds of systems?
   b. Which systems will require supplemental heating?

One way to determine what you know about your topic is to write a literature review — a written summary of the highlights of your early reading and note-taking. Even if you don't have to submit a literature review to your instructor, the literature review is an effective way to clarify what you know about your topic and how you might be able to approach it.

Once you have collected your data and, perhaps, also written a literature review, take time to interpret the information you have collected. By using specialized problem-solving strategies, such as those used in business and industry, you can develop powerful and creative insights into the problem you are planning to research.

With the problem clarified, you can then develop a plan for conducting the research. What research tools will be used? What methodology will be followed? Why is one method better than another one? Be sure to answer these questions before you begin your research.

Perhaps the most effective way to develop a research plan is to write a research proposal — even if you don't have to. A research proposal is a short paper in which a writer presents his or her plan for research. Typically, research proposals follow a standard format: background, statement of problem, proposed solution. The latter part of Chapter 5 presents a detailed approach to writing proposals.

CONDUCTING THE RESEARCH: USING THE LIBRARY

All researchers need to know how to retrieve information from libraries, using traditional search techniques as well as computer strategies. Some projects will, of course, require heavier use of library research methods than other projects.

As you read, take careful and systematic notes. Avoid using scraps of paper for jotting down notes. Instead, develop a routine system to help you organize and retrieve information when you need it. Chapter 6 provides the specifics.

CONDUCTING THE RESEARCH: GENERAL RESEARCH METHODS

Research methodologies differ from discipline to discipline. You need to determine what strategies are appropriate for your field. Clearly, all disciplines depend to some extent on a simple information-gathering strategy — letter writing. Chapter 7 explains how to plan and write letters so you get positive results.

CONDUCTING THE RESEARCH: PLANNING, CONDUCTING, AND ANALYZING SURVEYS

Some research methodologies — such as survey research, observational research, and experimental methods — are used primarily in the sciences. If these methodologies are appropriate for your topic, read Chapter 8 closely. Although surveys are rarely used in the humanities, many research projects involve learning from other people and all researchers could — conceivably — profit by the results of well-designed surveys. Consequently, if you are in the biological, physical, or social sciences, or even in the humanities, read this chapter to become familiar with the conventions of other discourse communities.

CONDUCTING THE RESEARCH: GATHERING INFORMATION BY INTERVIEWING

Interviewing can be an effective, efficient technique to learn what others think about issues, and you can learn how they behave in selected settings. To obtain good results from interviews, follow the systematic approach suggested in Chapter 9.

CONDUCTING THE RESEARCH: GATHERING INFORMATION THROUGH OBSERVATION

Like interviewing, careful observation can be an extremely useful strategy to gather information for your research reports. Chapter 10 explores the difficulties associated with observing carefully and then suggests strategies for gathering information for research reports through observation.

DRAFTING REPORTS

Research reports are often presented to instructors or employers in finished format, formats that rarely reflect the time and effort that went into the preparing the report. It is not surprising, then, that the reader of a research report rarely has any idea of the struggles writers had while drafting and redrafting.

Rather than trying to draft your research report all at once, try linking the research and drafting activities. In other words, as you complete parts of your research, write down notes and file them.

Chapter 11 suggests creating separate files for different sections of the research paper: Introduction, Methods, Results, Discussion, and Conclusion. Then, as you work on your writing, move to different files at any time — in no definite order. If you want, go directly to a section in the body, and do some prewriting and preliminary drafting there before drafting the introduction. Or write another section first. Your draft will grow incrementally. When you have completed all sections of the paper, reread them and incorporate transitions between one section and the next.

Writing often works best when you let it grow organically: draft a section one day, redraft a previous section, then move ahead to draft another section. Continue cycling through completed sections of your draft each time you work on a new section, revising and redrafting as necessary. Should you draft the visuals first and then draft the narrative? Or would it be more appropriate for you to draft the narrative first? The answer is, ''It depends.'' It depends on how visually oriented you are and on the topic you are researching. Do you think in pictures, numbers, or equations? If so, you may want to create visuals before drafting the narrative section of your research report. If you are more verbally oriented, however, you may always prefer to draft the narrative before the visuals.

What kind of topic are you investigating? If you are researching a topic that requires numerical data collection and analysis, preparing the tables or figures before writing the results section will help you focus your narrative on the key points from the data. Some topics demand that the writer pay more attention to the visual presentation of information than is necessary for other topics. Similarly, some topics require diagrams or illustrations. A report comparing two hypertext computer programs would be worthless without a diagram illustrating the inner workings of each program. On the contrary, some topics do not benefit from visuals. If you are arguing the philosophical merits of an ethical issue, visuals may neither help you write the argument nor help the reader understand it.

REVISING AND EDITING

When you are satisfied with the overall content and movement of your paper — the general organization and information — you are ready to revise for paragraphing, sentence structure, word choice, and visual display of text. Although much of how you proceed depends on individual preferences, you may want to do what experienced writers do: Pay attention to the global aspects of your drafts before turning to the finer details. Thus, you would focus on revising the content, organization, and structure before concentrating on spelling, mechanics, and style. Also, you would wait until your narrative is pinned down before revising graphs, charts, and other visuals.

Don't assume that you will automatically and intuitively examine everything that you need to check in your report. Use the revision guide list presented in Chapter 12 to guide you. Also, whenever possible, ask a colleague or a friend to read over your text. Even if you don't trust this person's editorial judgment, ask this person to identify passages that are hard to follow. By doing so, you may discover that, just because someone else is looking at your writing, you suddenly develop a sharper perception of your own work.

FINISHING UP

Finishing a research report involves considerably more work than finishing an essay. Since you will share your writing with other professionals, you will want to format it carefully. Formatting refers to the physical presentation on the page — the placement of lists, boxes, tables, text, and so on.

Of course, you must be sure that you have followed the appropriate style guidelines for your discipline. For example, you need to know whether your field follows the CBE (Council of Biology Editors) guidelines, the MLA (Modern Language Association) guidelines, the APA (American Psychological Association) guidelines, or some other style manual. To learn how specific journals interpret their style guidelines, consult several issues and read the editorial advice to prospective contributors.

Also, read several articles and observe how authors implement the disciplinary conventions in their articles.

Finally, you may want to attend to the physical production of your text as well as the overall formatting. Today, most writers opt to produce professional-looking reports with word processing software. Or, for some publications, writers produce research reports with desktop publishing packages. If you do not have access to a computer, however, you can still produce well-formatted research reports with a typewriter. Chapter 13 details an overall approach for the format and layout of your research reports.

Tips for Working on Research Projects

1. *Combine researching and writing throughout the process.* Don't do all your research first and then start writing. Write what you can when you can. If you are doing a humanities project, you might begin by developing a preliminary annotated bibliography; then you might draft an introduction; next, you might return to your bibliography and conduct more extensive library research. If you are conducting a science research project, you can draft the Methods section even before you begin your research — as long as you have clarified your research questions first.

2. *Take notes as you go.* In addition to taking notes on your topic, take notes on your process — are you confused about your research design? Should you ask your professor or supervisor to help you think it through? Where can you get more information?

3. *Allow the organization to emerge gradually.* Many writers develop the organization of their papers after they begin working on them. Don't think that you need to have the whole thing worked out in advance. And even if you do, let your outline change to reflect the growth in your thinking. When you write over time, your ideas change. If you let your outline constrain you, you will reduce your chances for having an effective paper.

4. *Develop a critical and reflective mind set.* When you read a source, read rhetorically. Ask, "Does the author have a bias?" Don't just assume that everything you read is an objective account.

5. *Talk to colleagues or classmates.* Writing should not be an isolated process. Nor should research be conducted in a vacuum. Talk to colleagues if you can. Let your colleagues help shape your thinking.

6. *Write progress reports.* If possible, write a progress report to your employer or instructor. Writing a progress report helps clarify where you are and where you need to go. It also allows your supervisor to provide you with suggestions for revision.

7. *Don't expect perfection.* Work to produce a shareable draft, not a finished product.

CONCLUSION

This chapter has given you some general guidelines to follow as you write your research reports. As you begin, decide what specific territory you will explore, what questions you will ask about a topic, what research tools you should use, and what focus you should take as you proceed. As you progress, determine how different chapters in this book can help you with different segments of your research. By reviewing and studying the specific chapters and sections within chapters, you will discover ways to make writing easier; at the same time, you will be developing writing skills that will help you in additional classes and throughout your career.

Keep in mind that professional-looking research reports do not just happen. They are the result of hard work, including preliminary investigation and ongoing inquiry, extensive periods of time to conduct the research, and a continuing reassessment of the evolving research report. Vital to that reassessment is seeking advice and guidance from others. In addition to seeking advice from your advisor or from a colleague, you can think of this textbook as a supplementary advisor. Unlike your advisor and colleagues, this book is available whenever and wherever you need it.

CHAPTER 4

Generating, Gathering, and Interpreting Initial Ideas

Ⅰn this chapter we cover

task analysis,
audience analysis,
exploring topic options,
selecting a topic,
generating ideas about the topic,
establishing a focus,
gathering initial information, and
interpreting initial information.

This chapter should help you get started on your research project. As you know, both the form and content of research reports vary from one discipline to another. The procedures to follow as you prepare to write, however, are quite similar. To write effectively, you need to develop your ideas, plan your research strategies, conduct the research, draft and redraft the report, and then, finally, revise and edit the rough draft. This chapter will focus on the beginning of your research project — the time when you need to develop ideas and pin down a topic.

When you start to work on your project, consider using the idea-generating or interpreting techniques presented in this chapter to help you select a topic. Remember that this chapter emphasizes ways to collect *initial* information. Subsequent chapters present research strategies that will help you investigate your topic through interviewing, observing, library searching, and other specialized techniques such as conducting surveys or observational research.

A LOOK AT YOUR TASK AND AUDIENCE

Task Analysis

First, your task. What have you been assigned to write, or what research project have you been asked to conduct and then write up? Even if your topic has been assigned to you by your professor or your supervisor you need to be sure that *you* understand what you are supposed to do. One of the best ways to determine the extent to which you understand your task is to take a few minutes and write an answer to the question, "What is my assignment?" More than likely, any misconceptions or ambiguities that you have will be revealed in your answer.

Be sure to check with your professor or your supervisor, however, to make sure that you fully understand the nature of the task. Some scientists and engineers have failed to realize that even though they are expected to complete technical research reports, their writing should not be exclusively technical. Even scientific reports need to establish some context; they need to indicate that the writer cared about the topic and that the reader ought to care. No topic exists just for its own sake. If something is worth writing about, indicate why other researchers would be interested in the topic. The following example from the introduction of a radiation-biology report illustrates the way scientific research should be presented in context:

> Recently an unknown radioactive substance was discovered in the drinking water supply of an elementary school located less than three miles from the nuclear-waste processing plant operated by Fraley Hazardous Wastes and Associates of Fort Collins, Colorado. Fearing a barrage of law suits from concerned parents, the local school board ordered a study to identify this unknown radionuclide and to propose alternate sources of drinking water.
>
> The purpose of this study is to identify the unknown radionuclide contaminant from a sample received from Fraley Hazardous Wastes and Associates using methods applicable to Geiger-Meuller counting systems. The objectives of this study are: (1) to determine the maximum beta particle energy, (2) to determine the half-life, (3) to identify the radionuclide, and (4) to determine the level of activity as of October 1, 1990.

In this example, the researcher explained not only how she conducted her experiment, but why the experiment took place — because it was important to locate the cause of contamination in a school's drinking water.

Another student, thinking that a report should contain only the technical side of the topic, wrote:

> To identify an unknown emitter, two characteristics of the sample should be determined: What radionuclide is in the sample? How much activity is present? Usually, detection is based on the type of emission, the energy of emission, and on the half-life of the radionuclide. Sometimes there is more than one radionuclide in the "unknown" and this information must thus be determined for each one. Characteristics must sometimes be determined if the three items listed above do not uniquely characterize radionuclides.

This student's introduction doesn't provide readers with the reason for the experiment — the fact that childrens' health was at risk because the water was contaminated. The report implies that the research has been conducted for its own sake rather than for the benefit of humanity. The writer seems to think that readers are only interested in the technical details of the experiment.

You need to be sure that you understand the task; you need a sense of how writers in the field report information and research results. Don't read just one or two sample documents or reports — examine several published over five or more years. As you read, notice how the others write. Also, observe how your colleagues react to the reports.

Sometimes the conditions or constraints within which you must operate can facilitate your writing process; at other times constraints can cause writer's block. To avoid problems, make sure that you fully understand the nature of your task.

Audience Analysis

Next, your audience. For whom is this research being conducted? In other words, who will read the report? What are these people like? What reasons might they have for reading this report? What context do they work in? How does the topic of the report affect them in that context? Don't begin conducting the research until you have answered these questions.

In the classroom, your instructor's assignment should help you understand your audience; but in the real world, your audience is unpredictable. Even though you may know who your readers are, there is no way to predict the multiple, changing factors that will influence how your readers will react to your writing. You may write a hard-nosed report about the environmental dangers of producing a product your company is considering manufacturing, only to learn that the chief executive of your company, who is sympathetic to environmental issues, has resigned. Then you may discover that your new boss is bent on proceeding, no matter what the environmental cost.

Nonetheless, to whatever extent possible, you need to understand the likely audience for your writing.

Try to visualize your readers. What do they look like? What do they say? Carry on an imaginary conversation with them. What kinds of questions do they have? Here are some questions you might ask yourself:

Who are my readers?

What are these people like?

Why are they interested in my research?

What is their attitude toward my topic?

What is the context of their interest?

Who clse would be interested in my research?

What are they likely to think of my research?

What questions are they likely to have about my research?

Technical writer and scholar David Dobrin has written extensively about the nature of the term "technical" in technical writing. Dobrin believes that writing is so much more than "merely technical information" (Dobrin 1989). To write well, a writer needs "background information" about the audience, not mere demographic data.

In the case of the radiation biology lab report described above, the professor carefully established a context for the assignment. Professor Leslie Fraley asked his students to assume the roles of radiation biologists working as professionals and serving on the review board for the journal *Health and Biological Sciences*. Students were told in advance that they would act as reviewers for one another's articles, just as they might be asked to do some day as practicing professionals. Yet many students did not think about their audience at all as they drafted their report.

Strategies for Task and Audience Analysis

1. *Task analysis*. Ask questions of your professor or supervisor. Check to see if your understanding of the assignment is the same as someone else's.

   a. *What is the purpose of your research report?* Instructive, persuasive, or merely informational — a historical record of what you did?

   b. *What are the stylistic or organizational requirements?* If you want to communicate information to a professor or to an employer, you sometimes have a good bit of flexibility. But if a journal in your field prescribes a specific format, then you must follow a prescribed format if you want to get your article published in that journal.

   c. *When are the due dates?* By knowing the due dates, you can pace yourself.

   d. *Will anyone look at the draft or collect any in-process notes with the paper?* Some instructors require students to submit note cards.

Some lab instructors require students to turn in lab notes. If your instructor requires such steps, make sure you understand the purpose of these notes.

2. *Audience analysis.* Understanding how your task relates to your audience and your audience's needs is critical to the planning process. Your audience expects you to write the way others write about similar topics in your field. To get a sense of your audience, ask and answer the following questions.

a. *Who are your readers?*

b. *Why are they going to be reading your report?*

c. *Do your readers' reactions matter?*

d. *What effect do you want to have on your readers?*

EXPLORING TOPIC OPTIONS

With task and audience under control, you are now ready to think about ideas. But what can you write about? What options do you have? You can determine the possible variations of the topic you might write about by answering the following kinds of questions:

What am I interested in?

What do I know about this topic?

What similar topics am I aware of?

What options do I have for conducting research on this topic?

Can I conduct research on a related topic?

For many writers, generating a topic and then narrowing the focus of the topic constitutes the most difficult part of the research writing process. But without a specific topic and a limited focus, you cannot move to the most important step in the early stages of writing a report: generating a research question or a thesis statement.

Rather than just sitting down at the computer and starting to write, researchers and experienced writers take time to reflect, time to gather their current thoughts on a topic and to begin to examine those thoughts critically.

Sometimes ideas seem to take on a life of their own, churning up a storm of thought that begins to take shape almost even before the ideas have been articulated. When writers work collaboratively on a project, much of the idea-generating can be the natural offshoot of preliminary discussion with someone or with several people about the topic; but even if you have to write independently on a project, the topic just automatically inspires you. On other occasions, however, writers need to force themselves into a reflective mode, almost tricking themselves into getting started on a project by using formal idea-generating strategies.

SELECTING A TOPIC

Much depends on whether you have free choice of topic or have been assigned one. Though you would prefer to have free choice of a topic, at some time in your academic, nonacademic, and career settings you will find yourself having to write about assigned topics. Let the following guidelines help you:

Either select a topic you care about or recast an assigned topic in a way that interests you.

Before selecting a new topic or recasting an assigned one, consider a range of possible variations of the topic that you might write about. Your second or third thought may turn out to be more promising than your first thought.

Before settling on a topic, see how much you know about it and how much you would need to find out in order to do a good job covering it. If you discover that the task of becoming familiar with your topic would be overwhelming, then consider a different topic (if you have free choice) or consider a variant of your assigned topic.

To determine how much you know about your topic, try rapid writing. Think about your topic for a few minutes. Jot down as many ideas as you can think of—in the form of a list. Then start writing in sentences. Keep writing for about twenty minutes. Then reread what you've written. If your writing is full of abstract and vague utterances without specific references, you probably know little about your topic.

GENERATING IDEAS ABOUT THE TOPIC

At the beginning of a research project, you will be doing many things simultaneously. You will read about your topic, take preliminary notes, talk to colleagues, and try some idea-generating strategies. Some techniques commonly used to generate ideas include

freewriting,

brainstorming,

patterned notes,

tree diagrams, and

working outlines.

By putting ideas on paper, you will see what you know and focus on generating additional information.

When you complete your research report, the structure will be linear, beginning with point number one, proceeding to point two, and so forth. The thinking that produces a linear organization, however, need not be linear. If you start with generating techniques such as freewriting, non-linear brainstorming, patterned notes, or tree diagramming, you can capture ideas, revise the order as you draft, and then put them into a clear, linear sequence at some point in your drafting process.

Freewriting

Freewriting means starting to write without a plan and seeing what emerges. When you freewrite, don't worry about thinking before you write. Just start writing. As soon as you think of something to get you started, write it down. Then keep writing. You will discover that it is possible to think and write simultaneously. The act of writing stimulates thought, and reading over what you have just written prompts you to write more (Figure 4-1).

One suggestion: turn off your internal editor. Don't correct style, grammar, or spelling errors as you work. Concentrate on putting ideas on paper or screen as fast as you can. Later, if you should want to use any of your freewriting, you can edit some or all of it, then cut and paste it into your draft.

Brainstorming

Brainstorming, like freewriting, stimulates ideas uncritically. So let your mind run free as you list your ideas on paper or screen. As you work, don't evaluate the items on your list; your objective is to exhaust your thinking and capture as many ideas as possible (Figure 4-2).

Patterned Notes

Patterned notes provide a visual way of presenting and linking key ideas. List key ideas in the center of the page and then build spokes of supporting ideas around them. This technique — sometimes called clustering — allows writers to discover how their ideas fit together or cluster (Figure 4-3).

Tree Diagramming

For tree diagramming, put the key idea at the top of the page or screen and then branch off into supporting ideas. Continue making subbranches for subsequent subpoints. This generating technique allows you to see your subpoints fit together to develop your main idea. By compressing and linking ideas on one page, you can see what you have accomplished so far and determine if you have gaps in your content or organization (Figure 4-4).

Mountain lions would make a good topic for a research paper, but what could I write about them. In recent years newspaper and magazine accounts suggest an increased incident or encounters with people. I wonder what the causes might be. Have any people been killed? If so, how many.

I wonder if the mountain lion population has increased since the turn of the century. What about their distribution? Are they found in only the West. I think I recall reading something about the Everglades species being in endangered or on the endangered species list. I should check that one out. How are the western species and eastern species related? I could do a research paper that looks at the taxonomy or species differences across the country. How much are they hunted? If so, in what states? I'd sure hate encountering one while out in the mountains, but I might. What if I do? What should I do? Could I develop a research paper around that topic? How realistic is the danger anyway?

How are the cats managed in the different states? What about hunting seasons? Do the state agencies limit the number of cats that can be taken in any one area? Year? If so, how do they regulate the species? What kinds of controls are used? Are more stringent controls needed? Perhaps I could argue a paper looking at the problems? What other kinds of things should I include? Maybe I should return to the idea of the increasing incidence in some areas. What are the causes? Implications for management practices? What limitations need to be placed on the population, if any? I need to think through this a bit more....

FIGURE 4-1   Freewriting

—Mountain lions are becoming a problem in the West
—Dig out TIME article with picture, parking lot, California
—Two young mountain lions tree jogger near Boulder, Colorado
—Home owners west of Loveland, Colorado, woman lets poodle out, hears cry, looks on deck, sees large mountain lion with poodle in mouth. Woman takes broom, goes out on deck, hits cat overhead with broom. Cat walks off into forest. Poodle never returns.
—Cats are becoming increasingly common in many areas, not shy, elusive, but bold.
—Few cases of humans being attacked, but a real concern.
—Why is this occurring?
    People moving into the mountains or rural areas where mountain lions have frequented historically. Deer attracted to areas of development since no hunting. Mountain lions find deer easier to catch, or attack.
—Need to dig out the number of cat attacks on humans in recent years? How many? Where? What are the circumstances?
—How can I assess the problem? Is it real? Growing? How good are my data?
—Wild mountain lion captured on campus by Colorado State University police about 4 a.m. in late August 1989. Young female wandered into Fort Collins and onto campus.

FIGURE 4-2   Brainstorming Notes for a Research Article on Mountain Lion Problems in the West

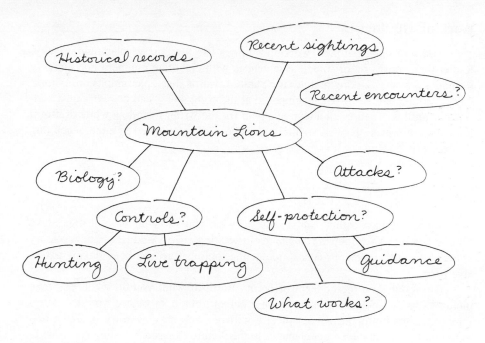

F I G U R E 4-3   Pattern Notes on Mountain Lions

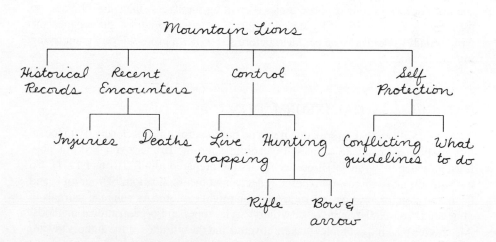

F I G U R E 4-4   A Partial Tree Diagram for a Research Report

Working Outlines

Unlike formal outlines, working outlines use a recursive planning strategy. Rather than consisting of complete sentences with elaborate numbering systems or Roman numerals, working outlines use phrases, words, lists, paragraphs in any mixture. Working outlines — when composed at the computer — can be rearranged continually until they represent a tentative plan for the writer to follow while drafting. Even then, however, the working outline can be easily readjusted by either recopying it or merely revising it with a word processor.

ESTABLISHING A FOCUS

Once you have a topic and a sense of what you know about your topic, take time to examine your focus. You can avoid wasting energy and taking unnecessary notes if you articulate your conception of the topic before you begin taking extensive notes.

To understand the concept of focus, think of what you do when you take pictures. As you prepare to photograph a person, place, or object, you first determine what the highlight of your picture will be. You may even try to frame that individual or object with other elements in the picture. Research writing is similar to photography in that researchers also need to focus — to establish the core of their research ideas.

One student in Dawn Rodrigues's class decided to do some research on how teachers could design flyers for public information workshops — on issues such as the environment, animal rights, drugs, and so on — at their elementary schools. The student also wanted to write about how to prepare a proposal for a grant to fund these public information projects. Dawn told the student that she really had two topics. If she just focused on one of those topics — creating the flyer — then she'd be able to focus better as she worked. By saving the grant proposal idea for another paper, the writer could work clearly on her ideas before she writes a proposal for a grant trying to fund her idea.

GATHERING INITIAL INFORMATION

You will not find information if you do not look for it. Consciously try to locate information and evaluate sources. Psychologist Jerome Bruner explained this phenomena when he wrote, "Discovery favors the prepared mind" (Bruner 1971). So put yourself into a discovery mindset; reflect about the implications of your topic and be on the alert for any possible subtopics you might explore. As you read journals in your field, consciously note other writers' style, tone, and organizational methods. Also notice the kinds of topics that are covered and the attitudes of the authors toward those topics. The following list reviews these suggestions and offers some additional advice for gathering information and ideas about your topic.

Gathering Information about Your Topic

1. Read academic journals and try to identify the kinds of questions writers might have asked themselves to generate the ideas in the articles.
2. Note how other authors define their topics. Analyze sections of sample reports to discover the kind of material you would need to fill each section of a similar report.
3. Ask discipline-specific questions about your topic. For instance, if you are writing about adolescent psychology and focusing on adolescent suicide, you might ask the following kinds of questions: Why do researchers feel that adolescents are distinctly different from other groups? How do some adolescents manage to cope? When are adolescents' problems most severe?
4. Finally, to gather ideas for your writing, listen to people around you as they work on projects. Try to establish whether there are any idea-generating strategies common to your area of employment. For instance, do people in the field ask one another the same sets of questions again and again? If so, jot down these questions and use them to interrogate your topic.

As you are looking at articles in your field for ideas, you should also use them for structural guidance. Look for any general patterns of organization or development. Patterns of organization sometimes help writers generate ideas. If, for example, you notice that many articles in your field tend to classify information, putting chunks of ideas into discrete categories, consider doing this to the information you gather about your topic. For instance, if you are researching ways to increase the amount of public involvement in the election process, you might discover categories where you can fit your ideas, such as advertising campaigns, public forums, and school-based efforts. In other words, by sorting your notes into different categories, you can organize your writing around these categories. When you have put your material into these slots, you will find out which categories need to be filled with additional information. You may even realize that you already know what you can put into those categories.

INTERPRETING INITIAL INFORMATION

After you have a specific topic and you have limited your focus, begin interpreting the information you collect. Some people do a terrific job collecting information — using such techniques as notes, surveys, and interviews — but they never critically examine and interpret their material. They miss an important part of the research process if they don't stop to *interpret* the information they are gathering. The process of interpreting involves making judgments about sets of information or data. By interpreting information, you force yourself to clarify your thinking about your topic.

Here are some strategies for interpreting information:

Ask key questions about the topic.

Locate and read current news stories about the topic.

Use the journalist's questions ("Who? What? Why? When? Where? and
   How?") to examine different aspects of the topic.

Look at the topic from different perspectives.

Use creative problem-solving strategies.

Beginning with Key Questions

Your initial questions about your topic might include:

What additional areas of the topic should I investigate?

What background information should I read?

Should I concentrate my information-gathering more on one area of the
   subject than on other areas?

You may need to do some library searching at this stage in the research process.
Chapter 6 provides guidance on how to find information in libraries. You may also
need to do a considerable amount of note taking as you locate sources.

Locating Current News Stories about the Topic

To clarify your attitude toward the topic, read widely. Newspapers, news magazines, specialized magazines, newsletters, and other publications are valuable
sources of information; so are television newscasts and radio news programs. You
should also scan trade magazines and professional journals in your field. Consider
attending professional meetings and conferences. Develop a questioning approach.
Be critical. And be creative.

In lectures on creativity, Dr. Roy Langford (late of Kansas State University) a
psychology professor, pointed out that a good writer could see a piece of string on the
sidewalk and build a story around it. The trick, Langford said, lies in looking at a
topic from a new perspective, in a new light, or in a different way.

Using "Who, What, When, Where, Why, and How"

When you are trying to interpret a general topic, ask "Who? What? When?
Where? Why? How?" These questions are often referred to as the "journalist's questions" because students in newswriting classes are expected to answer them in their
leads. The questions are just as appropriate for a research paper as they are for a
news story.

You can clarify your stance toward a topic by using the 5 W's. Consider the
massive Yellowstone Park fires of 1987. In 1972, the National Park Service imple-

mented a let-wild-fires-burn policy. The 1987 fires were the first major fires in the park following that decision. If you were asked to write a report about this event for a monthly meeting of the Sierra Club, you could ask:

1. *How* did the National Park Service's policy of letting fires burn come into being? *Why* did the Park Service change the policy?
2. *Why* aren't forest fires as bad as Smokey Bear has been telling us for some four decades?
3. *Who* is behind the management decision of letting the Yellowstone fires burn?
4. *What* are the environmental benefits?
5. *What* economic gains or losses follow forest fires?
6. *How* does the U.S. Forest Service staff a fire control base?
7. *How* does the U.S. Forest Service handle the logistics of getting fire fighters to the scene? Feeding them? Housing them?
8. *How* costly are forest fires to U.S. taxpayers?
9. *How* are fire fighters trained?
10. *Why* do fire fighters wear special clothing? *How* can that clothing protect them?

Literally hundreds of other ideas for research reports can be developed by asking questions related to the Yellowstone fires. With a questioning, critical attitude and the ''journalist's questions'' strategy to direct you, you can develop insights into your topic.

Looking at the Topic from Different Perspectives

Another strategy for critically examining a topic involves looking at the topic from different perspectives. Ask yourself how the following professionals would view a given topic:

An economist

A philosopher

An engineer

A medical doctor

A chemist

A physicist

A musician

An English professor

Because each discipline tends to ask different kinds of questions, you can often discover fruitful insights about your topic by looking at it through the eyes of a specialist in a different field.

Using Creative Problem-Solving Strategies

A creative problem-solving strategy may help you re-examine ideas related to your topic and develop new ideas and solutions for your problems. In *Applied Imagination*, Alex F. Osborn encourages people to come up with new ideas by using the following techniques:

Adapt the idea.

Modify it.

Magnify it.

Minify it.

Substitute new ideas for parts of the original idea.

Rearrange parts of the idea.

Reverse parts of the idea.

Combine parts of the idea. (1963, 286–87)

By trying such strategies, you can determine which strategies work for you. You'll also begin to see that certain activities help and others are counterproductive.

Using an Idea Notebook.   Keep track of your ideas for potential research papers and class assignments. To do so, take a tip from professional writers: keep an idea file or a notebook. Whenever you come across a useful idea, take notes and record the date, the source of the idea, names of experts, and any other relevant information. Record enough to help you search for additional material on the topic.

Consider how the student who was planning to do a paper on sex roles in Greek drama gained a different insight into her topic. She read the August 21, 1989 column of "Dear Abby" which carried a reader's inquiry about Damon and Pythias, two Greeks known for their devotion to each other (Coloradoan Choice Section 1983, p. B3). This got her thinking about gender issues and sexual stereotyping in Greek plays. She was interested in Greek literature, culture, and society, and decided that that question could be the kernel of an idea for a term paper. So she clipped the "Dear Abby" column, noted the date, publication, and page number, put it in her idea notebook, and added a question or two about the column.

Taking Stock of What You Know.   As a starting point for any research report, begin by writing down what you already know about the topic. Ask yourself: What do I know about topic X? List your responses as numbered points on the left side of a sheet of paper. Then ask yourself: How do I know Point 1? or What is my source of information for Point 1? Then continue asking the questions about each point that you have listed and enter your answers on the right side.

Table 4-1 shows how one student approached a topic. She was considering a research report that argued the benefits of wearing bicycle helmets. She began by asking, "What do I know about bicycle helmets?" She jotted down the list of items in

TABLE 4-1   Assessing Knowledge of Biking and Helmet Safety

Information	What is My Source of Information?
1. Bike accidents kill and injure.	Mother's friend's daughter died in bike accident, wasn't wearing helmet.
	Asked for biking laws at state driver licensing office; clerk made negative comments about biking and its dangers.
2. Bike helmets can save lives.	Newspaper accounts, people being hit last two months.
	Newspaper and television news accounts suggest some 1000 bikers are killed annually.
3. Helmets required of motorcyclists.	Mothers' friend's son biking to school when hit by a car, wearing helmet, crashed into windshield, no serious injuries.
	Newspaper articles and television news programs have reported safety factors of wearing helmets.
	Estimates are that 60% would not have died had they been wearing helmets.
	State law introduced, passed and then repealed, motorcycle accident death rate increased. Newspaper accounts over last year; logic of relationship? Is this evidence for the need for bicycle helmets?
	Professor's comment: "I make my living with my brain, so I wear a helmet."

the left column below; then she asked "What is my source of information about that item of information?" She listed her answers in the right column.

By developing a similar table and recording it in your idea notebook, you can help focus your thinking and, in turn, reconsider what you know. As a result, you will not only have grouped related ideas about a topic, you will also have identified possible sources of further information: recent newspaper articles and news magazines.

CONCLUSION

This chapter has suggested strategies to help you generate topics for your research projects. You should realize, however, that you can't expect any one kind of idea-gathering strategy to work all the time. Remember that each writing situation is different and that each writer has individual writing processes. By getting to know yourself as a writer and by becoming familiar with the research and writing tasks in your discipline, you will learn how to select the most appropriate generating strategies for a given situation.

After you complete one research project in a discipline, you will have a better idea of how to proceed in the future. Though you will no doubt have to spend a good deal of time on your first project, the time you invest will pay off in the long run. Workers who repeatedly produce the same kind of research report again and again develop the ability to work quickly and almost automatically. What has happened to them? They have begun to think like engineers or biologists or executives of a specific company. They have internalized the culture of the discipline. As a result of having read many reports in their field and discussed the reports with colleagues, their thinking strategies in that field have become automatic and their writing processes have adapted to the demands of the specific discipline. While you may never reach this level — or want to — the more practice you have, the easier such writing will come to you.

CHAPTER 5

Defining the Problem
and Planning the Research

This chapter introduces the concept of problem definition and the importance of establishing sound research questions related to your problem or to the question you are exploring. The suggestions will help you plan how you will conduct your research. Topics include

> defining the problem,
> developing research questions,
> developing a research plan, and
> writing a proposal (optional).

DEFINING THE PROBLEM

No matter what your field is or what topic you have chosen, you need to locate and define a problem or a research question to help clarify your reasons for conducting your research. This problem should be based on topics appropriate to your discipline. For example, in literature, a writer might write on the problem of determining authorship of Shakespeare's plays or on the question of whether authorship can ever be determined; in history, a researcher might explore the problem of determining who won and who lost a battle; or in engineering, a researcher might write about the problem of getting a robot to move an arm.

The word "problem" when applied to research refers to a slightly different concept than does the general definition of the word. A problem, according to the standard definition, is a difficult situation that you try to overcome. A research problem, however, is an identifiable area within a field about which either the researcher doesn't know the answer or to which no researchers have yet found the answer.

In college classes, you may be assigned research problems that have been treated before. But since you have not done the searching yourself, your instructor can allow you to re-examine problems or issues that have already been resolved. On-the-job research, on the other hand, typically involves researching uncharted territory. In both cases, unless you have a clear sense of the problem or question you want to answer, your work will be aimless and unproductive.

DEVELOPING PROBLEM QUESTIONS OR RESEARCH QUESTIONS

When you set out to conduct research, you need a clear direction so that you do not waste time and effort. The key to streamlining your research is to develop a clearly stated research question or research problem. This research question may be called your objective, your hypothesis, your purpose statement, your thesis statement, or something else, depending on your discipline and the kind of research you are conducting. The research question should

> guide your subsequent work,
>
> influence your information gathering,
>
> guide your data analyses, and
>
> influence your paper's content.

In essence, the research problem or question focuses your efforts, minimizes false starts, and saves time and unnecessary work.

When you begin investigating your topic, start with broad questions and, as needed, develop more narrowly phrased questions. For example, suppose you are interested in the economic impact of recent natural phenomena on society. You might do some preliminary library research on the topic. You might also recall the 1988 summer heat wave, when drought across the central United States resulted in parched corn fields and the predictions of increased food prices. Based on your reading and on your recollection, you would next write out your ideas and underline the key terms as shown below:

Research Questions

1. What is the *impact* of *drought* on *society*? (broad question)
2. What is the *impact* of *drought* on *Third World* countries?
3. What *impact* did the *1988 drought* in the *central United States* have on *food prices* for the *following 24 months*?

4. Did the *1988 drought* in the *central United States* increase *fresh fruit* and *vegetable prices* in the northeastern United States in the *24 months following the drought*?

How you define the italicized terms determines the direction of your research. Question 1 provides the opportunity for a broad, wide-ranging look at a multitude of issues and details surrounding the question around the world. Question 2 focuses the question on the less-developed countries. Question 3 centers on the United States, on food prices, and on a specified time period. Question 4 further refines the research activities by asking about the price increases of specific fruits and vegetables in a specified region and time period. But none of the questions explores the issue of what constitutes a drought. To fully research a topic, you must carefully define the key words (or the terms or variables) you use in your question. When you have clearly defined the term, you may find it necessary to change your research question.

Write your research questions down on paper, and then think about them. Change the key words and consider how the revision would change your focus. Try it now: change the key words in the above example and see what happens.

As you investigate a topic, discuss your proposed research question with your classmates, your instructor, or your professional colleagues. Doing so will help you focus your questions, direct your investigation, and resolve many difficulties.

DEVELOPING A RESEARCH PLAN

Planning will help you conduct research more efficiently and effectively. But before you begin to develop a research agenda, be sure you have identified and clarified your problem statement. Without a clear problem statement, you can't possibly know how to proceed with your task.

Rather than planning in your head, take time to write out a research plan. Consider such items as the requirements of the report, including due dates; how you will get started; what data collection or analysis you will do; what parts of the report you can draft early; when you will set aside time to complete the report. (Table 5-1 provides an outline that you can fill out to help you plan a report.)

What happens if you realize you can't complete the research in a realistic time frame? If this happens, you need to revise your problem statement and then rework your research agenda. By taking the time to write out your plans, you give yourself the opportunity to revise and reevaluate your task before it is too late.

Pay Attention to Style, Length, and Due Dates

You can plan more than content and time frame. You can also plan to use a specific style for your paper and to write a predetermined number of pages.

Style means different things to different people: personal style, editorial or stylebook style, typographic style, and idiomatic style are a few ways of describing what style means (Hill and Crochan 1977). Target your style to your audience. If your audience is an official one — an instructor at school or a superior in your company —

TABLE 5-1   Planning Matrix for a Research Project

Assignment

Due Dates

Startup Techniques

Data Collection Method(s)

Portions of Draft to be Completed Early

Time Frame for Research Activities

   Week 1

   Week 2

   Week 3

   Week 4

   Week 5

you may need to be more formal than if your audience is at the same level in your organization. For example, here are the opening paragraphs of two reports that discuss *Giardiasis*, a cold water protozoa that causes severe intestinal problems, including diarrhea, cramps, dehydration, vomiting, and related symptoms.

Literature Research Report on Giardia Outbreaks in Day Care Centers (Target audience: Parents)

> In recent years, day care centers across the country have been experiencing an increased number of outbreaks of many toddlers having diarrhea, cramps, and similar symptoms. Parents should not be too quick to label the sickness as flu.
>
> The children might be suffering from *Giardia*, an infection. *Giardia* is a cold-water protozoa that causes symptoms of diarrheal illnesses.
>
> Black et al. (1977) reported an increased frequency of outbreaks of *Giardia* in the day care setting. Some day care centers have experienced recurring outbreaks of the disease. Steketee et al. (1989) studied three outbreaks in a Wisconsin day care center and discussed the different control measures used.

Literature Research Report on Giardia Outbreaks Among Outdoor Enthusiasts (Target Audience: Hikers, Campers, Hunters, and Fishermen)

> Whatever outdoor activites people pursue in the mountains, they need to beware of ''beaver fever'' or ''beaver's revenge,'' as it is sometimes called.

Consider Bill, a Colorado State senior, who attended classes the last week of August, then took off for the Labor Day weekend. As he had done countless times before while fishing the North Platte River near Walden, Bill dipped his hand into the river for a drink of that cool, cold mountain water.

Little did he know that he would soon be struck with a severe case of "beaver fever."

By early October, Bill had lost four weeks of classes, and had been in the hospital twice as he fought bout after bout of diarrhea, cramps and other symptoms.

Finally Bill's doctor located the cause — Giardiasis.

Giardiasis is an infection from *Giardia*, cold-water protozoa, commonly found in what appear to be cool, clean mountains streams and lakes. Wherever beaver and muskrat live, *Giardia* often infect the water. Surveys indicate that 90 percent or more of beaver and muskrats carry and harbor the protozoa (Kahn 1975; Barbour et al. 1980; Wallis 1989).

To determine how to adapt your style to different audiences, ask yourself the following questions:

What will my primary readers expect?

What do my readers know about the topic?

Will my readers understand the terms?

Why would my readers read the piece?

How can my word choice, sentence structure, and tone be varied to suit these readers' needs?

Let your answers influence your information gathering and your report's organization, visuals, and language as well as its typographical style and layout.

Different Kinds of Style

Personal style, a writer's particular word choice and word placement, reflects a preference for writing naturally. Consider style as your writing's fingerprints, the characteristics of your text that distinguish you from other writers. *Stylebook style* refers to the rules that a given publisher, organization, or editor uses. (See Chapter 13 for illustrations of two citation styles and see Appendix A for a list of some common style manuals and references.) *Typographical style* reflects the use of typefaces, visuals, page layout, and other design considerations. For most research projects, you need not worry about typographical style except for format guidelines (See Chapter 13). When considering typographical style options, remember your reader. Are they classmates, lay persons, or professionals? *Idiomatic style* constitutes the accepted rules of grammar, syntax, and spelling. Some style manuals cover selected idiomatic style issues, while up-to-date grammar handbooks concentrate on modern conventions. When you are faced with solving idiomatic problems, first select the appropriate style manual for your field, and then study the style manual to see what grammar handbook the style manual recommends.

Some Cautions about Length

Length can be deceiving. Some instructors specify page count or word counts for assignments; others are not that specific. Page count is usually indicated in terms of a required number of double-spaced typed pages running between 200 and 300 words per page. With today's word processing programs and printers, a two-page, double-spaced assignment on one system might equal a four-page assignment on another system. If you have an approximate word count per page requirement, you can format your pages accordingly. Remember that word count does not necessarily reflect the quality of the writing. A 5000-word report may be poorly developed, lack focus, and be wordy, while a tightly edited, well-organized report on the same subject may run only 2500 words. If possible, have a short conference with your instructor or supervisor to discuss your idea, the project's size, and the timetable before you determine an appropriate length for your assignment.

A Word about Due Dates

Typically, you will know when your assignment — or a portion of it — is due. Once you know when a report is due, estimate how long it will take to complete the entire project. For example, assume you have to write a paper for a sociology conference on the topic "Drugs and Society." Assume further that the paper should include appropriate references from research journals; should be no more than fifteen double-spaced pages; and should be submitted in eight weeks. If you have at least a working knowledge of the topic, you might determine to allot about 6 to 24 hours for literature reviewing and between 4 and 8 hours for planning. Finally, you might decide to allocate between 16 and 40 hours for drafting, revising, and editing. To spread your work over ten weeks, you can work backwards from the due date:

Activity	Dates
Literature Reviewing	September 5 to 30
Planning and organizing	October 1 to 15
Drafting and revising	October 16 to 31
Polishing the final report	November 1 to 15
Final report due	November 17

Even with a timetable like this, problems can still arise, but by charting out a tentative schedule, you will at least have a sense of whether you are working fast enough.

WRITING A PROPOSAL

Professionals in almost every discipline are expected to write proposals for their research projects. Chemists write proposals to agencies seeking funding for their research. Artists' proposals seek funding for writing novels or developing collections of poetry. And professionals in social work direct proposals to federal agencies for applied research on such topics as Alzheimer's disease.

Proposals can be a valuable exercise for you, too. Although instructors do not always require student writers to submit proposals, students often prepare informal proposals on their own as a commitment to a research project.

Proposals are often routine steps in the process of getting funding for research. Funding agencies and potential benefactors need some way of determining who is worthy of a research award; the relative brevity of a proposal makes it an effective vehicle for such agencies to use as a screening device.

Instructors who require proposals do so for similar reasons. They want to evaluate not only the project itself but also the student's interest in and commitment to the project. They want to determine how much help a student will need.

But why would a writer draft a research proposal if he or she didn't have to? Proposal writing can help you think through the entire research process and force you to honestly assess whether you can complete your research as you designed it or whether the entire study needs to be revised and reconceived. Thus, even if you don't have to do a formal research proposal for a course, this section will help you see how a proposal can help you as well as the reader (the funding agency or the teacher).

Characteristics of Proposals

All proposals have some similarities:

They demonstrate a clear knowledge of the topic,
they explain the methodology, the plan for conducting the research, and
they assure the reader that the researcher is qualified to complete the
  project successfully.

Proposal requirements can vary widely. The two most common kinds of proposals are (1) the problem-solving or investigative proposal and (2) the research proposal (Table 5-2). The problem-solving proposal typically involves some kind of applied research. For example, architects may be expected to design a building, or consultants may be required to propose the scope and extent of services they propose to undertake. In contrast to problem solving proposals, proposals for research projects require that writers demonstrate an understanding of the research literature from which they derived their research questions. Each kind of proposal varies depending on the particular funding agency, discipline, or course project, but in general, the proposals tend to include standard components.

If you are proposing an in-depth literature review to answer your research questions, explain how you will search in the library and obtain articles from corporations and government agencies and sources. If you are collecting original information through interviewing or observing, explain the specific methods you plan to use.

When you propose a project that requires collecting original information, explain how you will collect the information, what specific kinds of information you

TABLE 5-2 Types of Research Proposals	
Problem-Solving Proposal	**Research Proposal**
Title	Title
Problem Statement	Purpose
Background	Literature Review
Scope	Methodology
Limitations	References Cited
Methodology	
Qualifications	
Call to Action	

will collect, how you will conduct the measurements, and how many people, animals, objects, or units you will measure. Then explain how you will analyze the information you collect. Remember that you will need to limit your data so that you have enough time to complete your data or information gathering, analyze or interpret your information, draft and revise your paper, and turn it in by the deadline.

Always be sure to write a strong justification for your research. Weak justifications often come from not fully understanding the problem, not having thought about the key concepts (variables), not having carefully developed the research questions, or not having reviewed enough of the literature to know what others have found in their investigations. To minimize such problems, dig into the literature, talk with professors and experts on the subject, and analyze the problem that you plan to investigate.

In some cases your professors or project managers can suggest how you can undertake the project with limited resources. In other cases, professors with an interest in your topic may have resources — laboratory space, equipment, supplies, computer time, and even limited funds — that you can use for your project.

By investigating the topic early, you will soon recognize whether or not you have the necessary background and skills to carry out the project that you are proposing. If you do not have this background, you will have to determine whether you can learn the necessary skills. Keep in mind that learning a new skill while undertaking a major research report gives you the opportunity to learn more than the topic itself, but approach the task with caution. Learning new skills can add a major time requirement for completing a project. The two lists that follow provide models for a problem-solving proposal and for a research proposal.

Model for a Problem-Solving Proposal

1. *Title*. Include an appropriate title that states the problem.
2. *Problem statement*.
   a. Include a succinct statement that outlines the details of the proposed project.
   b. Use specific details and explain what results you will produce — for example, a report or an article.

  c. Elaborate on the problem or note other research related to the
   project.

3. *Background*.
  a. Explain why the topic is important and support your reasoning. Shape
   the argument so that readers see the rationale for the proposed project.
  b. Answer such questions as: "Why is it important to conduct the
   study or carry on the assignment?"
  c. Provide specifics so that the reader sees the importance of your
   project.

4. *Scope*. Outline the project's scope. If your project is too large you
 won't be able to handle the assignment during the term. If the project
 is too small, you will not be able to produce an acceptable report.

5. *Limitations*. Discuss the limitations of the project's focus in answering the research questions. (Specifics may vary with the kind of project proposed, but often include the available time to collect information, the narrowness of the subject, the kinds and number of subjects
 to be studied, the funds available to cover expenses, the geographical
 area to be studied, or dozens or other limiting factors.)

6. *Methodology*.
  a. Explain the processes that you plan to use to gather the information that supports the thesis statement, answer the research questions, or achieve the stated objectives.
  b. Give enough information so that a funding agency, an employer,
   or an instructor can understand how the researcher will collect the
   needed information.

7. *Qualifications*.
  a. Explain why you can handle the proposed project.
  b. Present evidence of your prior experience studying the subject,
   using the methodology, or investigating similar subjects.
  c. Present a succinct sketch of relevant biographical information
   from your background to support your argument.

8. *Call to action*. Request funds for the project or permission to proceed.

Model for a Typical Research Proposal

1. *Title*.
  a. Be succinct.
  b. Give the reader a clear idea of your proposed research.

2. *Purpose* (Problem statement).
  a. Suggest either your initial research questions or describe the research problem that you will address.
  b. Include the key concepts (variables) that you propose to investigate.

3. *Literature review*.
  a. Provide a succinct literature review that builds the rationale for
   your research question.

    b. Identify the key concepts (variables) that will frame your research question.

    c. Demonstrate that you are aware of the recent research on your topic and the specific concepts you plan to investigate.

    d. Indicate the thoroughness of your literature review by the dates of the literature citations and kinds of literature cited.

4. *Methodology.*

    a. Tell what specific kinds of information will be collected and explain the research procedures (interviews, observational research, and so on). For an in-depth literature review paper, this section may include an explanation of how the researcher will obtain articles from corporations, government agencies, or other sources.

    b. Explain how the researcher will conduct the measurements, telling how many people, animals, objects, or units will be measured.

    c. Explain how this information will be collected and analyzed.

5. *References cited.* Give full citations to the literature cited within the proposal.

6. *Timetable.* Indicate target dates for completion of specific portions of the project.

7. *Budget.* Estimate the cost of materials, supplies, and other anticipated expenses. Such costs may include photocopies, paper, electronic computer searches, printouts, telephone calls, transportation costs, office supplies, as well as supplies and equipment for experiments.

You cannot usually develop a well-thought-out proposal in one sitting. So begin thinking about possible projects, jotting down ideas, and digging into the literature at least a week before your proposal is due, but preferably longer. Keep in mind that you may well experience false starts when you begin projects and find yourself having to change the focus of your topic or having to propose a new idea because your initial idea has not worked out. So start early and allow yourself plenty of time.

Further, recognize that you may need to refine and revise your questions after you have submitted your proposal. You may also need to gather additional information or reconsider the focus of your report. Realize, too, that once your proposal is accepted, you will probably have to continue to refine and revise and reformulate the proposal and the research questions. And remember that, although your initial literature review will provide the framework for your project, you should continue reviewing the literature as you work on your project.

Once you have your draft proposal, set it aside to cool. When you return to your draft, reconsider the entire proposal, including the size of the problem, your justification of the need for research on the topic, whether you have adequate resources to complete the project, and if you have the appropriate background.

If you've never written a proposal before, take time to read the two sample proposals that follow.

TO: Margaret Vota
    City College of San Francisco
FROM: Mary Caris
DATE: October 17, 1988
SUBJECT: Proposal for a formal report
AN EXAMINATION OF COMPUTER OPTIONS FOR THE SAN
FRANCISCO BAY COLLEGE ART DEPARTMENT

Problem Statement

This proposal will require investigating
what the art departments in other community
colleges are teaching in computer art; the
investigation will result in a formal report
informing interested members of the Art Department at City College of San Francisco (CCSF) of
the findings.

Background

The CCSF Art Department offers only two
courses, Graphic Design 35A and 35B, that include anything on computer-generated art. These
courses cover advertising and publishing. The
department plans to offer classes in desktop
publishing in conjunction with the Printing
Technology Department.

Advertising is a major example of the use
of computer art, but computer art has powerful
applications in such diverse fields as medicine
and space exploration. Animation is a popular
use of computer graphics that has fine arts as
well as commercial arts application. In Spring
1988, the Euphrath Art Gallery, located at

DeAnza College, hosted a major exhibition of computer art from around the world; it was a stunning show with emphasis on fine arts. I would like to see CCSF offer a class that explores how to do fine arts on the computer.

CCSF's Art Department plans to offer additional computer-related courses. Presently, the department has one MacIntosh computer. I don't know how many students are using it, but clearly more computers will be needed for an expanded computer art curriculum. In the meantime, we are losing students to other schools where they can obtain computer art training.

Scope

My study will research computer art classes being offered by other community colleges in the Bay Area. I plan to find out what kinds of hardware and software they are using, how many students are taking the courses, how many uses they can accommodate at one time (Are there labs for art students?), and the scope of the classes being offered. I will confer with selected CCSF art teachers about additional questions they would like me to ask.

Limitations

Because of time limitations, I expect this report will not be as complete as I would like. Since few Bay Area community colleges have districts or boards in common, it will be necessary to contact each college individually.

Because of financial consideration, I may limit phone calls to the 415 area code.

Methodology

The major part of my report will be based on information gathered by phone and personal interviews. I expect to view the facilities at several campuses and plan to observe one or two computer art classes while they are being taught.

Qualifications

Over the last two years I have taken several courses in Art and CIS departments at City College and I have enough background in art and computers to ask relevant questions. The kinds of questions I'll be asking will not require highly technical computer knowledge. Also, I know teachers in the Art Department who will be interested in this project and who might suggest questions for me to ask. I have had experience in interviewing people.

Call to Action

This study may also prove to be useful to faculty members in the Art Department. I hope that I will be allowed to write this report.

Editing and Revising Strategies of Five Professional Writers Who Compose on Computers

By Joan Zito

Purpose

I will explore how professional writers edit and revise texts composed on a computer. Specifically, I will explore how the terminal's display of text influences professionals' editing and revising.

Literature Review

Many writers and researchers agree that composing text on a computer is faster than using a typewriter or writing longhand (Beck & Stibravy, 1986; Fluegelman & Hewes, 1983; Dauite, 1986; Zinsser, 1983). Writers can compose ideas on a computer quickly, because they know they can easily return to revise and edit copy, including correcting spelling errors, deleting sentences, and rearranging paragraphs. They do not need to retype whole pages to make their changes.

Although composing on a computer may be faster, revising can be slow and difficult (Fluegelman & Hewes, 1983; Zinsser, 1983; Lutz, 1984). Krull & Rubins (1985) estimated that the standard video display terminal shows about 1100 characters on the screen at one time. In contrast, 8.5 × 11 inch paper with normal margins and 36 lines contains almost 3800 characters.

Fluegelmann & Hewes (1983) and Zinsser (1983) say that the limited text display of a VDT makes it difficult to get a sense of flow when rethinking and reorganizing the text. College students have difficulty locating information, detecting errors, and reading their texts (Haas & Hayes, 1986), and clerk-typists proofread on-line text slower than they proofread hard copy (Gould & Grischkowsky, 1984). Case (1985) reported that computers increase unnecessary revisions. Writers "fool around too much" with the text because they know they do not need to retype entire pages when they revise a section.

Novice writers (Collier, 1983; Dauite, 1986), college students (Beck & Stibravy, 1986; Haas & Hayes, 1986), and clerk-typists (Gould & Grischkowsky, 1984) have been the subjects of most on-line editing and revising studies. Sommers (1980) and Flower et al. (1986) report that novice writers revised text differently than experienced writers did.

I found only one study that investigated experienced writers. Lutz (1984) compared how experienced writers compose, edit, and revise at a computer with how they work with pen and paper. The data included the amount of time needed to do the task, the number of words edited, number of words per sentence, and the total number of changes made in each text.

I found no research on how professional writers edit and revise text as they compose on a computer. Therefore I propose a case study of how five professional writers compose on a computer. Specifically, I will investigate how they revise and edit with computers and with pen and paper, as well as their perceptions of the difficulties, if any, they experience while composing on the computer.

Methods

I will interview five professional writers about their composing, editing, and revising practices. For this study editing will mean correcting spelling, punctuation, and simple grammatical errors. Revising will mean reconceptualizing ideas and organization through rearranging sentences, paragraphs, and major sections.

For my interviews I will develop questions that determine the following:

1. Writing style or approach
   a. ''Dumping'' or freewriting—entering ideas into the computer as fast as they are generated without correcting errors.
   b. Brick-Laying—Completing and polishing the entire idea, sentence by sentence or paragraph by paragraph, before developing the next sentence or paragraph.
2. Editing preferences
   a. On-line or hard copy? Why?

    b. When—while composing or after? Why?

3. Revising preferences

    a. On-line or hard copy? Why?

    b. After composing each idea, paragraph or pages, or more than a page?

4. Proofreading aids

    a. Use of spelling checkers

    b. Use of grammar checkers

5. Other

    a. Years of computer experience

    b. Hours of computer use per day

    c. Preference of display VDT

    d. Lines of text displayed

    e. Sizes of screens they have worked on (Standard 20 to 24 line screen)

    f. Size of page (single page; double page; more than two pages)

Timetable/Budget

Each survey will take about 30 minutes. I will begin the surveys next week and complete them by March 12, 1988. Under that timetable, I will complete my final report by April 18, 1988. Photocopies of journal articles, paper, and telephone calls will cost less than $15.

Literature Cited

Beck, C. E., and Stibravy, J. A. (1986). The effect of word processors on writing quality. Technical Communication, 33(2), 84-87.

APA

Case, D. (1985). Processing professional words: Personal computers and the writing habits of university professors, College Composition and Communication 38 (1), 66-68.

Collier, R. M. (1983). The word processor and revision strategies. College Composition and Communication, 34 (2), 149-155.

Daiute, C. (1986). Physical and cognitive factors in revising: Insights from studies with computers. Research in the Teaching of English, 20 (2), 141-159.

Flower, L., Hayes, J., Carey, L., Schriver, K., and Stratman, J. (1986). Detection, diagnosis and the strategies of revision. College Composition and Communication, 37 (1), 16-54.

. . .

CONCLUSION

This chapter has suggested ways to begin your research: (1) you need to define your problem; (2) you need to develop a research plan; (3) you need to develop research questions; and (4) you should consider writing a research proposal. By working out most of the difficulties in your research early in the process, you'll be able to enjoy conducting the research and writing the finished report.

CHAPTER 6

Conducting the Research: Library Searching and Other General Information

This chapter introduces the essential elements of any writer's research processes and gives some important information every researcher should know:

> library research strategies,
> effective reading and note-taking strategies, and
> ethical and legal issues: plagiarism and copyright.

No matter what discipline you are in, you will need to know how to conduct library research. Knowing how to conduct a search of the literature or the key information related to your topic is a critical part of learning how to write an up-to-date research report in any field.

Basic library research — knowing how to locate essential books, articles, or other sources — isn't all that difficult to learn. To begin, you need to get to know your library and its resources. Then you need to develop a literature-searching strategy. Finally, you need to learn how to read critically and take notes efficiently. The first part of this chapter provides an overview of the library and some of its resources. It also provides you with specific guidance on how to develop effective literature-searching strategies for your professional writing needs. The latter part of the chapter introduces reading and note-taking strategies. At the end of the chapter you will find potentially valuable information on plagiarism and copyright law.

LIBRARY RESEARCH

To use a library effectively, the first thing you need to do is understand the big picture — the library's layout, organization, and resources. At some schools, all library resources are in one building. At other schools, they are scattered across campus. Larger campuses, such as the University of Wisconsin-Madison, have separate undergraduate and graduate libraries. In addition, many campuses have specialized libraries devoted to specific subjects: music, architecture, humanities, engineering, biology, and medicine. Some campuses also have departmental libraries and reading rooms.

Get to know the configuration of your library or libraries. Check near the main library entrance for orientation literature, audio-visual aids, announcements of workshops, computer-orientation programs, and other helpful aids. Introductory pamphlets typically give locations, hours, floor plans, and holdings. Use these pamphlets to find information about the following:

Card catalogs

Reference areas

Periodicals reading areas/rooms

Government publications

Check-out desks and offices

Computerized card catalog and online systems

Networked card catalogs

Commercial computerized data bases

While you're touring the areas, look for additional literature that can help you with your searching, and consider saving the material in a notebook of library resources. As you gather material, add it to your notebook; you will find it extremely helpful as you search for materials for different research projects.

Finding a Book or Periodical

As you get to know your library, the first thing you should do is learn how to find a book or periodical on a specific topic. Card catalogs usually contain major divisions — author, title, subject, or combinations thereof — while the electronic card catalogs are organized around words, names, titles, or call numbers. Before searching the stacks or the on-line catalog for a book or periodical, you need to know whether your library uses the Library of Congress cataloging system or the Dewey decimal system.

The *Library of Congress* classification system separates all knowledge into 21 categories and assigns each to a letter:

Letter	Subjects
A	General works
B	Philosophy-religion
C	Auxiliary sciences of history
D	History (except American)
E–F	History of America
G	Geography, anthropology, folklore
H	Social sciences
J	Political science
K	Law
L	Education
M	Music
N	Fine arts
P	Language and literature
Q	Science
R	Medicine
S	Agriculture
T	Technology
U	Military science
V	Naval science
Z	Bibliography and library science (Cornell 1987; Kansas State 1987)

In contrast, the *Dewey decimal system* divides all knowledge into 10 different categories from 000 to 900:

Number	Subjects
000	General works
100	Philosophy
200	Religion
300	Social sciences
400	Language
500	Pure sciences
600	Technology (Applied science)
700	The arts
800	Literature
900	General geography & history (Katz 1979)

After you locate a book or periodical, fill out a call slip or find it on the shelf and check it out. Only after you have mastered the basics of using a library — including knowing how to check out a book — are you ready to conduct systematic research.

LIBRARY SEARCHING

When conducting library research, a writer searches for a body of existing information on a given subject. The difference between hit-or-miss searching and strategic searching can mean the difference between a mediocre report and an excellent one.

Beginning the Search

If you are new to a topic, you'll probably want to begin by becoming familiar with general resources, such as articles in current newspapers and magazines. To find citations to possible articles, first check the *Readers' Guide to Periodical Literature, The New York Times Index*, and *The Wall Street Journal Index*. Alternately, try using a computerized data base specifically designed for general searching, such as *Info-Trac* or one of the CD-Rom systems such as *Newspaper Abstracts ONDISC*.

General reference sources can also be a useful starting point for library searching. Consult *Sheehy's Guide to Reference Books* and major bibliographies covering your subject. (If you can't find a useful bibliography, ask your reference librarian for help.) Such bibliographies usually cover major topics and cite books, reports, magazine articles, journal articles, videotapes, microfiche, microfilms, government publications, and other forms.

After you have generated a preliminary list of sources, you will be able to identify some related terms or descriptors used in materials related to your topic. For a complete list of descriptors related to your subject, check the *Library of Congress Subject Headings*. Often located near the card catalog or in the reference area, this handy reference identifies the subject headings for your topic, notes related terms, and provides the relevant Library of Congress call numbers. Such information can help you determine what terms to use in your search. Later, as you learn more about your topic, you can narrow its focus.

After you have conducted your preliminary search — and have read the materials you have uncovered — you may need to revise your research question (Chapter 5). When you are satisfied with your research question, continue searching until you have read and taken notes on a sufficient number of sources. The following list suggests questions to help guide your literature search.

Questions to Guide Your Literature Searching

1. What is your topic? (State your topic in broad terms and define it.)
2. Can you locate some overview references (general reference works about your topic) to learn more about what has been written on your topic?
3. Can you narrow your topic?
4. What are the Library of Congress subject headings for your general topic or for your narrowed topic?
5. What specific bibliographies are available on your topic?

6. Does the card catalog include any books on your topic?
7. Does your topic require recent information from periodicals? If so, note the location of these periodicals.
8. Determine whether your library subscribes to these periodicals. If it doesn't, can you obtain copies of articles through inter-library loan?

Conducting An Advanced Literature Search

After you have narrowed your topic and isolated a few key sources, you should develop an advanced literature-searching strategy.

When you conducted a literature search for papers in basic composition classes and other freshman-level courses, you probably used newspaper articles, textbooks, popular magazines, encyclopedias, and other generalized publications. As you write more advanced research reports for different discourse communities, in both the classroom and on the job, your readers will expect you to use primary and secondary literature sources — specialized books and monographs, trade magazines and newspapers, and academic journals. Why? Readers in different discourse communities know that the information in such publications has usually undergone a careful review by the editors and has often withstood a critical review of other members of that discourse community.

The key to finding appropriate articles in specialized periodicals is to use the abstracting journals and indexes and their electronic counterparts on CD-Roms and commercial electronic data bases. *Readers' Guide to Periodical Literature* and Info-Trac cover both the more generalized and the special-interest magazines, while abstracting journals and indexes and their CD-Rom counterparts cover thousands of specialized topics. Use these specialized abstracting journals and indexes and their CD-Rom counterparts, and you will usually find citations to relevant articles in trade magazines, academic journals, government publications, and other specialized publications.

As you find each source of information, be sure to record the bibliographic information on bibliography cards that you develop for the sole purpose of organizing your information (see Figure 3-2, page 32).

As noted in Figure 3-2, indicate related subjects at the bottom of your cards as a guide for additional literature searching. When you enter this information, do so carefully and fully, and be sure that you understand all information you record.

Developing Search Strategies

You will not be able to conduct a comprehensive literature search on your topic without an efficient search strategy. What is a search strategy? It is a plan that you develop for identifying and reading key sources on your topic. Effective searching involves more than finding the two or three books listed in the card catalogue about your topic. Productive searching involves reading key articles in your field, checking reference sources, talking with professionals in your field — and *noting the source of your information* on bibliography cards.

In the past, librarians often assisted with computerized literature searches. But now with computerized card catalogs a common feature of many university libraries, it is important that researchers learn how to conduct their own searches. The critical issue in electronic library searching is redefining the topic of your research report so that you can be sure to find related literature. You cannot just tell a computerized searching program to find all the references on a given topic and assume that the list you retrieve is complete. The key to effective literature searching — whether manual or electronic — begins with a clear research question and a list of related terms. A clear research question on the topic of user documentation might be: Has effective user documentation led to greater profits for specific vendors? Related questions might be (1) Have standards emerged for online documentation? for hard-copy documentation? (2) Do standards continue to change? (3) Are those companies who value effective documentation developing a larger share of the market?

Guidelines for developing a search strategy are presented in the following list; the guidelines are then put to use in a sample search, illustrated in the second list.

Guidelines for Developing a Search Strategy

1. Start with a broad topic. See how much your library has available on that topic.
2. Generate a list of related topics. Search to see if the related terms of these topics lead to any other available sources.
3. Narrow your search topic and related terms.
4. Identify the relevant abstracting journals, indexes, CD-Roms, and other electronic data bases.
5. Continue redefining the terms of your search. Literature on your topic may be indexed according to terms that you haven't yet begun to use in your search.
6. Search manually as well as electronically.

An Illustration of a Sample Search

1. *Research questions for a broad topic: Computer documentation*
   a. Are there any standards emerging?
   b. Do different authors agree on some issues of documentation?
   c. Is online documentation preferred to hard-copy documentation?
   d. Is hypertext documentation the most effective kind of documentation? What standards are emerging for hypertext documentation?
2. *List of related topics*
   a. computer documentation standards
   b. relationship between computer documentation and profits of specific companies
   c. examples of companies that value documentation
3. *Narrowed list of related terms*
   a. software documentation
   b. end-user documentation
   c. online documentation

4. *Relevant publications and data bases*
    a. *Psychological Abstracts*
    b. *Communication Abstracts*
    c. *Uncover*
    d. *ERIC*
    e. *PsycLit*
    f. *Social Science Index*
5. *Revised terms of search*
    a. Use new terms as you search separately for information on online documentation and on technology profits in order to develop a sense of the state of the art in documentation and to get a sense of how to learn whether a computer company will make a profit.
    b. Combine topics to find articles that connect both parts of your topic: documentation and profit in the computer industry.
6. *Manual and electronic search*
    a. Browse in the stacks. You may find valuable information in unexpected places.
    b. Talk to experts in the field. Ask if you can read their unpublished papers.

DEVELOPING EFFECTIVE READING AND NOTE-TAKING STRATEGIES

As you collect information related to your topic, read carefully and take good notes. If you developing efficient strategies for reading and taking notes, you will save valuable time for other facets of your research. Be sure to learn how to: (1) evaluate your sources critically, (2) read for different purposes, (3) read different subjects in different ways, (4) read with a questioning attitude, and (5) take notes sparingly and judiciously.

Record your notes on notecards or develop another systematic way of collecting information. If you include paraphrases, summaries, and carefully selected quotes from your sources, you will have all the information you need when you begin to write your paper. By taking time to put ideas into your own words as summaries or paraphrases, you reduce the chance of accidental plagiarism.

Evaluating Your Sources Critically

Once you find a potential source, you are only partway there. You need to evaluate its usefulness for your research report and to note that information on your bibliography card. To begin, ask

Does this source provide the information you need?

Is the information new to you?

Does the source provide in-depth coverage?

Is the information recent?

To answer the first question, flip through the source materials to determine their scope. If the source is a journal article, review the abstract. If it is a magazine article, review the lead or opening paragraphs and summary. If it is a book, lengthy report, or conference proceedings scan the table of contents, chapter overviews, and summaries. Look carefully at the tables, graphs, charts or other illustrations, because they often highlight key information.

Next, compare the information given with what you already know about the subject. If the source presents new information for you, assess its depth of coverage. Keep in mind that some publications are directed to general readers with no specialized background, while others are meant for readers with some specialized background, and still others are written for readers with highly specialized backgrounds. Generally, the more specialized the audience, the more in-depth the content and the higher the qualifications of the writers.

Look for biographical sketches, bylines, credits, abbreviations of academic degrees, or descriptions that follow the bylines. Or look for short biographical sketches or résumés of the authors in the front matter or back matter and review that information carefully.

Do the writers have special backgrounds on the subject? In newspapers and more general publications, many writers or reporters are generalists — they write on any topic assigned to them. In more specialized publications, like many trade magazines, writers have some expertise on specific topics. In highly specialized publications, like academic journals and a few trade magazines, the writers have several academic degrees and years of professional experience in working on their subjects.

As a rule, the more specialized the author's background, the more in-depth and specialized the information in any given citation. Thus, if you were doing a research report on cholesterol, and found relevant articles in *The New England Journal of Medicine*, *Nursing 91*, and *Prevention Magazine*, you would need to carefully consider the authors' credentials as you assessed the information given. Researchers with medical degrees, and often Ph.D.s, usually write articles for the *New England Journal of Medicine*; nurses with bachelor's, master's, and doctor's degrees usually write articles for *Nursing 91*, while general assignment reporters, writers, and freelancers write articles for *Prevention Magazine*. Similarly, the coverage by the first two publications provides more in-depth treatment than the third mass-circulation magazine does.

Consider, too, the recency of the information. For some assignments, articles and books published ten, fifteen, or even fifty years ago may still be invaluable; for other assignments, such articles would be hopelessly dated and hence worthless. Put yourself into the following two situations and think about the time elements you would have to consider in evaluating your sources:

1. Imagine that you are taking a folklore class and you are interested in medicines that Appalachian Mountain residents used to treat colds. Chances are that articles spanning the last 100 years or more might provide useful information.

2. Assume you are in physics class and doing a paper on superconduc-
tors. If you are trying to determine the most recent developments, any
literature more than four to six weeks old may be dated. In the late
1980s, physicists worked nearly around the clock, slept in their labs,
and made major advances in compounds that could conduct electricity with virtually no loss at higher temperatures. The media reported
advancement after advancement — often only days apart.

When you assess a potential source, begin with a questioning attitude and let
what you know about the topic and the questions given above guide your reading of
that source.

Reading for Different Purposes

When you decide to read a specific source, read for different purposes. Early in
your literature reviewing, read to acquire a general understanding of the topic; later,
read for specific information you need. Always think about why you are reading a
particular piece and ask, ''What is my purpose for reading this source?''
You usually read for four purposes:

To develop a general understanding of the subject,

To identify the key points,

To learn specific details, or

To find other literature.

Reading to Develop a General Understanding.   Read the title, abstract or overview, subheads, and conclusion, if present. Study any illustrations. If you don't know
the terminology, look up the words. Let the following questions guide your reading.

Sample Questions for Critical Reading
1. What can I learn from this reading?
2. What assumptions does the author make?
3. What are the bases of the author's conclusions?
4. Does the author agree or disagree with other authors? Why?
5. Does the content agree with what you know about the topic?

Developing such questions helps guide your reading so that you look for valid, usable
information.

Reading to Identify Key Points.   Look for clues that indicate writers' key points,
and use the clues to help you find them. In books, look for overviews, summaries,
and highlighted materials. On highly specialized topics, some books contain what are
sometimes called executive summaries — brief overviews for busy executives or pro-

fessionals providing a quick look at the main points of the entire book. In many books, chapter titles and subtitles highlight the major divisions and the key points of the chapter. In some books, bullet lists emphasize key points and alert you to coming information. Lists may be numbered or unnumbered. Numbered lists often provide clues to the more important information or to the preferred sequence of activities. Books sometimes provide marginal notes to the right or left of the body of text. Such marginal notes emphasize the more important information.

In articles, look for summaries, abstracts, conclusions, title or headlines, subtitles or subheads and lists. Well-written titles summarize the main idea of the article or give a good idea of the breadth and depth of the article. Headings and subheadings can identify the skeletal structure of an article.

Reading to Learn Specific Details.   In contrast to reading for a general understanding, when you read for specific details you search for particular kinds of information. For example, one of our students, a psychology major, was writing a research paper on the research techniques used in studying problem solving. She focused on protocol analysis, a technique in which test subjects talk aloud as they think through a problem. Specifically, she wanted to know how many subjects had been used for protocol analysis techniques. So she read articles looking for the sample size, trying to determine the number of people used in different studies. Another student, an environmental health major, was developing a research paper on techniques to control radon gas, the radioactive gas that can be found in houses; some scientists believe that it may cause between 20,000 and 30,000 deaths annually from lung cancer. She searched the literature looking for techniques to reduce radon; she also wanted to learn how to estimate the amount of radon reduction that would result from each technique. When she first read the articles, she looked for the different techniques, such as sealing cracks in the foundation, adding ventilation systems, and installing air-to-air exchangers. Then she looked for specific estimates of radon reduction using each technique.

The message behind these students' experiences is this: Let the question driving your paper and your knowledge of the subject influence what you read when looking for specific details. In many cases you need not read an entire article.

Reading to Find Other Sources.   As you read any material, always look for information that will lead you to other literature. When reading popular publications and trade magazines, note the names of any researchers, specialists, or titles of books, articles or other literature that might be useful for further digging.

When reading through the scholarly literature, look carefully at the references, bibliographies, and literature cited. Such a check often identifies sources that you might not find in your library search. Another useful way to identify potentially valuable sources for your paper is to let one article lead you to other sources. Note in which journals other articles on the topic were published; check them, and you are on your way to finding additional, useful information.

Read Different Subjects in Different Ways

Scientific and technical articles that report the findings of a study are often organized functionally: (1) Title and authors, (2) Abstract, (3) Introduction — literature review and the research questions, (4) Methodology — how the researchers gathered the information, (5) Results — tables or figures and major findings, (6) Discussion — implications of what the research means and its relation to other studies, and (7) Conclusions. Different publications label the sections differently.

To read such articles, scan the title, read the abstract, and study the conclusions. Then ask, "What was the purpose? What was the method? What are the key findings?" Your answers should tell you whether or not you need to read the full article. If you decide to read the full article, read the introduction, with its literature and research questions, carefully. Then ask, "What was the researcher's rationale for the study? What was the key question addressed? Why did the research address this question?"

When you read the methods, ask, "How did the researcher collect the data/information? What limitations, if any, did the researcher impose on the project?" Before you read the entire article, review the research question and look at the tables and figures. Then ask, "What would I conclude from the data?" Then read the results and ask, "What did the researcher find? Do I agree with the findings? Why or why not?"

When you read the discussion, remember that researchers are interpreting their data based on their prior knowledge of the subject, the limitations of the study, and their findings. So ask, "How did the researchers interpret the results? What meaning did the research put on the findings?" Some researchers speculate about future studies and suggest additional points that need investigation. Finally, read the conclusion, and ask, "What are the major findings? Does the author place any limitations on the data? Does the author make any recommendations concerning future studies?"

Read with a Questioning Attitude

Whatever you read, read with a questioning attitude. Just because something is in print does not make it accurate, true, or real. Always question sources and evaluate them carefully. As a starting point, ask

Who produced the publication?

What is the source of a publication's content?

Consider each question more closely.

Who Produced the Publication?   Publishers influence their publications by setting editorial policy and by selecting the editors and writers. Spend a few minutes reading a recent issue of each of three newspapers: *The New York Times*, *The Christian Science Monitor*, and *The National Enquirer*. Speculate on the reasons for the topics covered in each source, the different depth of coverage and treatment of the same item in the different papers, and the publisher's influence in each newspaper.

Scholarly publications are published by commercial publishers or professional societies. Such publishers often have editorial review boards and peer review systems that rigorously screen articles before they are printed. In the peer review process, researchers submit copies of their articles to a publication's editor. That editor then sends copies of the article (without the author's name) to other researchers known for their expertise in the subject matter. Based on their specialized backgrounds, these researchers then review the theoretical development and content of the article, the research methods, the findings, the inferences drawn, and the quality of the writing. As a result, many articles are rejected and most of the others are rewritten before they are published.

Many major book publishers practice a similar peer review process. In college textbook publishing, for example, the acquisition editor asks other professors to review manuscripts following selected guidelines. Many texts undergo several critical reviews and numerous revisions before the book is published.

What is the Source of the Publication's Content?   Whenever you review a publication, ask yourself, ''What is the basis or foundation of the information presented?'' Does the information come to the authors from reviewing other literature? making observations? interviewing other people? In all cases, determine whether the information reported is fact or inferences.

Consider the following. In spring 1988, a Mississippi preacher called for the resignation of the producer of Mighty Mouse animated cartoons and the vice-president of CBS's children's programming division. The preacher, Rev. Donald Wildmon, observed an April 23, 1988, episode in which Mighty Mouse reached under his cape, pulled something out, sniffed it, and regained his normal posture. Rev. Wildmon claimed Mighty Mouse was sniffing cocaine. The cartoon's creator, Ralph Bakshi, said his hero was sniffing flowers (Associated Press, June 10, 1988).

When you critically read literature, look carefully for the facts and the inferences based on those facts. And keep in mind that inferences vary with individuals' backgrounds.

Take Notes Carefully

Two philosophies emerge on the subject of taking notes. One argues that you should read the materials in the library, assess their potential value, and take the needed notes on your first reading. You photocopy your sources only when you live far from the library, plan to use a table, illustration or other detailed data, cannot check out the references, or have another compelling reason (Zimmerman and Clark 1987). The other philosophy argues that you find the article, scan its contents, and assess its potential. If the piece looks promising, you photocopy it. Later, you carefully reread the material, think critically about it, and make any needed notes. Proponents of the second philosophy argue that you may not know the value of literature until you are well into the project. Thus, taking detailed notes too early wastes time because you may not need the item. They also argue that you may have to retrace your steps to the library and look up the material again, so why not photocopy and file it to save time and effort later?

Further, they argue that you need a copy in order so to check details and assess content more carefully. Of the two philosophies of note-taking, the first appears more common in the humanities, the second in scientific and technical fields.

When you photocopy material, add the complete citation to the first page of your photocopy: author, date, publication, publisher, location, page numbers, and other relevant information that is needed for bibliography cards (Figure 3-2) and full citations. If you are copying several articles, staple or clip all the pages of each article together. When you have several sources, do not shuffle and mix pages or you will have problems later.

As far as the form goes, some students use standard note cards, other students use half sheets or full sheets of 8½ × 11 paper for notes, and a few now take notes directly on disk while working on their personal computers. Some students write out their notes longhand, while others type them. When you prepare notes, be sure to retain a reference to your bibliographic card for each note card you use (Figure 6-1). If you have been able to identify subtopics, you can put only one or two key ideas related to a specific subtopic on a card, sheet of paper, or computer screen, then you can shuffle and rearrange your cards as you organize your research materials.

Lap-top computers will help taking notes in the library too. With such a unit, you can enter your notes directly onto disk and print out them later on note cards.

When reviewing literature, keep your purpose in mind and take notes as needed to help you when you begin writing. As you take notes, try to paraphrase or summarize your sources. Include quotations from the original selectively.

Paraphrasing.   Paraphrasing involves rephrasing a short section of text in your own words, following the order in which the ideas occur in the original text. When writing, always credit your paraphrased passages with the appropriate bibliographic citations — footnotes, endnotes, author-date references — for the style you are following even though the words are your own. When you are paraphrasing a passage, Crews and Schor (1985, 467) suggest that you keep the same order of ideas and level of details; Whitten, Horner and Webb (1990) suggest that your recast should be about the same length as the original. Always use your own words and credit your source.

Summarizing.   Summarizing means putting someone's ideas into your own words, without following the original order of ideas. It is possible to summarize an entire essay or an entire book in a few paragraphs. Generally, you summarize when you need to boil information down to its essentials. You do so because the original is not succinctly written, is poorly written, is too long to quote, or because you can more effectively summarize the material in your own words. When summarizing any text, read through the passage and then ask yourself the following questions:

Locke, Spirduso, & Silverman (1987)

p. 21 LS&S suggest short, "gentle introduction," that uses general terms, but prepares readers for the detailed accounts that follow."

p. 21. "... The trick in these opening paragraphs of the introduction is to sketch the study in bold strokes of major constructs without usurping the function of the more detailed sections that follow."

FIGURE 6-1   A Sample Content Note Card

What are the author's main points?

What information do you need?

What material can you delete and still make your point?

How can you best summarize the information? (Zimmerman and Clark 1987)

A careful reading, as suggested earlier, can help you summarize. If you are reviewing an article or report that covers an empirical study, read the abstract, summary, and conclusion carefully, and then ask yourself the following questions:

What are the study's findings?

What methodology was used? (In other words, how were the data/information gathered?)

Did the author note any limitations?

Did you note any additional limitations?

What information is relevant to your project?

Think over the questions and give answers in your own words. Try to summarize and boil down the information to only the essentials that you need to make your points. If you talk aloud, you often summarize the information you learned.

Quoting Sources.   Sometimes you will want to use only a quotation or a portion of a quotation from your source. If you want to use only a portion of a quote, try to incorporate the quote into your paraphrase or summary. Indirect quotes are really summaries or paraphrases of what someone said. For example, Locke, Spirduso, and Silverman (1987,16) point out that proposals function as communications, plans, and contracts (Figure 6-1). When using direct or indirect quotes, work carefully to make sure that you do not misquote your sources. A photocopy of the original helps so you need not recopy your notes again when writing your paper.

Different disciplines use information in different ways. Look carefully at the literature in the humanities and you will see that authors often use more and longer direct quotes than in the scientific literature. In the scientific and technical literature, writers depend heavily on paraphrasing, summarizing, and boiling the information down to a sentence or two. If you are writing a research paper in the humanities, study carefully how the literature you are reviewing uses quotes. Likewise, if you are writing a research paper in the sciences, study carefully how authors handle quotes in their articles. If you expect to be quoting material directly, be sure to include quotations on your note cards.

CONSIDERING ETHICAL AND LEGAL ISSUES: PLAGIARISM AND COPYRIGHT

When you are developing research papers, careful note-taking can help you avoid committing plagiarism and violating the copyright law. Plagiarism entails taking someone else's intellectual work — ideas and creativity — and presenting it as your own (Drum 1986, 241; Zimmerman and Clark 1987, 374; Whitten, Horner, and Webb 1990). Sometimes, the plagiarist violates the Federal Copyright Law.

Some people plagiarize out of ignorance; some plagiarize deliberately. Under pressure to finish an assignment, individuals may take another person's work, retype it, fail to credit their source, and claim the work as their own. Still others change a word here, a word there, recast a phrase, alter the presentation order, or massage the original in some way, and then suggest the work represents their effort. In doing so, they cheat themselves out of a chance to learn, to think, and to grow intellectually.

What is plagiarism? While working on another book, coauthor Don Zimmerman uncovered a potentially plagiarized piece. A friend gave him a photocopy of a short, humorous critique of selected phrases from scientific writing. The piece, supposedly written by a student in a professional major, had appeared in a student magazine in the early 1980s. Don thought the student's piece would lighten his book, so he telephoned the author, whom we'll call "Sam." He asked if Sam would be willing to give permission to use his article. "Gladly," Sam agreed, "But do credit me and give me a copy of your book."

Some four months later one of Don's students, Linda, handed him a photocopy of a humorous piece on science writing. She had obtained her photocopy while working as an intern at a major corporation in a Southern state. Don instantly recognized the similarity to Sam's work. Linda's photocopy credited C. D. Graham, Jr., writing in *Metal Progress*, (1957), a trade magazine, as its source (Graham 1957, 75–76). After class Don rushed back to his office to compare Linda's photocopy with Sam's article. Compare these excerpts yourself:

Sam's 1980s copy:

It has long been known . . . I didn't look up the original reference.

Metal Progress 1957 copy:

It has long been known that . . . I haven't bothered to look up the original reference.

Sam's 1980s copy:

Thanks are due to Joe Blotz for assistance with the experiment and to George Frink for valuable discussions. . . . Blotz did the work and Frink explained to me what it meant.

Metal Progress 1957 copy:

Thanks are due to Joe Glotz for assistance with the experiments and John Doe for valuable discussions. Glotz did the work and Doe explained what it meant.

Not only did the wording of several of Sam's items appear similar to those in the 1957 *Metal Progress* piece, but the ordering of entries appeared similar, too. The statistical probability of Sam ordering his entries in the same order as the *Metal's Progress* piece is 1 chance in 7 million. Neither piece appeared in Don's final book.

Often those who deliberately plagiarize think their readers will not recognize their act. Surely, they tell themselves, no one will spot their little deed among the millions of articles, reports, books, and other documents. But almost certainly others will eventually learn they have plagiarized. Once the deed is uncovered, action follows swiftly. Plagiarized pieces may lay hidden for decades only to emerge later in a person's career.

In the 1988 presidential campaign, Senator Joseph Biden's character came into question some 23 years after he had reportedly plagiarized five pages from a law review while he was a first-year law student (Kraus, Clifton, Fineman, and McCormick 1987). News reporters then carefully followed Biden's speeches and checked the accuracy of his content and the extent of his borrowing phrases and ideas from others without attribution (Kraus, Clifton, Fineman, and McCormick 1987). Biden soon dropped out of the presidential race.

University and college policies on punishing plagiarism, a form of academic dishonesty, vary widely among campuses, ranging from flunking the assignment through dismissal from school. Off campus, when found out, the plagiarized deed results in a loss of credibility, damaged careers, and possible loss of jobs.

Keep good, detailed notes; know from where you developed your ideas and credit those sources fully; and make sure your notes include full, adequate, and accurate citations. If you are unsure about whether to cite a source, do so; it is better to err by providing too many citations than too few.

Often you will face a dilemma when trying to determine whether to credit an idea. That is where reading widely and a thorough literature review can help. Are the ideas widely known and held in common among professionals in a particular field? Do the same ideas emerge time and time again? If so, you might use the idea without crediting the source, but it is a judgment call that you'll need to make. To be safe, credit your sources. As already noted, paraphrasing and summarizing provide two ways to use other authors' ideas and avoid plagiarism — if they are handled carefully and credited fully. Paraphrasing requires putting the original author's ideas in your own words in a passage of about the same length. In contrast, summarizing requires boiling the original ideas down to a limited number of words. But remember: paraphrasing and summarizing require citations.

Copyright: The Legal Issues

If you plan to use copyrighted materials in a research report that will be published in a journal, magazine, book, thesis, dissertation, or other publication, you must seek permission from the copyright holders.

Interpretations vary. For example, the student edition of the *MLA Handbook*, specifically cautions students,

> In quoting in a work intended for publication — a thesis or dissertation, but *not* a term paper — the writer must be fully aware of the copyright law and the needed permission to reproduce materials from some sources (Gibaldi and Achtert 1980, 138–39).

Major style manuals and publishers' guidelines vary on word counts and other criteria that determine when you should seek permission to use copyrighted materials. But most agree that lengthy quotes or the use of a major portion of copyrighted texts, tables, figures, or similar illustrations require obtaining permission and crediting the sources. For materials in the public domain, you need not obtain permission, but you should credit your sources. Webster's *Standard American Style Manual* (1985, 302) explains public domain:

> Material in the public domain includes, but is not limited to, works published before the twentieth century and also public records and federal and state government publications.

Study the appropriate style manuals and carefully apply their guidelines when using copyrighted material.

The notion of copyright emerged over the centuries to protect the property rights of those who produced creative works. The Copyright Act of 1976 established copyright as a federal law and extended these rights to written documents, software, photographs, tables, figures, illustrations, music, recorded performances, software programs, books, magazines, journals, and other publications. The law groups works into

> Literary works;
>
> Music works, including any accompanying words;
>
> Dramatic works, including any accompanying music;
>
> Pantomimes and choreographic works;
>
> Pictorial, graphic, and sculptural works;
>
> Motion pictures and other audiovisual works;
>
> Sound recordings (François, 1982, 682).

Keep in mind that copyright covers the *form* of the presentation, not ideas or facts. Consider the basic introductory textbooks in psychology, sociology, economics, or composition. Your instructors review dozens of similar books before selecting the texts for their courses. The texts usually include similar content and ideas, but the organization, format (page design, typefaces, and layout), as well as presentation style, wording, and other specifics vary widely.

The 1976 Act protects the creators' rights to their work. When individuals create something, they own it. For works created after January 1, 1978, the Copyright Law carries protection for the life of the creator, plus 50 years. The companies can copyright such materials for 75 years from publication date.

The 1976 Act protects creators' efforts and enables copyright holders to receive money — economic gain — if a commercial market exists for their efforts. And commercial markets do exist for copyrighted works. For example, *Time* (1988) reported that the song *Happy Birthday to You* generates some $1 million in royalties annually for its copyright owners, the Birch Tree Recording Group.

François (1982, 681) explains coverage for older copyrighted materials:

> For works created prior to January 1, 1978, the initial twenty-eight year protection remains in effect, but the new law in most instances extends the renewal period to forty-seven years (for a total of seventy-five years' protection) instead of a maximum forty-six years' protection.

Once the copyright period expires, works go into the public domain; they may be used without permission.

How Do You Register Materials?

Under the 1976 Law, you need not copyright the work. However, registering for copyright clearly establishes a work as the creators' property and fixes the date of its creation. Should creators not register the work, proving that they created the work may be difficult.

A work qualifying for registration must be original and in a fixed tangible medium, such as print, electronic recording, photographic or other visual technique. It must also carry the date and a copyright notice. The copyright notice itself may take one of three forms: © (the letter C in a circle); the word "Copyright" or the abbreviation "Copr."; for phonorecordings, the form is the letter P in a circle, ℗ (Zimmerman and Clark 1987, 369).

Registering a copyright requires writing to the Copyright Office, U.S. Library of Congress, Washington, D.C. 20559, and requesting the appropriate forms. Formal registration entails filling out the forms and sending them, the registration fee ($10 in 1989) along with two copies of the published work. The copyright office then registers the work and returns the completed forms to the creator.

Can You Use Copyrighted Materials?

You use copyrighted materials under three provisions: (1) "Fair use," (2) Copying, and (3) Obtaining permissions or licensing. The 1976 law spells out some provisions and provides other general guidelines enabling the courts to determine the permissible use of copyrighted materials.

The Copyright Act does not clearly define fair use, but focuses on (1) the nature of the use — whether to make a profit or for nonprofit or educational purposes, (2) the nature of the work used in relation to the whole, (3) the amount of the work used, and (4) the impact of the use upon the potential market or value of the copyrighted work (CBE Style Manual Committee 1983; 17 USC 107; University of Chicago 1982, 115). The law acknowledges fair use of a copyrighted work; uses that are not infringements of copyright include: criticism, comments, news reporting, teaching, scholarship and research. The law leaves the detailed interpretation of fair use up to the courts.

Your use of copyrighted works for many common assignments usually falls under fair use. As of January 1989, no one has brought suit against a student for infringement of copyright for using copyright materials as part of classroom assignments (Drechsel, personal communication, 1989).

Photocopying machines abound in university and college libraries and by their presence they provide ample opportunity for photocopying materials. The copyright law acknowledges teaching, scholarship, and research as examples of fair use but it leaves vague the issue of reproducing copyrighted works. François (1982,691–692) reported on an ad hoc committee on Copyright Law Revision of education associations along with representatives of the Authors League of America and the Association of America Publishers, Inc. developed photocopy guidelines. Specifically, Francois reported that ''in their professional work teachers or research scholars can make or use a single copy, without charge, of:

A chapter from a book

An article from a periodical or newspaper

A short story, short essay, or short poem

One chart, graph, diagram, drawing, cartoon, or picture from a book, periodical, or newspaper (1982, 692).

CONCLUSION

This chapter has provided the basics of library research and has suggested ways to help you read critically and take notes carefully. Not only will you use these basics for gathering information for literature review research reports (Chapter 14) but in many disciplines you will combine library research with one of the other research methodologies covered in the chapters on writing original research reports (Chapter 15) thesis statement research reports (Chapter 16) and problem-solving research reports (Chapter 17).

Even though your discipline may not rely heavily on a particular methodology, you might want to read about that methodology anyway. Sometimes research tools from other fields can help researchers to develop creative insights into their own topics.

CHAPTER 7

Gathering Information Through Writing Letters

This chapter presents a simple but powerful strategy for gathering information for research projects in all fields — writing letters to appropriate sources. The chapter first explains what kinds of literature can be acquired through correspondence, then details how to write those letters, and finally suggests how you can become a more effective letter-writer. The chapter includes

an overview of the kinds of information available,

strategies for determining whom to address your letter to, and

advice about what your finished letter should look like.

WHAT IS AVAILABLE?

Private businesses, government agencies, universities and colleges, associations, institutes, and other organizations produce thousands of pieces of informative literature annually. One way of organizing this vast amount of information was presented by Professor Thomas N. Trazyna of Seattle Pacific University; he divided organizations and their methods into 16 categories (Trazyna, 1986) as illustrated in Table 7-1.

TABLE 7-1   Types of Organizations and Their Publication Methods

1. *Inventors, Small Firms*
   internal reports
   patents
   new reports
2. *Corporations*
   internal reports
   proposals
   publications for sale
   patents
3. *Small Publishers*
   reference books
   catalogues
   specialty newsletters
4. *Large Publishers*
   trade lists
   internal publications
   journal management offices
5. *Lobbies/Professional Associations*
   membership publications
   trade publications
   convention reports
   position papers
6. *Charities/Churches*
   newsletters
   newspapers, annual reports
   magazines
   commission reports
7. *Foundations*
   publishing offices
   annual reports
   catalogues
   information offices
   project reports
8. *Think Tanks* (companies such as RAND, SRI, MITRE, etc.)
   internal reports
   articles, books
   publications for sale
9. *University Departments*
   internal reports
   articles, books
   funded research projects

10. *University Research Centers*
    journals
    monograph series
11. *Federal Government*
    reports
    books
    minutes
    newspapers
    catalogues
    data bases
    contract reports
    information centers
    specialized libraries
    research centers
12. *State Governments*
    Similar to federal government in range and complexity
13. *Local Governments*
    reports
    newspapers
    newsletters
    manuals
    minutes
14. *Extra-Governmental and Quasi-Governmental Agencies*
    reports
    newsletters
    books
    information offices
    conference proceedings
    suggested legislation
15. *Regional Governments* (regional water, transit, and power agencies)
    reports
    annual reports
    membership lists
16. *International Government* (United Nations Agencies, Treaty Associations, Common Market, World Court, etc.)
    range of publications similar to U.S. Federal Government

Source: Thomas N. Trayzna, "Research Outside the Library," *College Composition and Communication* 37, 2 (1986): 217–23. Copyright 1986 by the National Council of Teachers of English. Reprinted by permission.

The available information includes news releases, patents, proposals, reports, books, papers, articles, and other publications. Organizations develop many of these publications for both internal and external use; you can often obtain them with a simple letter of request. Organizations will, however, be unwilling or unable to give you certain specific kinds of information. For example, do not expect private businesses to provide information about their product development, their market research, or personal information about their employees.

In contrast, government and private organizations will usually provide all but classified information, if they have the information readily available. But seldom will they devote extensive time to collecting data for you because of limited staff for such efforts.

TO WHOM DO YOU ADDRESS YOUR LETTER?

Most libraries have a selection of *Who's Who*s and other professional directories that usually list individuals' addresses. An alternative strategy is to review the telephone directories kept by your library. Many directories have not only organizations' street addresses, but many also include a map showing the zip codes for the community. Thus, a careful check of the telephone directory can produce the complete address. Other printed resources for addresses include trade, business, and organizational directories.

If you're not sure where to start looking for names and addresses, review these directories: *Directory of Directories*, *Directory of Information Services*, *Guide to American Directories*. As their names suggest, these directories provide the tool for locating other, more specific directories and information sources on business and commercial firms.

Across the country, many organizations publish area directories. For information linked to a specific region or locale, look for local, state, and regional directories covering business and manufacturing. In some cases the publishers may be commercial firms; in other cases, universities and government agencies publish directories. For example, the University of Maryland Library's information pamphlet, "Industry and Corporation Directories," lists the following:

> *Metropolitan Washington, D.C. Manufacturers Directory*
> *Directory of Maryland Manufacturers*
> *Directory of Women-Owned Businesses: Baltimore-Washington Area*

Depending upon the directory, you can find such information as names, addresses, size of organization, number of employees, kind of products or services, and much more. You can often find similar directories for many regions, states, and localities. Check the library's card catalog or online computer system; if you can't find help, ask your librarian.

Finding Names and Addresses

Periodically some government agencies publish information guides and directories to their units and employees. Libraries may have copies of such directories and information guides. If not, call the government agency and ask for the directory you need.

Some specialized directories include information about individual employees or members.

Businesses and Organizations.   If you are interested in finding names and addresses of people in nation-wide businesses and organizations, check national directories such as:

Directory of Corporation Affiliations
Million Dollar Directory
Dun & Bradstreet
Standard & Poor's Register of Corporations
Directors and Executives
Trade Names Directory

Specialized Directories.   Periodically, many associations, groups, and other organizations publish membership directories. Here's a brief list of such specialized directories:

Business Organizations and Agencies Directory
Conservation Directory
Encyclopedia of Associations
Gale's Directory of Publications
Polk's World Bank Directory: North American Edition
Sheldon Retail Directory of the United States and Canada
The Foundation Directory
Literary Market Place

Directories of Individuals.   Several directories list names and biographical data on professionals:

American Men and Women of Science
Who's Who in America
Who's Who in Art
Who's Who in Banking
Who's Who in Canada

Who's Who in Ecology
Who's Who in Engineering.

To find background information on a specific individual, first determine in which directory to search and then find the specific name. If you know the professional field under which an individual's name might be listed, check your library's card or online catalog for biographical directories in that professional area. When you find a directory, check it for the individual's name. If that approach does not work, consider using a commercial electronic search of the biographical directories. For example, the *Biography Master Index* lists some 3 million references to biographical information in some 700 biographical directories (Directory of Online Databases 1989).

WHAT SHOULD THE LETTER OF REQUEST FOR INFORMATION LOOK LIKE?

You will find that letters are more effective if they: identify key people by name and title; use a professional-looking format; include key information; use a personal style; and allow the respondent time to reply. The following sections give you some strategies to use for each of these important components of gathering information by letter writing.

Identify and Write Key People by Name and Title

Carefully written letters to public relations specialists and subject matter specialists in government agencies, businesses and industries, and other organizations usually produce current information on many topics. Whether you are writing to the public relations department or seeking information from a specialist, your letter often receives quick response if you write to a specific person by name.

When you review literature, be alert to names, organizations, and addresses. When you encounter them, write them down. If you can't obtain the name and address from the literature, check your library for professional and organizational directories, or call the organization or business.

When writing, address the receiver appropriately as Mr., Mrs., Ms., or Dr. You can also use Professor, Director, Chair, Coordinator, Supervisor, or another appropriate occupational title. Use such occupational titles to avoid the problem of trying to figure out whether some names, such as Dale, Carol, and Marion are male or female.

Use a Professional-Looking Format

Used properly, the letter format and layout suggest a serious, interested inquirer. Used sloppily, they suggest an individual who doesn't care. So use a standard business letter format such as the block style (page 100) or the semiblock style (page 101). The block style does not use paragraph indentions and eases your typing task. The semiblock style uses indented paragraphs and the return address, complimentary close, and signature blocks on the right.

For your letters, use a good 20-pound bond weight white paper and standard # 10 business envelopes, 4⅛ by 9½ inches. Don't use erasable bond papers, because ink smears and smudges easily on them. Type your letter or compose it on a personal computer and then print it on a letter-quality or laser printer. Make sure the type is dark, bold, clear, and easy to read.

Use Standard Postal Zip Codes

To speed your letter on its way, use the U.S. Postal Service's standardized state abbreviations and the appropriate zip codes. Some organizations now use the long nine-digit zip codes. If they are available, use them.

Here are the standard state abbreviations:

State	Abbr.	State	Abbr.
Alabama	AL	Montana	MT
Alaska	AK	Nebraska	NE
Arizona	AZ	Nevada	NV
Arkansas	AR	New Hampshire	NH
California	CA	New Jersey	NJ
Colorado	CO	New Mexico	NM
Connecticut	CT	New York	NY
Delaware	DE	North Carolina	NC
Dist. of Columbia	DC	North Dakota	ND
Florida	FL	Ohio	OH
Georgia	GA	Oklahoma	OK
Hawaii	HI	Oregon	OR
Idaho	ID	Pennsylvania	PA
Illinois	IL	Rhode Island	RI
Indiana	IN	South Carolina	SC
Iowa	IA	South Dakota	SD
Kansas	KS	Tennessee	TN
Kentucky	KY	Texas	TX
Louisiana	LA	Utah	UT
Maine	ME	Vermont	VT
Maryland	MD	Virginia	VA
Massachusetts	MA	Washington	WA
Michigan	MI	West Virginia	WV
Minnesota	MN	Wisconsin	WI
Mississippi	MS	Wyoming	WY
Missouri	MO		

A SAMPLE LETTER IN BLOCK FORMAT

Sam Jones
2525 Overlook Road
State College, PA 16801

September 15, 1992

Dr. Sam Jones, Director
Radon Research Laboratory
U.S. Department of Energy Laboratories
Denver, CO 80666

Dear Dr. Jones:

In preparation for a term paper that I am writing for my environmental health class here at Pennsylvania State University, I
learned that your laboratory has been investigating alternative
air exchangers to reduce radon levels in homes.

From a news article, apparently based on a news release from
your laboratory, I learned that you were to have completed your
tests as of July 1, 1991. Has your laboratory completed its
testing and technical report on the research results?

If so, would you please provide me a copy of your report by
November 1? If not, do you have any preliminary results that
you can share with me? In that way I can use your information
as I draft my paper the week of November 15-22.

Thank you for your help.

Sincerely,

Bill Murray

A SAMPLE LETTER IN SEMIBLOCK FORMAT

Sam Jones
2525 Overlook Road
State College, PA 16801

September 15, 1992

Dr. Sam Jones, Director
Radon Research Laboratory
U.S. Department of Energy Laboratories
Denver, CO 80666

Dear Dr. Jones:

In preparation for a term paper that I am writing for my environmental health class here at Pennsylvania State University, I have learned that your laboratory has been investigating alternative air exchangers to reduce radon levels in homes.

From a news article, apparently based on a news release from your laboratory, I learned that you were to have completed your tests as of July 1, 1991. Has your laboratory completed its testing and technical report on the research results?

If so, would you please provide me a copy of your report by November 1? If not, do you have any preliminary results that you can share with me? In that way I can use your information as I draft my paper the week of November 15-22.

Thank you for your help.

Sincerely,

Bill Murray

Include Key Information

Effective letters begin with an opening paragraph that explains the purpose of the letter: for instance, a letter might begin by explaining that you are writing a research report on topic X. Your letter might then summarize what you have found about the topic and give your specific reason for writing. Next, you might include detailed, specific questions that take the reader's reaction into account.

A letter should not expect too much of the recipient. For example, do not write a general all-purpose letter such as the following:

```
I am doing a project on technical communication
for a technical writing class at X college or
university and I am wondering if you could give
me a list of important technical communication
articles.
```

Rather, to achieve results, an effective letter should be specific:

```
    As a student member of our department's
committee to consider establishing a technical
communication major at X university, I reviewed
your program's description in the Society of
Technical Communication's Directory of Programs
in Scientific and Technical Communication. Your
program interests us, and we would like to know
more about

1. How you manage to attract students to your
   program,
2. How you screen potential applicants, and
3. What qualifications you seek in professors
   to teach in your program.

To have our report ready for our College's Pro-
gram Review Committee on May 1, could we have
your response by April 1?
We appreciate any help you can provide.
```

General inquiries, such as the request in the first example, leave readers in a quandary. They feel obligated to answer their mail, but such letters carry telltale messages: (1) The writers do not know how to use the library, (2) the writers have not bothered to read any of the literature, (3) the writers have not sufficiently narrowed their research question, and (4) the writers are too lazy to do the work themselves. Answering letters takes time and in today's busy world, people do not care to respond to letters that communicate such messages.

People respond more positively to letters that contain definite questions, are addressed directly, and are focused on the topic. Write such focused letters and you will increase your chances of obtaining quick, clear responses. Such letters reflect well-conceived questions showing that you understand your subject, have reviewed the literature, and consider the addressee a knowledgeable person.

Use a Personal Style

When writing, speak simply, directly and personally. Write so the person addressed thinks of your letter as a polite request from a friend who needs a favor. Simple, direct writing helps carry your message and minimizes confusion. Further, direct writing helps you avoid a stuffy tone that carries an undesirable message.

Once you have a printed copy, check carefully for grammar, spelling, and format problems. If you detect any problems, redo the letter. That's where the word processor makes writing easy, since you need not retype the entire letter.

Give Your Recipient Time to Respond

Request information early in the term so you won't put undue pressure on the recipient of your letter and so that you will receive your answer in sufficient time to incorporate the information into your assignment. *Plan on a three to four week period between when you write your letter and when you receive a response.* If you don't receive a reply within three weeks, a polite follow-up letter often produces results.

CONCLUSION

You may be wondering how information collected from various sources can help your research project. Perhaps an example will illustrate the value of writing to appropriate sources early in the life of a project.

When Ed Carpenter needed information on how to reduce levels of household radon, a letter to the U.S. Environmental Protection Agency in Washington, D.C., brought him copies of the latest research reports — copies he could not obtain from his library's government publications collection. From reading those reports he found out about air-to-air exchangers — mechanical devices that exhaust polluted air, bring in fresh air, and save energy while significantly reducing radon levels.

In interviewing experts, Ed learned that NuTone manufactured one of the leading air-to-air exchangers. In trying to find information about the NuTone units, he called local heating and air conditioning suppliers, but none carried the units. One salesman told Ed that NuTone's headquarters was in Cincinnati. A trip to the library and a review of the Cincinnati telephone book (many libraries have telephone directories of major cities) produced Nutone's address and zip code. So Ed wrote the company's marketing division explaining his problem and asking for information on the company's air-to-air exchangers. Two weeks later Ed received the company's sales and technical literature on air-to-air exchangers.

The message is this: done well, carefully written and formatted letters can help you gather needed information; the information you gain by this method can supplement your other research methodologies.

CHAPTER 8

Planning, Conducting, and Analyzing Surveys

Over the years, social scientists — sociologists, psychologists, market researchers and others — have developed ways to enhance the survey process. This section capitalizes on their expertise and suggests practical ways to use surveys for research papers.

As an information-gathering technique, students and professionals in many different fields use surveys: A wildlife management major surveys homeowners around a lake to determine the lawn damage from grazing Canada geese; a sociology major develops a questionnaire to learn about college students' views on abortion issues; a recreation science graduate student surveys hikers planning trips into Yellowstone's back country. This chapter first provides an overview of surveys and then explains how to do the following:

plan the survey,

conduct the survey, and

analyze and interpret the survey data.

AN OVERVIEW: WHAT IS A SURVEY AND WHY SHOULD YOU USE ONE?

A survey is a process of collecting information from a group of people about a specific subject. The survey process consists of preparing a questionnaire, sampling the population, collecting the data, coding and analyzing the data, interpreting the results, and incorporating the findings into your research report.

Why do researchers conduct surveys? Surveys are used to learn about such things as people's attitudes, opinions, or knowledge of a topic. Politicians use surveys to gauge the public's position on political issues; educators use them to evaluate educational programs; health officials use them to assess public awareness of health issues; businesses use them to assess potential markets for products; and hundreds of organizations use surveys in day-to-day decision making and evaluation.

Before you prepare and conduct a survey, ask, "Will a survey provide the information I need?" At times, the information you need already exists. So begin by reviewing the literature on your subject and interviewing subject-matter experts. If you find you do need a survey, you will at least know something about the subject and can therefore develop a better survey.

PLANNING THE SURVEY

If you decide to do a survey, you need to answer the following questions:

1. What kind of survey will you use?
2. What do you want to learn as a result of doing the survey?
3. Who do you plan to survey?
4. How will you analyze your data?
5. How expensive will it be?
6. Do you need to seek permission to conduct the survey?

Thinking about such issues early minimizes problems later.

What Kind of Survey Should You Use?

Surveys fall into three kinds: (1) self-administered surveys, (2) telephone surveys, and (3) personal-interview surveys. Each has its advantages and disadvantages. For self-administered surveys, you give or mail the questionnaire to the respondents and ask them to fill it out. For telephone surveys, you call respondents and ask them questions over the telephone. For personal-interview surveys, you contact the respondents and ask them questions from the questionnaire in a face-to-face setting.

For many projects, you will find the self-administered questionnaire the quickest way to collect data. A class or group meeting often provides a useful setting for using a self-administered questionnaire. In such a meeting, you can easily survey 50 people in 30 minutes, but do keep limitations in mind. When you have a class or group complete a survey, you cannot generalize beyond the respondents' answers when you write your report.

An example of a specific survey may help you understand the benefits and the challenges involved in developing a good survey. Assume that you are using a survey to determine what homeowners know about radon — the radioactive gas that seeps into many homes and may cause 30,000 deaths from lung cancer annually. Assume further that you are collecting responses from 75 people attending a public meeting on radon control techniques. Remember that you can write *only* about the 75 people who attended the meeting and completed your questionnaire. You cannot generalize to all homeowners in your community. Why? You do not know if the people attending your meeting are similar to or different from other homeowners. They may be especially health conscious; they may be avid do-it-yourselfers; they may be better educated than most other homeowners; or they may have several or all of these characteristics.

If you want to generalize, consider sending a mail questionnaire to a *random sample* of the population you want to study. Random, in the statistical sense, means that each person in the population has the same probability of being selected for the survey — not an easy matter to work out. Even with a random sample, you must have a high response rate, so that you can generalize to the whole population. (The details of preparing a systematic random sample are presented in a later section of this chapter.)

Telephone surveys provide the opportunity to collect generalizable data too. They can be based on random samples, or they can be group-specific. By using telephone interviews, respondents do not need to read and fill out a questionnaire, response rates can be higher, and you can collect information from a widely dispersed population. When doing telephone surveys, try to complete all interviews within a week so that you can maintain a consistent approach to your topic. Be prepared to devote a large block of time to this task. If you plan a 20-minute telephone interview of fifty people, you can easily spend 20 to 30 hours collecting data. Disadvantages may emerge with telephone interviews, however. You may have trouble obtaining the telephone numbers of some individuals; the cost of long distance calls for widely dispersed respondents might be high; and some people will refuse to answer your questions.

Personal, face-to-face interview surveys provide an opportunity to probe deeply, ask more questions, and observe the respondent. But the disadvantages of face-to-face interview surveys include not finding people at home, in their offices, or at the interview site; respondents' refusals to be interviewed; and the time required to complete the interviews. For a 30-minute survey of 50 people, you could easily invest 50 or more hours collecting data.

What Do You Hope to Learn?

Before you begin drafting questions for your survey, write down your objectives — decide what you want to accomplish. When you are through, think about what kinds of decisions will you make as a result of the information you obtain. What kinds of data do you need to make those decisions? What kinds of conclusions might you draw? Will you be making any recommendations? Such an approach clarifies your thinking and tightens your focus on your problem.

In preparation for this book, Harcourt Brace Jovanovich conducted a national survey of professors who incorporated writing into their courses. The rationale was to determine the assignments given most often, how instructors wanted their students to gather information, and the problems the students encountered in completing the assignments. Selected objectives included

1. Identifying the courses using writing assignments and the kinds of written assignments that instructors use;
2. Ascertaining the diversity of requirements for the different kinds of written assignments;
3. Assessing the kinds of writing and information-gathering problems that students face and how instructors help their students overcome the problems.

The information gathered, along with data from literature reviewing, personal interviews, and telephone interviews helped shape this book. Clearly establishing your objectives gives you direction for your survey and keeps you on track for your research report. So write down your general objectives and then develop specific objectives from which you can draft your questions. Because of the complexity of writing questions, a later part of this chapter examines those problems.

Whom Will You Survey?

Two questions arise when you consider who you might survey:

1. What is your population?
2. Do you plan to conduct a census or to use a sample of the population?

What Is Your Population?   When you plan a survey, consider who you want to survey. Think about the characteristics of the people you would like to have answer the questions. If you would like to know what students at your school think about abortion issues, define the kinds of students you want to interview. Do you want to know about all students at your school? Only female students? Only male students? Only students of a specific religious denomination? Each group may give you different results. Remember too that the population you study depends upon all of your objectives, not just a few of them.

Do You Use a Census or a Sample?   Once you specify the population, consider whether you should conduct a census or sample the population. A census is a complete enumeration of all units — everyone — in the population. A census of a small, clearly defined group, such as those attending a particular class on a specified date, is possible. But suppose you wanted to survey students on a campus of 5,000 students.

A complete census would be demanding, time-consuming, and wasteful. Furthermore, you would not be able to contact all students because some would be on campus only an hour or two a week, others might have left school, and still others would not be at home when you tried to contact them. The major problem with a census thus centers on the issue that seldom, if ever, can you contact everyone in the population. As a result, you have no way of knowing if the students you missed would have answered your questionnaire differently from those that you interviewed. Thus, you could not generalize to the whole population. Finally, the cost in both time and money would be unrealistic.

By using a sample, you need not talk to everyone in the population. You can concentrate on interviewing a few people selected by either a purposeful or random sampling. For purposeful samples, you identify the desired characteristics and survey a limited number of people. Purposeful samples often provide specific insights into a population, but as with a census, you can neither generalize to a larger population nor determine the accuracy of your results.

When you want to generalize to a specified population, use a random sample. You can design your method of random sampling in various ways. One way is to conduct a systematic random sample. Assume that you can obtain a complete list of all 5,000 students enrolled at your school and that you want to survey 50 of them. Divide the size of the sample into the population to obtain a sampling interval; in this case 5,000 divided by 50, gives an interval of 100. Then using a table of random numbers from a standard statistics book, select a random number between one and 100.

Assume that the number is 78. It represents your starting point. Taking the list of 5,000 students, count to number 78. That student represents the first person to survey. Using an interval of 100, you would then pull the name, address and telephone number of every *kth* student; in our case, you would sample every 100th (kth) student name — numbers 78, 178, 278, and so forth — until you have 50 names. Standard statistics books detail other sampling methods.

When using a random sample, you can specify the sampling error, i.e., how closely your sample reflects the larger population. For example, the evening newscasts of the major television networks often report survey results. The announcer usually closes the news story by reporting a sample size and the survey's accuracy, such as, "In our national survey of 1255 registered voters, 49 percent favored candidate X and 50 percent favored candidate Y. Our survey was accurate within 3 percentage points." This means the actual percentages for the population are within plus or minus 3 percent of the reported percentages for 95 out of every 100 samples taken of that population.

Lists from which you sample can create problems. Assume that you want to survey bicycle riders on your campus. How would you sample bicycle riders? Does your campus require students and staff members to register their bikes? If so, you could ask the department handling the registrations to provide you with a list of registered bicycle owners. But does that include everyone who rides bicycles on campus? What about people who fail to register their bikes? Is the list current? Perhaps the clerks maintaining the list are months behind in entering names. These and other problems create so-called "dirty lists," incomplete or outdated lists of the population. When you use a list, make sure that it is complete, up-to-date, and accurate. If you use a less than ideal list, avoid generalizations.

Determining the sample size often turns out to be one of the more difficult decisions you will face. For creating purposeful samples, no clear guidelines emerge, but you should ask enough people to see if patterns emerge in the responses. Often a sample of only 15 to 25 people will begin to show similarities in their responses.

For random samples, the problem of guidance becomes more complex. Costs often become the limiting factor on determining sample sizes, but the sampling scheme, the kind of study and the potential attrition rate may also influence many researchers' decisions (Wimmer and Dominick 1987). Up to a point, larger sample sizes reduce the sampling error — the larger the sample, the more likely it is that responses will represent those of the entire population. But increasing the sample size often does not decrease the sampling error enough to offset the added costs.

To illustrate, assume you conduct a random survey of 25 students from your school and find that 45% favor abortion and 55% oppose abortion. The sampling error in this case is about 20%; this means that 45% $\pm$ 20% (25.2% to 64.8% of the population) favor abortion, while 55% $\pm$ 20% (35.2 % to 74.8% of the population) oppose abortion. If you sample 50 students and find the same 45/55% response, the sampling error drops to about 15%. Sample 100 students, and the sampling error drops to about 10%. Sample 250 students, and the sampling error drops to about 6%; sample 500 students, and the sampling error drops to about 5%; sample 1000 students, and the sampling error drops to about 2%. Not only does the sampling error change with the sample size, it changes with the percentage of responses to questions. A lengthy discussion of the issue goes beyond the scope of this text. To determine the sample size needed for your research, see a standard statistics text or check with a statistician.

How Will You Analyze Your Data?

Think about how you will analyze your data before you collect it. For small sample sizes (n = 25 to 50), you can hand-tabulate responses to a dozen questions, but if you add more questions, increase your sample size, or compare one group against the other, you will need to turn to computerized statistical packages. To find what is available on your campus, check with your computer center, computer laboratories, or the computer and statistics departments. Select programs that provide percentages (frequencies), cross tabulations (a comparison of one question against another), and other statistical tests. Common programs include the SPSS (Statistical Package for the Social Scientists) and SAS (SAS 1985; Norusis 1987).

How Much Will Your Survey Cost?

How much will it cost to conduct a survey? The answer depends upon the kind of survey, the length of your questionnaire, your sample size, and data analysis. Furthermore, some costs are fixed and others are variable. You can reduce the fixed costs by typing the questionnaire, coding your own data, and handling the data analysis yourself. You can control the variable costs by reducing questionnaire length, limiting the sample size, and restricting data analyses.

Plan to type questionnaires or typeset them with a desktop publishing system. If you don't have a personal computer, check with your company, school, or community for computer laboratories with word processing and desktop publishing facilities. Some schools often provide such services free, while some student centers or unions and commercial copy centers charge a minimal rental fee. Printing costs increase as you add questions to your questionnaire and increase your sample size. With careful planning and a short questionnaire, you might duplicate the questionnaire for only pennies per respondent.

To estimate costs, determine the number of pages for your questionnaire plus the cover or advance letters, and then estimate the number of people you plan to sample. Plan to print at least 10% more questionnaires than you need. For mail surveys, print twice as many questionnaires as you need, plus an additional 10%. Why? To obtain a high response rate, use three mailings: an initial questionnaire mailing, a follow-up postcard, and a second questionnaire mailing. Once you have determined the number of pages for your questionnaire and the number of questionnaires you need, obtain price estimates from local photocopying services or printers.

For mail surveys, postage adds another cost. To determine the mailing cost per questionnaire, prepare a packet: questionnaire, cover letter, and the stamped, addressed mailing and return envelopes. Weigh the packet. Then weigh the return envelopes and a completed questionnaire. To determine a mailing budget, add the mail costs of two packets, the return mail costs, the post card cost, and then multiply that figure by the sample size.

Beyond the questionnaire, the cost of telephone surveys includes the costs of sending respondents a letter about the survey in advance, the expense of telephone calls (local and long distance), and salaries for interviewers.

Do You Need Permission to Administer Your Survey?

Because of possible abuses of humans in scientific studies, many colleges and universities, and some private and public agencies, require that research involving humans be reviewed so that the research will not harm anyone. On many campuses, human subjects committees require students and professors alike to submit draft cover letters and questionnaires to them for review.

CONDUCTING THE SURVEY

An ideal survey would be one in which you clearly establish your objectives; obtain a clean, usable list; draw a random sample of appropriate size; develop and pretest the questionnaire; collect the data; generate a high response rate with a low sampling error; and then generalize back to the larger population. Of course, you will rarely have such an ideal setting for your research. You will find your funds and time limited. Further, populations may not be easily reached without major costs. Therefore, carefully consider your resources and available time, and proceed accordingly.

If you have a less-than-ideal setting, but one where, nonetheless, you can collect usable data, limit your generalizations when you write your report. Such surveys will produce interesting and enlightening results even though they are not comprehensive.

Survey research involves many steps. The researcher needs to do the following:

1. Develop appropriate objectives,
2. Check the survey design to avoid common pitfalls,
3. Order and arrange questions carefully,
4. Develop appropriate cover letters and advance letters,
5. Pretest the survey/questionnaire and letters, and
6. Produce and print the survey/questionnaire.

How Can You Develop Appropriate Objectives?

Begin by first considering your objectives and then specifying a list of detailed objectives. Ask, "What do I want to learn from this survey?" Keep in mind that surveys can give you respondents' information and misinformation on topics; their attitudes, opinions, perceptions, and viewpoints; and their past, present, and future, self-reported behaviors.

Think about the information you will need to write your report and make sure that your objectives will produce that information. Once you have the objectives, consider whether you want to ask open-ended or closed-ended questions. For open-ended questions, respondents answer the questions in their own words. For closed-ended questions, respondents select between the choices you provide.

On the Harcourt Brace Jovanovich survey of English professors, two subobjectives focused on (1) the need to know the kinds of writing problems instructors observed in their students, and (2) the strategies instructors used to help students overcome their problems. We used two open-ended questions:

What are the major writing problems that your students face?

_____

_____

What strategies have you found that help students overcome these problems?

_____

_____

Open-ended questions allow diverse responses, but summarizing the answers may become difficult and time consuming.

In our survey we designed closed-ended questions to ascertain other objectives: (1) How common computerized card catalogs were, (2) The number of students attending the selected schools, and (3) Instructors' perceptions about the importance of word processing skills. From these objectives emerged various questions, including the following one:

Does your library have a computerized card catalog?

_____ No   _____ Yes

Not only is this a closed-ended question, but it is a dichotomous question — one in which respondents have only two choices. In contrast, multiple-response questions would look like these:

About how many students are enrolled at your college or university?

_____ Under 4,999   _____ 5,000–7,499   _____ 7,500–9,999

_____ 10,000–14,999   _____ 15,000–19,999   _____ More than 20,000

How would you rate the importance of having word processing skills prior to students' taking your writing classes?

_____ Not at all important   _____ Not very important   _____ Important

_____ Very important   _____ Extremely important

Keep in mind that you need a range of responses so that you can begin to understand the variations within your population.

How Can You Avoid Common Pitfalls in Survey Design?

When you design your questions, be especially cautious about problems created by using words with multiple meanings, double-barrelled questions, leading questions, and questions with overlapping categories.

Avoid Multiple-Meaning Questions.   When drafting questions, select your words carefully and use language your respondents will understand. Keep in mind the respondents, their knowledge level, and the terms they use to describe the subject. For example, a survey on fishing might ask,

Some people fish for pike and others do not. Do you happen to fish for pike?

_____ Yes   _____ No

The problem centers on the word "pike." Different fishing enthusiasts call different species of fish "pike." So you would need to use a better term — walleye, northern pike, pickerel — or recast the question. Here, drawings could help distinguish between fish species.

For a survey of banking practices of students you might ask,

> Some respondents tell us they have written bad checks and others say they never have. Have you ever written a bad check?
>
> _____ Yes   _____ No

The problem centers on what constitutes a "bad check." To different people, it may mean, writing a check on an account with insufficient funds; writing a check on a closed account, or forging someone else's name to a check. Just because you are familiar with certain terms and define them in a particular way, do not assume that your respondents use them the way you do.

Avoid Questions that Create False Data.   When writing questions, consider whether your respondents have thought about the survey topic. Some people answer questions to be polite even though they have not thought about the topic. Consider:

> Under the Federal Communications Commission's fair comment ruling, television stations must give equal time to opposing sides on a political issue. Do you favor or oppose the ruling?
>
> _____ Favor   _____ Oppose

If this question were asked of the general population, few respondents would know of the ruling, and fewer yet would have thought about it. But they might have answered "favor" or "oppose" anyway. By asking such questions, you create false data. To minimize this problem, ask screening questions, such as

> Some people have heard of the Federal Communications Commission's fair comment ruling and other people have not. Have you heard of the ruling?
>
> _____ No   _____ Yes
>
> If yes, do you favor or oppose the ruling?
>
> _____ Favor   _____ Oppose

Avoid Double-Barrelled Questions.   Double-barrelled questions ask two questions at once. Suppose a survey of a gardening club's members asked,

> As a home gardener, do you use herbicides and pesticides?
>
> _____ Yes   _____ No

A respondent may use herbicides but not pesticides or may use pesticides but not herbicides. The question does not allow for such answers, and you cannot distinguish which question the respondent answered.

Avoid Leading Questions.   Leading questions telegraph, suggest, or tell the respondent how you would like them to answer a question. For example,

> Don't you favor the outlawing of trapping animals for their fur?
>
> _____ Favor   _____ Oppose

Not only is this a leading question, but some respondents have not thought about trapping animals, nor do they care.

Avoid Questions with Overlapping Categories.   Questions with numeral responses are prone to overlapping categories, such as

> How many students are enrolled at your college or university?
>
> _____ Under 5,000   _____ 5,000–7,500   _____ 7,500–10,000
>
> _____ 10,000–15,000   _____ 15,000–20,000   _____ More than 20,000

In rare circumstances when enrollments would fall exactly at 5,000, 7,500, 10,000, 15,000, or 20,000 students, respondents would not know which category to chose. So use responses with distinct categories:

> About how many students are enrolled at your college or university?
>
> _____ 4,999 and under   _____ 5,000–7,499   _____ 7,500–9,999
>
> _____ 10,000–14,999   _____ 15,000–19,999   _____ More than 20,000

How Should Questions be Ordered and Arranged?

Begin with general, non-threatening questions, move on to your main or key questions, and put the sensitive questions last. Sensitive questions include those about age, income, education, and other demographic characteristics. To determine possible sensitive subjects, interview a few members of the population that you will survey. Finally, check to make sure that questions early in the questionnaire do not supply respondents with answers to later questions.

In addition to determining the proper order of questions, make the physical layout — the arrangement of the questions on the page — easy to follow (see the sample questionnaire that follows). Clearly separate the questions and the response categories so that respondents will put their responses in the right places. Finally, make sure that the arrangement provides a logical flow.

A CLEAR, WELL-LAID-OUT QUESTIONNAIRE

Control Number 891-_____-_____

1. I'm currently a _____ Freshman _____ Junior _____ Sophomore _____ Senior _____ Grad _____ Other

2. My current major is _____

    2-a. (JT majors only): What is your concentration (option)?

    _____

    2-b. (JT non-majors only*):

    _____ Hoping to become a JT major

    _____ Undecided about becoming a JT major

    _____ Not planning to become a JT major

3. If you can, please estimate your present typing speed in words per minute: _____ Words per minute

4. Have you ever had any hands-on experience with a computer?

    _____ No (Go to Question 5.)

    _____ Yes (Go to Question 4a.)

    4-a. What kinds of things have you done with computers? Check as many as may apply:

    _____ Word processing

    _____ Data entry

    _____ Data analysis

    _____ Library searches

    _____ Game playing

    _____ Other: _____

    4-b. About how much time had you spent using computers for word processing? (Just give a reasonable estimate.)

    _____ None (Go to Question 5.)

    _____ A few hours at most

    _____ May be 10 to 30 hours

    _____ More than 30 hours, but under 50 hours

    _____ 50 hours or more

    4-c. How did you <u>mainly</u> learn word processing on a computer? (Check one response only):

    _____ Self-taught with manual

    _____ Taught by friend, co-worker, etc.

    _____ Took a specialized course or workshop in word processing

    _____ Learned in another course

    _____ Other: _____

*Technical Journalism.

How Can You Develop Effective Cover Letters and Advance Letters?

Cover letters and advance letters legitimize surveys and increase responses. Succinct, well-developed letters often overcome a respondent's reluctance to participate in a telephone, personal interview, or mail survey. Cover letters (see the sample on page 118) accompany mail and self-administered questionnaires and ask participants to help with the study. Cover and advance letters should tell potential respondents the salient points about the study, explain how their names were selected, promise confidentiality of responses, and encourage a quick response. Professional researchers usually use letterhead stationery and have a director or other official sign the letter. An advance letter also says that an interviewer will contact them within a week and seek their help with a study. Advance letters should arrive a few days before the interviewer telephones or knocks at the door.

How Should You Pretest the Questionnaire?

Once you have the questionnaire and letters polished, select one or two people who are knowledgeable on the subject and who have a good understanding of the target population. Ask them to read the letters and complete the questionnaires, and then ask them about their reactions to the questionnaire, including specific questions, and the cover or advance letter. Consider their comments and recast the questionnaire and letters as needed. Next select five or six people representative of the target population and administer the questionnaire. Then query them as you did the people in the first pretest. Correct any problems and repeat your pretests using the revised questionnaire.

If you plan to use a computer program to analyze your data, prepare the computer program, enter your pretest data, and make your computer runs. Thus you can debug the computer program and review the pretest data. By pretesting your data analysis, you need only replace the pretest data with your survey data and run the program.

What about Production Techniques?

A neat, clean-looking questionnaire makes the task look easier to the respondents, so invest the time to type your questionnaire neatly, or typeset it with a desktop publishing system. Whatever system you use, prepare a clean master and then have your questionnaire photocopied or printed, depending upon the number of questionnaires you need.

When printing your questionnaires, keep in mind that it is less expensive to have extra questionnaires printed on the first run than to have a second printing. Most likely, you will use the extra questionnaires when developing a code book (discussed in the next section), training interviewers, and coding data.

SAMPLE COVER LETTER

January 23, 1989

JT210 Students
Spring 1989

Department of Technical
Journalism
Fort Collins, Colorado 80523
(303) 491-6310 or 6319

Dear JT210 Student:

We are seeking your help to enhance the teaching of News-writing in the computer laboratory.

Specifically, we're conducting a study that will: (1) obtain a basic measure of your writing processes, grammar, and spelling; (2) find out how to best orient students to word processing and writing on computers; (3) assess how much you improve your writing, spelling, grammar, and mechanics during the semester.

We need your help. We would like you to volunteer for the next 45 minutes or so to complete a questionnaire. Your responses will in no way reflect on your grade and your answers will remain confidential.

If you're willing to take part in this study, please complete the attached questionnaire. If not, please let your instructor know, so you can proceed with an alternative classroom activity for the next 45 minutes or so.

We sincerely appreciate your help.

Sincerely,

Don Zimmerman
Professor

ANALYZING AND INTERPRETING SURVEY DATA

Wrapping up your project requires analyzing and interpreting the data. Be careful here, as little errors can create serious problems. You need to do the following:

1. Analyze your data and
2. Interpret your data.

How Should You Analyze Your Data?

Simple frequencies or percentages will serve well for small class projects (Table 8-1). In some cases you may want to compare students' responses to questions. For example, Table 8-2 shows the attitudes of respondents with and without computer and word processing experience.

A basic question centers on whether you should hand-tabulate your data or use a computer program. The answer depends upon the number of questions on the questionnaire, the number of respondents who completed usable questionnaires, and your research objectives. Generally, you can hand-tabulate questionnaires to obtain frequencies or percentages for a small number of responses and a short questionnaire. But when you need cross tabulations and a more sophisticated statistical analyses, you should use computer programs, such as SPSS or SAS. Some programs have good manuals, self-guided tutorials, videotapes, or other self-teaching materials. On many campuses computer departments, computer centers, and statistical laboratories offer classes, and consultants can help you with your problems. But before you can conduct the computer analysis, the data must be in a form the computer can analyze.

To prepare the data for computer analysis, convert the answers to a numerical code the computer can manipulate. Use the columns for the questions and one or more rows for each respondent's answers (Figure 8-1).

TABLE 8-1   Percentage of Students Reporting Computer Experience before Taking Basic News Writing in a Computer Laboratory

Kind of Computer Experience	Frequencies[a] (*n* = 118)
Word processing	35%
Data entry	15
Library searches	25
Game playing	75

[a]Some students had multiple computer experience.

TABLE 8-2   A Comparison of Attitudes toward Computers and
Word Processing

	Prior Word Processing Experience?[a]	
	Yes	No
Attitude item	(*n* = 85)	(*n* = 35)
Word processing will make writing easier.	2.25	3.75
Using word processing reduces spelling errors.	2.75	3.50
Using word processing reduces grammatical errors.	1.75	2.00
Learning word processing will help my career.	1.00	1.00
Learning word processing will be hard.	4.75	2.25
Learning to use a word processor will be fun.	2.50	1.75
I write very well.	2.00	1.50
I write better than most students at my grade level.	1.50	1.75
I make a lot of spelling errors when I write.	2.00	2.25
I make a lot of grammatical errors when I write.	2.00	2.25

[a]Respondents rated each item on a 1 to 5 scale, with 1 being "strongly agree" and 5 being "strongly disagree."

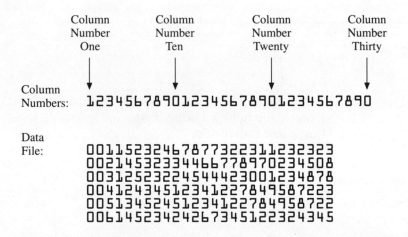

FIGURE 8-1   A Sample Coding File

Here is a question and its code book entry:

Questionnaire

25. Some respondents tell us they like using automated banking machines, while other respondents tell us they do not like using the machines. Would you say you strongly dislike, dislike, don't care, like, or strongly like using automated banking machines?
_____ Strongly dislike _____ Dislike _____ Don't Care
_____ Like _____ Strongly like

Code Book

Column   Question and response categories

Q. 25. Some respondents tell us . . . Would you say you strongly . . .
In column 50, code the number for the respective response.

50   1 = strongly dislike
              2 = dislike
              3 = don't care
              4 = like
              5 = strongly like
              8 = not applicable
              9 = not ascertained/no answer to question

If respondent Number 1 marked "strongly like," you would enter a 5 in column 50; if respondent Number 2 marked "strongly dislike," code a 1 in column 50. Figure 8-1 provides a sample code file. If some respondents do not answer a question, or if some questions are not applicable to some respondents, you need to add a coding scheme to handle the data. In the above case, 8 indicates not applicable and 9 indicates not ascertained. Some questions require two, three, or more columns for coding. In such cases, you need to adjust the coding scheme to fit the number of available columns.

The basic approach in coding data requires that you specify each variable (question), tell the computer what the columns and rows mean, and indicate the needed statistics. Begin data analysis with a listing from the code sheets; enter the data; and print out the data to check for missing items, missing codes, and other problems. Next run frequencies or percentages, and examine them. If desired, run a cross tabulation—i.e., tabulate one variable or question against another. Software manuals provide specifics for such procedures.

How Should You Interpret Your Data?

Once you have your frequencies, cross tabulations, and statistical tests, you can then interpret your results. But be careful; common interpretation errors include (1) overgeneralization of data, (2) false extrapolation, (3) disregard for dispersion, (4) inappropriately selecting cases, and (5) making technical errors.

Overgeneralization means making broad statements unsupported by your information. Suppose you used a random survey of freshmen and sophomores on your campus and you found that 75% prefer Brand A computers over Brand B personal computers for word processing. You cannot then simply generalize that all undergraduate students prefer Brand A computers over Brand B. Why? You did not survey juniors, seniors, and graduate students, nor did you survey students on other campuses.

False extrapolation means extending numerical values beyond the limits of your data. Suppose you conducted an experiment to see if intensive grammar review improves students' grammatical knowledge. Suppose you find that 2 hours of drill a week improves final test scores by 4%, 3 hours of drill a week improves final test scores by 6%, 4 hours a week by 8% and 5 hours a week by 10%. You cannot then say that 10 hours of drill a week would improve test scores by 20%. You would have made an inference beyond the limits of your data.

Disregard for dispersion means ignoring the range of responses. Assume that you are taking a criminology course and that your class has randomly surveyed students on your campus about capital punishment. When summarized, the survey results showed that 50% of all students support capital punishment. But a closer look at the data shows that the percentages of students favoring capital punishment were: 70% of the freshman, 60% of the sophomores, 50% of the juniors, 40% of the seniors, 30% of the graduate students. Clearly, reporting a simple 50% leads to a misinterpretation of the data.

Inappropriately selecting cases can lead you astray, too. Assume that you used a survey to collect data in an experiment that evaluated the impact of computerized grammar and spelling checkers on students' spelling and grammar knowledge. Let us say you tested students at the beginning and the end of the term. When reviewing data, you noticed that students who scored above 80% on the first test scored 95% on the second test. If you focus your discussion on students scoring 80% or above on the first test, you have inappropriately selected cases. Students scoring below 80% may or may not have improved as much as students scoring above 80% on the first test.

Technical errors (usually mathematical, data entry, or statistical errors) easily creep into data analysis. Thus you need to work carefully and check your work closely. As you conduct a survey you will begin data analysis and develop a feel for the data. Suppose you have surveyed students on your campus and your analysis shows your respondents averaged 35 years old. Only if your campus draws an unusually high percent of older students should such a figure emerge; so recheck your data carefully. A slip in coding, an error in the computer analysis, or other slips could have produced your false results.

When interpreting data, keep in mind that you are trying to determine what the data mean. Thus, you must make sense out of the numbers obtained. Careful interpretation begins with fully understanding your objectives, study design, sampling design, data analysis, and their limitations.

CONCLUSION

Survey research may be your primary research technique, or it may be just one of several data-gathering strategies you employ as you work on your research project. If you do use several research methodologies, using "triangulation," you look at your research questions from different research perspectives, thus assuring that you have a more comprehensive view of your topic. However you use them, surveys can be useful and powerful research tools.

CHAPTER 9

Strategies for
Effective Interviewing

Interviewing — a structured process of questioning others — provides a valuable technique for gathering information for research papers and other classroom assignments. Through interviews you can gather information that is not available through observation or by reading the literature; capitalize on people's knowledge, skills, and expertise; and ascertain opinions, attitudes, perceptions, and facts.

This chapter

explores the foundations of interviewing,

details the one-on-one personal interviewing process,

details the telephone interviewing process, and

suggests how to assess the information gained.

THE FOUNDATIONS OF INTERVIEWING

First, consider interviewing from a social perspective: people occupy different positions — professors, presidents, supervisors, college students, coaches, trash collectors, bicycle enthusiasts, and so on. By thinking about the positions people hold, the setting of the interview, and how the interaction might proceed, you can ask better questions, clarify responses, and reduce erroneous information.

When explaining interviewing, Professor Steven H. Chaffee, chair of Stanford's Department of Communication, says that certain expectations, problems, and conditions recur in each of three social categories — potentates, experts, and the general public (Chaffee 1975). Potentates include: administrators, presidents, chairpersons, politicians, supervisors, and others in power positions. Experts include: accountants, ornithologists, meteorologists, sculptors, pianists, engineers, and other subject-matter specialists. The public, in this context, are people without expertise on the subject matter of the interview.

Although Chaffee developed his concept to help budding journalists understand interviewing, it can also help you with your interviews. When preparing for an interview with potentates, Chaffee suggests that you prepare general questions to learn what is on the potentates' minds, because they often take control of the interview. Thus, your task becomes one of guiding the interview to produce the information you want.

Interviewing experts also calls for careful planning; you need to prepare structured and detailed questions. As you prepare your questions, learn the basic terminology in the expert's field. Learn enough about the subject so the expert does not need to explain the basics; for example, you would not want to ask a nutritionist to explain the basic food groups.

When interviewing the general public, take time to explain the reason for including them in your research. People are more likely to take your questions seriously if they feel their answers matter. Also, always adjust your approach, speech, and dress to fit the interview setting. How you dress can influence the degree of cooperation a person gives. A business suit or a fancy dress would not be appropriate for on-site interviews of Iowa hog farmers, nor would dirty jeans and an army field coat be appropriate when interviewing people attending an opera. Not only what you wear, but also how you talk influences your results. You would need to use different terms to talk with street people in San Diego than you would use when interviewing prep school students in New England.

No matter what kind of person you interview, you are asking that individual to give up time to help you; thus, do not ask time-wasting questions. You can avoid such questions by familiarizing yourself with the topic before conducting the interview.

Understanding and Accuracy — The Desired Outcomes

When you interview someone, you are seeking information about that person's knowledge of, attitudes toward, or perceptions about a topic. Your task becomes one of developing an accurate, clear understanding of the respondent's responses, knowledge, and thoughts on your topic. This requires, in some cases, detaching yourself from your own perspectives, viewpoints, attitudes, and prejudices.

Assume that you're working on a class assignment for a report that argues for gun registration. Assume further that you think hunting barbaric, and that you believe it inhumane to hunt deer, elk, bear, and other big game. Finally, imagine that you favor gun registration. To obtain the viewpoints of others, you plan to interview members of local hunting and fishing clubs. Some members may belong to the National Rifle Association; therefore, most, if not all, will oppose gun registration. What should your approach be? Try to be objective and to listen actively to their reasons and justification for opposing gun registration. Objective interviewing centers on developing a clear, accurate understanding of your respondent's knowledge, attitudes, or perceptions.

THE PERSONAL, ONE-ON-ONE INTERVIEW

When preparing for an interview, think of the process as comprising three activities: (1) preparing for the interview, (2) conducting the interview, and (3) following up the interview.

Preparing for the Interview

Adequate preparation makes the difference between useful, productive interviews and useless, time-wasting activities. Preparation includes

Establishing a clear purpose,
Familiarizing yourself with the subject,
Setting up the interview, and
Preparing the questions and the interview focus.

Although the sequence appears linear, you might be preparing questions at the same time as you familiarize yourself with the subject and you are setting up your interviews. Furthermore, at any point in the process you may find yourself needing to clarify your purpose, to gather additional background information, or to set up more interviews.

Establishing a Clear Purpose.   First, establish a clear reason that will guide your interview. A muddled purpose wastes both your time and the interviewee's. Let us say that you are working on a research paper focusing on the issues of teenage pregnancy in the local community. Ask yourself, "What do I mean by the local issues? City? County? Local school district issues?" What kind of questions might you ask? How serious locally is the issue of teenage pregnancy? Do local health departments have any programs to combat teenage pregnancies? If so, what are the programs? What educational or health programs does the local school district have to reduce teenage pregnancy? Is the approach positive? Negative? What kinds of topics does the program concentrate upon? Do the programs work?

Suppose that, based on your literature reviewing, you have learned that one of your school's professors is a national expert on education programs designed to reduce teenage pregnancies. In such a situation, you may be able to gather information that has not been reported in the literature. To help yourself, write a specific statement that summarizes what you know from the literature, then determine what information and/or clarification you hope to get from the interview.

Preparing for the Interview.   First, familiarize yourself with the topic. Read relevant literature so that you know the terms and terminology your respondent will use; you will then have a general understanding of the topic. If you are preparing for a research paper on teenage pregnancy and are trying to determine the impact of teenage pregnancies, dig out the most recent national, state, and local statistics. If you find a lower teen-pregnancy rate in one community than in another, plan to ask interviewees to explain why the rates are lower in some communities than in others. If you are focusing on programs to reduce teenage pregnancy, plan questions to learn how programs differ and why some programs work better than others.

Setting Up the Interview.   As you read about your topic, note the backgrounds of the writers, where they work, and their professional expertise. For example, if you are exploring a topic such as trends in the real estate market, and you are developing a local focus, you would want to interview local experts. In what offices, departments, or organizations might you find them? In what kinds of jobs or positions would they work? Or assume that you are interested in the direct marketing of condominiums. In your literature review, you note articles by experts in college architectural and marketing departments, chambers of commerce, real estate professional organizations, professional builders' organizations, banks, savings and loan companies, and law offices. You will want to check with organizations like these for the names of such people in your area. For example, you might call the appropriate college departments, explain your project, and then ask which professors you should interview. Efficient, cooperative secretaries can help you to identify the right professor to interview.

When you call for an appointment, explain your topic and say why you want to interview the specific person. Ask for an appointment at a convenient time in a week or so. Then double-check the time, day of the week, date, location, and the way to find the office. Take notes and pencil in the time, date, and location of the appointment on your calendar. If you schedule the interview more than a week in advance, call back a couple of days before your interview to double check the time, date, and location. Doing so politely reminds the interviewee of your scheduled interview.

When the day of the interview arrives, give yourself plenty of time to arrive at the location. Schedule your travel time so you arrive about five minutes early. Locating some buildings and the offices within them can be especially difficult, so allow enough time to find your way to the designated building, correct floor, and right room.

Preparing Your Questions.   Most personal interviews rely on open-ended questions; avoid "yes," or "no" responses by asking questions that will encourage lengthy answers. In other words, do not ask, "Do you agree with the Utah legislature's law restricting abortion?" Instead, ask "Can you tell me your attitude toward

Utah's recent legislative decision?" or "Can you give me your opinion as to why the legislature voted overwhelmingly to restrict abortions?" Open-ended questions give respondents the opportunity to share their thoughts and provide details that are not in the literature. For a research paper on aid to developing countries, you might ask an expert, "A number of experts now question the effectiveness of some development programs. Based on your experiences, what makes an effective development program in a Third-World country?" Keep in mind that you can ask questions that elicit different kinds of answers — factual information, attitudes, perceptions, insights, or observations.

When preparing for an interview, write out your questions and arrange them in order from general to specific. Many skilled interviewers suggest opening with general questions and then moving to in-depth, detailed questions. If some of your questions will be controversial, save them until you've asked your general questions. Depending on the subject, respondent, and questions, plan to ask 15 to 30 questions during a 30 minute interview.

Conducting the Interview

Arrive about five minutes early, let the secretary or the expert know you have arrived. When you are asked to sit down, try to take a seat so you can look directly at the person you will be interviewing. Then spend a couple of minutes explaining your interest in the topic. Once you have established rapport, explain why you selected the individual for an interview, ask your general questions, and then move on to your specific questions. When asking such questions, be prepared for adverse reactions — anger, fear, resentment, or other negative reactions — and plan in advance how to handle such reactions.

As respondents answer your questions, concentrate on what they say, how they say it, and carefully consider what they mean. Try paraphrasing your interviewee's comments. Begin by saying, "As I understand it, you are saying," and then give your paraphrase. Doing this reduces the length of the response, cuts to its essence, assures that you understand the response, and helps you remember it. If you plan to tape-record your interview, be sure to get the interviewee's permission. Do not rely exclusively on the tape recorder, since tape recorders do fail. Therefore, take notes as well.

During the interview, keep your questions and notes as unobtrusive as possible, but do keep the interview moving along so you can cover all the necessary questions. Do not feel that you have to ask the questions in the order in which you have listed them; try to let questions emerge naturally from the conversation. If the respondent strays from your topic, return to the topic by saying, "I have several additional questions about topic X that I would like to ask." Then ask your next question. As you work through your list, keep an eye on the clock and plan to end your interview on time.

Some 10 minutes before the end of your interview, check your notes and your paraphrasing of quotable items. Then review the key points to make sure that you have accurately recorded what you learned and to make sure you've asked all your questions. You may want to clarify a few points that you plan to quote in your report. If so, read the quotation back, and ask if that accurately represents the point made. As you close the interview, be sure to ask for copies of any reports, articles, or other printed material your interviewee said would be provided. Finally, ask if you can call back to double-check points, if needed.

Taking Notes: Practical Tips from the Pros

When taking notes, many journalists use small reporters' notebooks, about 4″ × 8″, and felt-tip pens. That notebook size allows unobtrusive note-taking, while felt-tip pens allow you to write more quickly. Reporters seldom use secretary's short-hand, but they do use abbreviations; drop articles — "a, an, the;" abbreviate terms; and drop unneeded words to shorten their notes. Using such an approach requires transcribing notes immediately after the interview, because memory fades quickly.

If you do plan to tape record an interview, remember that you may need to transcribe the interview; also keep in mind that transcribing a tape recording takes twice as long as the initial interview. Remember too, that some interviewees find tape recorders threatening and will tense up, will not talk freely, or will refuse to be interviewed.

When you use a tape recorder, use one with a footage counter and fully charged or new batteries, and carry spare batteries and tapes. Before the interview, practice changing tapes and batteries, and always test the recorder to make sure the unit works properly.

If permission is granted to tape an interview, place the tape recorder between you and the person being interviewed, and turn the microphone so it will pick up both your question and the respondent's answer. Then begin your interview. When your respondent makes quotable statements, note the reading on the footage counter and the time. In that way, you can later fast-forward to the spot, listen to the quote, and write it out. Finally, do not forget to take notes on paper during the interview.

Following Up the Interview

After you have left the interview, spend a few minutes reviewing your notes, filling in missing details, writing out full quotes, and deciphering your abbreviations. Think about what happened during the interview and record any information that you did not write down at the time. Also jot down your immediate reactions and observations about the interview.

Avoiding Common Problems

When you interview people, you may encounter such problems as finding that you are interviewing an inappropriate person; arriving at the wrong place, time, or date; having distractions during the interview; or interviewing an unwilling respondent.

To prevent spending time in interviewing inappropriate persons, screen potential interviewees in advance. When you seek people to interview, identify subject-matter specialists on your topic. That will go a long way toward eliminating interviews that create problems. When you call to set up an interview, explain your research project and ask some preliminary questions to ascertain whether the person knows your subject. Let the answers determine whether you need to do the interview.

To avoid mistakes, always verify the time, date, and location when you set up the interview. If you do not know how to find the location, ask; then write the directions on your calendar. Always check your calendar for such items before the interview. During the interview, outside noise, telephones ringing, and other people interrupting can increase the interview time, distract the interviewee, and create other problems for you. If distractions become a problem, ask if you can return at a more favorable time, or ask to move to a place where you will not be interrupted.

When an interviewee refuses to answer your question or displays uncooperativeness, reassure the respondent that you have a sincere interest in his or her responses. Doing so may often turn the interview in your favor.

By asking respondents for reports, articles, and other documentation you can often overcome a selective memory problem. Sometimes you can ask for those materials as the need arises during the interview. In other cases, you might wait until near the close of the interview to request such materials.

INTERVIEWING BY TELEPHONE

Today's sophisticated telephone system can be an efficient tool to help you interview people around the world — if you approach your task seriously. Unlike the person conducting a one-to-one interview, however, the telephone interviewer has the distinct disadvantage of not being able to see the respondent. Furthermore, the interviewee can end the interview by hanging up. So establish rapport quickly to ensure that the interviewee will cooperate with you. The best approach is to prepare thoroughly for your interview.

Preparing for Your Interview

To prepare for a telephone interview,

1. Obtain the person's telephone number,
2. Develop and write out your questions, and
3. Call the interviewee and conduct the interview or schedule a future time for the interview.

Obtaining Telephone Numbers.   You can obtain many telephone numbers from telephone and professional directories, directory assistance, and organizations' receptionists. Many libraries have telephone directories for major cities in either printed or microfiche formats. When you search for telephone numbers, keep in mind that you may need to look under different subjects, titles, and categories to find the telephone numbers you need.

Developing Your Questions.   For telephone interviews, plan to ask fewer questions than you would in a face-to-face interview, and try to avoid long, complex, involved questions. Although you can sometimes justify longer interviews, try to keep most telephone interviews under 15 minutes.

Conducting the Telephone Interview.   Conducting the telephone interview involves using one of two approaches. In one approach, you call individuals without advance notice, tell them you have some questions to ask, and conduct the interview at that time. For the second approach, you call the individuals you want to interview, explain that you want to interview them, and then schedule a convenient time to conduct the interview. Return the call at an agreed-upon time and date.

When you first call, identify yourself and explain the reason for your call; pose your questions clearly; take notes carefully; rephrase or repeat items that you plan to quote; give your complete address if you are requesting that information be sent to you; and thank the individual for his/her help before you hang up.

Afterwards, follow through with the usual procedure of reviewing notes, adding comments and information as needed. In addition, be sure to write the respondent a short letter of thanks.

ASSESSING THE INTERVIEW INFORMATION

After the interview, you need to assess what you have learned—and that is not an easy task. Entire books are devoted to assessing information, evaluating data, and analyzing statistics. The next few paragraphs touch on some of these issues and suggest a questioning approach to guide your assessment of what you have been told. Be cautious and skeptical about what you have learned.

Start with general questions:

What was the source of the information?

What was the basis of the information you were given?

What kind of information did you learn?

What corroborating evidence did the interviewee provide?

How does the information you received agree or disagree with what you
    knew about the topic before the interview?

What Was the Source of the Information?

When you start to assess information, consider the information source and the kind of information you have learned. Why did you interview the person in question? How did the person establish his or her expertise? How long has the person been an expert? What are the person's unique qualifications? Are those qualifications relevant to the information you sought?

Suppose you interviewed a researcher from Fantastic Gardening Corporation about the company's new product, Humongous Grown 25. Based on her research, the researcher found that adding Humongous Grown 25 to the soil increased sweet corn growth by 90% in the company's experiments. In addition, you interviewed a horticultural researcher from your local agricultural school, who reported that Humongous Grown 25 boosted sweet corn production by 5%. In both cases, question what the researchers were measuring and how they were measuring it. What did Fantastic Gardening's researcher mean by "growth" versus the horticultural researcher's "production"?

What Is the Basis of the Information?

Let your answers to the following questions guide your assessment of the information: How did the person come to know what he/she told you? Was it through years of practical experience? Was it through education and specialized degrees? Was it through years of study? Was the information based on a one-time observation? Multiple observations? Reports from other people? Experiments?

Consider the awakening of health consciousness among many people about the time they turn 40; they become more concerned about taking care of their bodies. Suppose you were doing a research report and interviewed a recent health convert, who reported an increased energy level following weight loss and a regular exercise program. How would you assess this person's report of an increased energy level? In contrast, assume that you interviewed a medical researcher who told you that 90 percent of the 500 subjects in a weight loss and exercise programs reported a higher energy level after six months. How would you assess these reports of increased energy levels? In the first case you have a sample size of one, in the second a sample size of 500. But even more important, what do all subjects mean by "an increased energy level"? What does that mean? To whom? In what ways did the researchers measure it? Interpret it?

What Kind of Information Did You Learn?

Did you seek facts, personal observations, inferences, attitudes, opinions, expert judgments, or still other kinds of information? Was what you were told based on fact or inference? If you were given statistical data, do not let statistics and numbers overwhelm you, but look critically at the data. Ask how concepts were defined and how the data were collected, analyzed, and interpreted.

Consider one commonly reported statistic: "Some 90% of the population have had a homosexual experience." When given such information in an interview, probe deeply to understand the statistics better. Ask: What do the terms mean? In these cases, what does "a homosexual experience" mean? Likewise, ask: How were these data collected? What population was studied? How large was the population? How many people were sampled? How many people were studied? Was the study replicated?

What Corroborating Evidence Did the Interviewee Provide?

Did the interviewee provide additional information that helped support the information you were given? Were you given any reports, citations, or references to literature that might help confirm the information reported in the interview? Did the interviewee suggest that you talk with others, mention other experts, or suggest literature to review?

How Does the Information Align with What You Knew?

When given new information, you instinctively compare what you are told with what you already know. Thus, good preparation for your interview will help you considerably. By preparing thoroughly for the interview, you build a background that helps you ask better questions, and, just as important, this background knowledge helps you assess what you are told in the interview. So, do not forget to ask yourself, "How does what the interviewee told me compare with what I knew about the subject before the interview?"

If the new information does not agree with what you knew previously, do you know why? If not, ask and probe deeply so you can learn the reasons for the difference and better understand the information you have gained. Even if the information agrees, probe deeply to learn the reasons for the agreement and to gain a deeper understanding of the topic.

CONCLUSION

In this chapter we have given you detailed guidance on how to become a productive interviewer. We have also suggested how you can analyze and assess the results of your interview. We have not, however, been able to suggest how you might incorporate your interview data into your final research report. Only you can make that judgment. By taking stock of all the information you have gathered, you can begin to sift and sort. What you include depends on your individual preferences and on the specific needs of your readers.

CHAPTER 10

Gathering Information
by Observation

T his chapter discusses observation, a research meth-
odology useful in many disciplines. How you use observation depends on your specific research project. If your goal is to publish the results in a prestigious scientific
journal, you will need to be much more systematic in your observation than if you are
conducting informal research for a college course. This chapter includes

general principles of observation,

factors that influence observation,

common observational strategies,

casual versus systematic observation, and

threats to validity.

INTRODUCTION

When Bruce Bury, a scientist for the U.S. Fish and Wildlife Service, goes into
the field to collect snakes, lizards, turtles, and other reptiles, he goes alone. Why?
When trying to observe reptiles, he hears them before he sees them. When he takes

other people with him, they make too much noise, and he cannot hear the animals he is studying. Bruce observes by hearing—he has learned the sounds that reptiles make.

Everyone makes hundreds of observations daily. Most of the time, we observe casually; few of us are systematic as we gather information. In contrast, scientists, whether in the physical, biological, or social sciences, make systematic observations. Earl Babbie (1982, 21), a social scientist, points out that observation forms one pillar of science; the other is reason. He later points out that observation alone does not equal science, but science requires making sense of information gathered through observation.

Babbie and some other scientists use the term "observation" in a broad sense and include diverse observational techniques—physical observation, experiments, tests, evaluations, and other techniques. Still other scientists, such as Fassnacht (1982, 27), define "observation" narrowly. They exclude tests, interviews, questionnaires, and experiments from the conceptualization of observation. The following discussion first uses "observation" in its broad sense and then distinguishes among the different kinds of observation.

GENERAL PRINCIPLES OF OBSERVATION

Observation includes seeing something, making note of what you have seen, and then interpreting the results. Suppose that while you are studying at your desk, you look up and glance across the room. You notice something moving. You look again and you recognize the movement—it's a spider crawling up the wall. Depending upon what you know about spiders and your attitudes toward them, you might grab a magazine and squash the spider. Or you might capture it for further study.

Around the clock, you are bombarded with sounds, smells, sights, tastes, and other stimuli. If you responded to all such stimulation, you would soon be overwhelmed. In order to live in a stimulus-rich world, you must develop a defense mechanism, a selectivity, by focusing your attention only on specific items and ignoring others. And that focus influences what you see.

Consider dollar bills. You see them frequently, and yet, how well do you observe them? What is pictured on the back of a dollar bill? What is in the left-hand circle? What is at the bottom of the pyramid? Can you translate the letters into a number? What is it? Most people do not observe dollar bills critically (Gombrich 1972). Why? They don't need that information.

If you are like most people, you observe selectively. Economic development officers often use selectivity to get the attention of community leaders. The officers hire out-of-town photographers to photograph cracked sidewalks, trashy streets, abandoned vehicles, broken street lights, missing traffic signs, and other decay. When the community leaders see the slides, they are devastated—their community does not look that bad! But it does to many nonresidents. By focusing on certain elements, some people see one thing; by focusing on other elements, others see something else.

FACTORS THAT INFLUENCE OBSERVATION

Many things influence selectivity: your frame of reference, education and training, expectations, and orientation. Frame of reference includes all of the experiences you bring to the setting. It is the sum of everything you know, what you have done, and your experiences. Grombrich (1972) raised a series of questions about NASA's plaque on the Pioneer spacecraft. Consider Figure 10-1. What does it communicate to you?

Now read NASA's explanation. Did your frame of reference give you the background to understand the plaque?

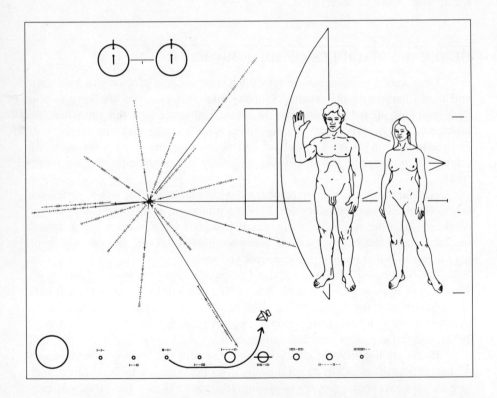

F I G U R E 10-1   The Drawing Engraved on the Plaque Attached to the Pioneer Spacecraft

NASA'S NEWS RELEASE EXPLAINING THE PLAQUE: 25 FEBRUARY 1972

Manned Space Center, Houston, Texas

Pioneer F Plaque. — The Pioneer F spacecraft, destined to be the first man-made object to escape from the solar system into interstellar space, carried this pictorial plaque. It is designed to show scientifically educated inhabitants of some other star system — who might intercept it millions of years from now — when Pioneer was launched, from where, and by what kind of beings. The design is etched into a gold-anodized aluminum plate, 152 by 229 mm (6 × 9 in.), attached to the spacecraft's antenna support struts in a position to help shield it from erosion by interstellar dust. The radiating lines at the left represent the positions of the 14 pulsars — cosmic sources of radio energy — arranged to indicate our Sun as the home star of the launching civilization. The "1-"symbols at the ends of the lines are binary numbers that represent the frequencies of these pulsars at the time of the launch of Pioneer F relative to that of the hydrogen atom shown at the upper left with a "1" unity symbol. The hydrogen atom is thus used as a "universal clock," and the regular decrease in the frequencies of the pulsars will enable another civilization to determine the time that was elapsed since Pioneer F was launched. The hydrogen atom is also used as a universal "yard stick" for sizing the human figures and outline of the spacecraft shown on the right. The hydrogen wavelength — about 8 inches — multiplied by the binary number representing "8" shown next to the woman gives her height — 6½ inches. The figures represent the type of creature that created Pioneer. The man's hand is raised in a gesture of goodwill. Across the bottom are the planets, ranging outward from the sun, with the spacecraft's trajectory arcing away from Earth, passing Mars, and swinging by Jupiter.

Keep in mind that your education and experience have prepared you to make critical observations, make inferences, and solve specific problems. Their education helps medical doctors to observe carefully when they examine a patient. They note the patient's weight, height, blood pressure, smoking, drinking, and other behaviors. They then ask about physical symptoms, emotions, feelings, and pain. Based on the information learned, they then order X-rays, blood tests, EKGs, glucose tolerance tests, ultra-sounds, urine analyses, and other tests. With the additional information, they refine their diagnosis. Other professionals also develop their observational skills: accountants, agronomists, auditors, auto-mechanics, editors, farmers, musicians, and hundreds of others.

Experience influences your expectations and observations. Assume that you live in the Eastern United States, have not traveled in the West, but have read popular articles about the West, purchased calendars, and seen movies set in the West. From these sources, you may have been led to expect mountains and coniferous forests to cover the region. They don't. If you drove Interstate 70 west to Denver, you would travel through some 150 miles of farmlands, ranches, and prairie from the Kansas line. Or assume that you took Interstate 80 across southern Wyoming; east of Cheyenne you would drive through prairie and farmlands — most of it a treeless plain. To the west, you would drive through high mountain deserts covered with sagebrush and inhabited by jackrabbits, prairie dogs, and antelope.

Not only do your expectations influence observations, but your orientation influences what you see as well. Your position, location, time, and date can affect what you see. Consider an example. If you want to hear elk bugling — sounding their mating call — you might decide to visit Rocky Mountain National Park, some 70 miles northwest of Denver, during the rutting season in early October. If you arrive at Horseshoe Park, a large meadow just west of the Fall River entrance to the National Park, after 9 a.m. and return to Denver by 5 p.m. for dinner, chances are you will not hear any elk bugling. But if you arrive by 4 p.m. on a weekday, and if you park your vehicle at the Sheep Lakes overlook and stay there until 8 p.m., you will greatly increase your chances of hearing elk bugle. Repeat the trip on a Saturday evening, though, and dozens of people will crowd the area and reduce your chances of hearing any elk.

By knowing how your frame of reference, education and training, expectations, and orientation influence your observation, you can enhance both your casual and your systematic observations.

COMMON OBSERVATIONAL TECHNIQUES

Observational strategies include casual and systematic techniques, either of which can be done directly or indirectly (unobtrusively or without the observer's knowledge). Direct systematic observation can use personal observation, participant observation, and experiments. As you consider each observational approach, keep in mind that each academic discipline has specific observational guidelines. Some fields use indirect and direct unobtrusive observations that serve well for descriptive, exploratory studies, while other fields use systematic observation and experimentation and provide a more rigorous approach for making inferences.

Each observational strategy has advantages and disadvantages, which may vary from one academic discipline to another. Further, some disciplines rely on some observational techniques more than other disciplines. The following paragraphs highlight the advantages and disadvantages of each technique. (Figure 10-2 provides an overall scheme for discussing observation.)

Systematic Observational Strategies

Direct Observation.   Direct observation may be either personal, participant observation, or experimental. *Personal observation* is a strategy in which nothing stands between you, the observer, and the observed people, animals, or objects. You are in

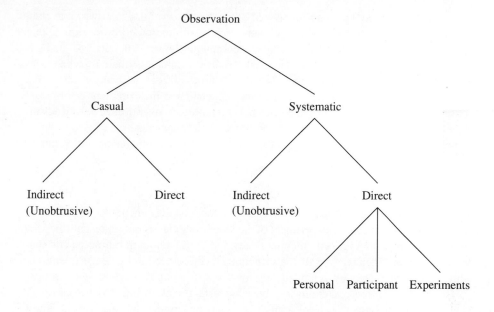

F I G U R E 10-2   A Strategy for Organizing Observations

the setting, but you do not interact with anyone or anything. You record what you
have seen immediately after the observation (Fassnact 1982, 27; Wright 1988).

An obvious drawback is that the observer's presence may influence what is
being observed. Visit any zoo, and you will soon see the animals watching the people
watch them. Another drawback focuses on how the observational time period and the
observational location are selected; as we pointed out earlier, different times and
locations give different results — and yet, watching people and animals is often the
only way of learning more about their behavior and reactions. Still another problem
is that what you observe and how you observe may change over time. Despite their
limitations, personal observations provide firsthand data, enhance the understanding
of the problem, and can help to define relationships. Time may be the major cost
associated with such observations.

In *participant observation*, observers become part of the group and take part in
group activities, while at the same time they are observing the group. Babbie
(1982:210) divides participant observation into participants-as-observers, observers-
as-participants, and complete observers. Participants-as-observers take part in all
activities, but make clear to the group that they are conducting a research project.
Observers-as-participants acknowledge being researchers but do not themselves participate — much like newspaper reporters covering events. Complete observers watch

the group, but do not take part in any activities; the observer doesn't overtly explain his or her real reason for being present. For example, when co-author Dawn Rodrigues observed one of her colleague's computer classes, students assumed she was in their class merely because she needed to use computers, when in fact she was the researcher. This technique too can suffer from the effects of being measured; a bias in the selection of the time, place, and subjects; and measurement errors from observers changing what and sometimes how they observe over time. The key advantage is that observing over a long period of time minimizes reactive effects of being observed. For many of your research topics, the only cost would be the time required to make observations.

Experimental Observation.   In different classes, you may encounter two different kinds of experiments. The experiment of the laboratory classroom represents the kind of experiment with a known outcome or results. Here you learn a process and thus enhance your understanding of the principle. In the other kind of experiment, the kind often conducted by scientists, the outcome is unknown. Here scientists are searching for answers and exploring cause and effect relationship. Does X cause Y? For example, assume you have apple trees in your garden and you want to know whether spraying insecticides reduces worms or maggots in your apples. First you refine your question to ask:

> Does spraying at the pesticide rate and intervals designated on the insecticide container reduce the infestation of apple maggots?

Assume the manufacturer recommends spraying just before bloom opening and at two week intervals thereafter until two weeks before harvest. You have two Golden Delicious, two Jonathan, and two Granny Smith apple trees. You number your trees one through six and you then flip a coin. If it comes up heads, you spray the odd numbered trees. If it comes up tails, you spray the even numbered trees. Consider the trees sprayed as the treatment group; those that you do not spray as the control group. When you harvest the apples, you count the number of wormy apples from each tree, calculate the percentage of wormy apples in both groups, and run the appropriate statistical tests. At that point you can infer whether spraying reduces apple maggot infestation, but the careful scientist would replicate the study several times before making inferences.

    The logistics — space, equipment, subjects, and need for clearances — often create some of the greater disadvantages of experiments. Depending on the discipline and the research question, the costs can become overwhelming for many student projects. The advantages include the increased rigor for making cause and effect inferences and the availability of a solid body of literature to guide you in many disciplines.

Indirect Unobtrusive Observation

Unobtrusive observation means observing indirectly or looking for artifacts, evidence, or signs left behind by whatever you're studying — people, animals, equipment. You observe without disturbing or influencing your subjects. Webb, et al. (1973) in their classic book, *Unobtrusive Measures: Nonreactive Research in the Social Sciences*, focused on social science research, but the concept works in other fields as well. Consider these examples:

Chinese jade dealers noted the difference in pupil dilation as an indicator of potential buyers' interests in different stones, while Darwin, in 1892, noted pupil diameter as an index of fear (Webb et al. 1973:2). Restaurant chefs observed the kinds and amounts of different foods customers leave on their plates as an indicator of the popularity and quality of different dishes (Roscia 1988). Wildlife biologists used pellet — i.e., feces — counts to estimate deer, elk, sheep, and rabbit populations (Davis 1963). To determine levels of radon, the radioactive gas trapped in some buildings and homes, researchers have developed charcoal canisters and alpha track-etch detectors.

Hundreds of creative ways can be developed to gather unobtrusive observations on the phenomena under study. All provide valuable information, but you would be wisest to couple the information gathered through unobtrusive observation with data collected in other ways. Nachimias and Nachimias (1987) encourage triangulation — using two or more methods to collect data — to minimize the risk of reaching erroneous conclusions.

CASUAL VERSUS SYSTEMATIC OBSERVATION

Systematic observations are planned, have a specific, clearly defined purpose, and are usually well organized and clearly directed. Simply, a systematic researcher sets out to make specific observations and is guided by predetermined criteria. In contrast, casual observation lacks the criteria and rigor of systematic observation.

Data collected casually may not fully represent the situation, and such data often reflect the biases the observer brings to the setting. But casual observation may provide an inexpensive way of collecting data and beginning to develop an understanding of the subject being observed.

Casual observations produce useful information for describing what is happening, exploring a new problem, and trying to enhance your general understanding of a topic. Casual observation often provides the foundation or ground work for subsequent, rigorous, systematic observations. To understand casual observation, imagine that you attend college in a small community, you are taking a sociology class, and you are assigned a paper on "cruising," a teenage, Saturday night ritual of driving cars up and down Main Street. You arrive at about 7 p.m. and you note few teenagers cruising and you position yourself in the middle block of Main Street. By 9 p.m., however, teenage drivers jam Main Street, honking their car horns, stopping to talk, making catcalls, whistling, and racing their cars' engines. You take a few notes and head home by 11 p.m. On Sunday, you think about what you have seen, and you conclude that cruising appears to be a harmless teenage activity. You support your conclusion with your observations.

In contrast, one of your classmates reaches a different conclusion. She arrives at about 10 p.m. and positions herself near three taverns at the north end of Main Street. She sees four fights, five auto collisions, five possible drug sales, and three arrests. Before she heads home about 1 a.m., she jots down some notes. On Sunday, she thinks about her observations and concludes that cruising is strongly associated with crime and other activities that endanger teenagers. When she writes her paper, she supports her conclusion with her observations. In both cases, you and she made casual — and very different — observations.

Empirical sociologists — those who collect data through experimental observation to gain a better understanding of social activities — would proceed very differently from both you and the other student. First, they would review the literature to determine how cruising has been defined and studied and whether it has any relationship to crime. Next, they would follow a systematic approach: (1) develop a theoretical foundation, (2) propose a research question or hypothesis that identifies specific behaviors, (3) plan a methodology suggesting how and what to observe, (4) devise a sampling scheme, and (5) select the appropriate statistical analyses, if needed.

You can use either casual or systematic observation. Casual observation can build a general understanding of what you plan to study, while systematic observation, the hallmark of science, provides more specific, detailed information. Both casual and systematic observation can provide useful insights into a problem or topic.

Strategies for Casual Observations

General guidelines for casual observation center on learning about the subject and developing an idea of what you would like to observe. You will need to learn to recognize specific points and to separate the usual from the unusual.

Once you learn what to look for and how to look for it, you can observe more efficiently and effectively. When Don Zimmerman was a teenager living in Eastern Kansas, his father, his brother, and he trapped beaver along rivers, streams, and lakes. During those years he learned to spot beaver sign: cut bushes, fell trees, dams, flooded fields, mud slides, lodges, peeled cuttings, and burrows. Now, a glance along the banks of streams as he drives across bridges often lets him spot beaver activity.

Or consider a patrol officer on duty. After midnight, a patrol officer spots a car with only one headlight. He stops the driver, asks him to walk a straight line, to say the alphabet, to close his eyes and touch his nose, and more. Based on the observed behaviors, the patrol officer then decides whether to detain the driver and administer a blood test to determine alcohol content. Here, the patrol officer's observations began casually but move to a more systematic approach.

In the first case, Zimmerman had learned to spot the clues that signal beaver activity. In the second case, the patrol officer has learned what clues signal a potentially drunk driver. For any observational task in a discipline, learn what clues to observe by reviewing the literature, talking with experts, and practicing observation. For many assignments, casual observations will serve you well, but for others you will need to make systematic observations.

Strategies for Systematic Observation

Systematic observation requires developing and using guidelines to direct your observations. To make systematic observations,

1. Familiarize yourself with the problem, issue, or topic for which you will be doing the observations;
2. Develop one or more specific questions, objectives, or hypotheses to guide your observations;
3. Define the concepts, variables or factors you plan to observe;
4. Develop an appropriate way to measure (observe) the concepts, variables, or factors; and
5. Select an appropriate way to record your observations.

Familiarize Yourself with the Literature.   Start with a thorough literature review to help you: (1) understand your topic, (2) learn the successful and unsuccessful approaches others have used to study your topic, (3) identify the appropriate observational strategies, and (4) provide insights to help you ask the question and direct your investigation.

Refine Your Question.   Systematic observation requires developing a clearly defined question. For some courses, you can use broadly defined questions; for other courses, you will need narrowly defined questions. Consider a broad question, such as, ''Do bicyclists violate traffic laws on campus?'' This question would direct you to observe many different locations where traffic law violations occur: running stop signs, speeding through stoplights, riding on sidewalks, riding on closed streets, and riding without reflectors or lights after dark.

In another case, you would need a narrowly defined question to direct your observations. Assume you are taking a psychology class and you are interested in reactions to traffic control signs. You notice newspaper reports of increased collisions between bicyclists and pedestrians on campus sidewalks. When you talk to the campus police, you learn that they have asked the maintenance shop to install bicyclist traffic control signs on three sidewalks within the next four weeks. You have plenty of time, so you review the psychology and communication literature on warning messages and people's reactions to them. You also interview the campus safety officer.

Based on your background, you draft your question, ''Do the 'No Bicycle Riding' signs along sidewalks A, B, and C reduce the number of bicyclists along those sidewalks?'' The question suggests a change might occur—i.e., a reduced number of sidewalk bicycle riders. Therefore, you will need to observe bicycle traffic on sidewalks A, B, & C at different times of the day and days of the week both before and after the signs go up. With that data, you can calculate bicycle traffic before and after the installation of the signs, calculate the change, if any, and make inferences.

Define the Concepts, Variables, or Factors.   Before you can make valid observations, you need to define what you will be observing. When you develop your question, you have begun to identify what you plan to measure by simply naming it. But you may also need to develop a specific, detailed definition of the concept before you really understand what you are setting out to observe.

To illustrate, consider the bicycle question again. What do you mean by bicyclists? Do you mean the number of bicyclists riding on the sidewalk? What do you mean by riding on the sidewalk? Will you consider individuals who dismount and walk their bikes along the sidewalk as bicyclists? What about an individual who rides the bicycle some 50 yards or so down the sidewalk and then dismounts? Is the individual who walks past the sign and then stands on one pedal and pushes her bicycle considered a bicyclist?

The issue centers around precisely defining what you will observe and what will help you determine how to measure what you will observe. Too often people argue about an idea or a term when they are talking about entirely different things. So be precise; the more specific you can define what you plan to observe, the more easily you can measure it.

Determine an Appropriate Measure.   Once you define the concepts, variables or factors, you will need to figure out how to measure them. Two major considerations emerge: (1) What observational techniques should you use? (2) What units of measurement should you use?

For the first question, consider direct measurements, unobtrusive measurements, experiments, or combinations thereof. For many assignments, both direct and unobtrusive measurements will work well.

For the second question, measurements vary widely across the disciplines. In some fields, you have millimeters, centimeters, decimeters, meters, kilometers to measure distance; grams, decagrams, hectograms, and kilograms to measure weight; degrees Celsius to measure temperature; and seconds, minutes, hours, days, months, and years to measure time measurements.

In other fields, such as the social sciences, humanities, business and education, you may need to devise a measurement. Here researchers must first define the concepts — attitudes, knowledge levels, behaviors — and then devise the measurement units. Social scientists call the first concept explication and the second operationalization. Operationalization entails developing a finite way to measure the concept. For example, you might operationalize cruising as the number of cars with teenagers driving past a particular intersection on main street. Or you might count the number of cars stopping and groups talking per block.

Design an Appropriate Recording Technique.   Once you know how you will measure the concepts, select an appropriate recording technique. Common, useful techniques include

> Field and laboratory notebooks and journals,
> Checklists, and
> Equipment.

Field and laboratory notes, notebooks, and journals provide a permanent record of observations. Use them to record your observations and to give you insights to your study. The size and format of such material vary widely among professionals. Journalists often use reporters' notebooks, spiral bound $4 \times 8''$ pads with 70 or so pages. They cradle them in one hand and write with the other hand, with the heavy cardboard back and front providing a rigid support for writing. Some students use $4 \times 6''$ or larger note cards, number the cards, punch a hole in one corner, and insert a large ring to keep the cards together. Other students find $8.5 \times 11''$ or $4 \times 6''$ yellow pads useful for notes, while still others use 8.5×11 inch typing paper, or half sheets for taking notes.

When taking notes, use waterproof ink, and take the notes periodically while you are observing. At the very least, take notes immediately after you have finished your observations. Do not delay until the next day; if you do, you will quickly forget useful details. Whether you use reporters' notebooks, note cards, or note pads, transcribe your notes once you have returned from the laboratory or field. Consider typing the notes out, making a backup copy, and storing it in another location.

For some projects, a field or laboratory notebook, journal, or diary provides an excellent way to record details and observations in a permanent record. The approach entails providing key details and summarizing essential information.

Checklists can ease observational tasks and recording. When developing checklists, include: who did the observing; where it was done — give location and description; when it was done — date and time; and the observational techniques used. The example below illustrates a checklist for observing behavior in a computerized writing laboratory. The observers used a one-way window to observe selected students in assigned seats.

CHECKLIST FOR COMPUTER LABORATORY STUDY

Part I Background on Observation

Observer (print name): _____

Date: _____ Begin Time: _____

Class: _____

Section: _____ End Time: _____

Row & Seat Number(s) observed: _____

Part II Observations Made

Directions: Use tally marks (llll) to record the number of times each behavior occurred for each student.

			Seat Number		
Observations	One	Two	Three	Four	Five
Asking others					
Instructor	___	___	___	___	___
Lab Assistant	___	___	___	___	___
Other students	___	___	___	___	___
Searching instructions					
Used quick reference	___	___	___	___	___
Used index	___	___	___	___	___
Used table of contents	___	___	___	___	___
Using system					
Restarted system	___	___	___	___	___
Removed disk	___	___	___	___	___
Re-entered story	___	___	___	___	___

General Narrative (Provide general narrative of your observations, use the back of the checklist, if needed):

If you use *electronic or optical equipment* to record observations, know how to operate the equipment, and check it to make sure it runs properly. Always check the power source — for instance, the batteries — to make sure it will function throughout the observations. If you use a tape recorder, put new or fully charged batteries in the unit and start with a new tape. Be sure to carry spare batteries and extra tapes, should your batteries fail or your tape run out. Still and video cameras can provide useful photographic records too. If you use cameras, always familiarize yourself with them and test them before you begin your observations. If you use computers and software programs to measure and record data, familiarize yourself with the system, test it, and know how to trouble-shoot the system before you begin using it.

When you collect data, develop a routine so you do not misplace your field notes, laboratory notebook, checklists, recordings, or films. Always store them in a safe place. Whatever recording technique or equipment you use, always make back-up copies — photocopies or additional disk copies — and store them in a safe spot.

Too often novices depend upon their memories, and their memories fail them. Remember, "The strongest mind is weaker than the palest ink" (Mosby 1963:22). Accurately recording information is important in many day-to-day settings. Police and fire department dispatching offices record all incoming calls. Doctors dictate their observations of patients, and a medical secretary then transcribes the dictation into the patients' medical records.

Researchers use various types of recording equipment and a number of different techniques. A University of Wisconsin sociologist videotaped canoeists on northern Wisconsin rivers to determine the frequency of their use of the rivers (Heberlien 1976). A biologist studying bobwhite quail in the Flint Hills of Kansas recorded his data — temperature, wind velocity, light intensity, date and time — on file cards (Dick 1967).

THREATS TO VALIDITY: AVOIDING ERRORS IN SYSTEMATIC OBSERVATION

To minimize erroneous inferences, scientists use a variety of research designs, replications, and other strategies. Over the years, scientists have developed research techniques designed to rule out alternative explanations, so-called threats to validity.

Threats to validity are factors other than the one being studied that might explain the results. Social science research methodology textbooks usually provide a lengthy discussion of experimental design and the threats to validity (Babbie 1982; Nachimias and Nachimias 1987). For a detailed discussion of experimental designs and validity, see Campbell and Stanley (1963), and Cook and Campbell (1979).

Replicating a study — that is, repeating a study several times and finding that the results are similar — helps build a stronger case for making inferences. If the results come out differently, then careful scientists begin to question the cause and effect relationship. Triangulation, or obtaining data in different ways, further enhances the basis for the inferences made. For example, a study designed to assess the effectiveness of how using word processing, spelling, and grammar checkers might use data gathered in several ways: (1) personal observations of how students write on the computer; (2) experiments comparing students using computers and writing software with students without computers and software; (3) diagnostic examinations designed to evaluate the effectiveness of specific software on students' grammar and spelling; (4) analysis of students' writing samples, and (5) interviews of students about their writing at the beginning, middle, and end of the term.

Being aware of common errors helps you avoid them. Observation is imperfect for many reasons, chief among them being what you bring to the setting, the way you observe the setting itself, the way you record data, and the inferences you make about the data. The key to minimizing errors lies in carefully collecting information, sorting out your observations from your inferences, double-checking your efforts, and comparing your observational data with other data through triangulation. Keep in mind that comparing information (data) gleaned from other techniques against what you gained from observation helps you assess the quality of all information. Interviewing, literature reviewing, and other information-gathering techniques can provide supporting information for your assignment. If you encounter information that conflicts with yours, carefully assess both data sets. Report both and then discuss the potential explanations for the differences.

Realize that your background and experiences, expectations, physical abilities, and emotions may color what you see. Recognize that the way you observe influences what you see or don't see, and that each observational technique has certain limitations. Keep in mind that such limitations may include time, location, perspective, duration, and other factors, as illustrated with the cruising example. The limitations of participant observation may include failure to note events and behaviors, or forgetting to complete field notes. For experiments, limitations include: a limited budget, limited time, or small sample size, among other factors. Remember that the environment, too, can distort your observations. If you are observing people or animals, keep in mind that your presence might change their behaviors. In addition, some errors in observation occur because the researcher records information inaccurately or uses faulty equipment. Other errors occur because the researcher makes incorrect inferences.

For example, a researcher may select one conclusion or position over another as a potential explanation of the occurrence, without acknowledging alternate possibilities. In international development, poor farmers often do not practice modern farming techniques. Frequently development specialists conclude that poor farmers lack a knowledge of modern farming techniques and implement a program to make the farmers aware of modern practices. In reality, any of a multitude of economic, political, and societal factors, or combinations thereof, might explain why farmers do not adopt the modern farming practices.

Still other inconsistencies occur when data do not support the points being made. For example, if a health official argues that the anti-drunk driving program has reduced highway deaths by an overall average of 25% for the last five years and ignores years when the data do not support the program, he is not being consistent. A closer look at the data might show that for two out of the last five years, highway deaths were actually 25% above the average; the conclusion is not consistent with the data.

CONCLUSION

We can provide you with only a general overview of observational strategies, since different approaches to observational research are sanctioned by each discourse or disciplinary community. This chapter, however, does give you a starting point. For additional information consult the references listed in the References and seek help from subject-matter specialists in specific disciplines.

CHAPTER 11

Drafting the Research Report

This chapter covers what is often called the drafting stage of the writing process. Unlike many textbook authors, we see drafting as an incremental process rather than as a separate stage of the research-writing process. Experienced researchers write portions of their research reports while they are conducting their research; they do not wait until they have completed it to write it up.

In this chapter we present

an overview of the concept of drafting,

an explanation of the incremental process for drafting,

suggestions on how to proceed as you draft with a word processor,

advice on how to organize your ideas,

suggestions on how to draft visual information, and

information on how to write a progress report.

DRAFTING: AN OVERVIEW

After collecting information, generating ideas and developing a plan for organizing them, a writer is ready to draft. A writer can draft while simultaneously conducting research, or a writer can take notes during the research process and draft later.

Drafting refers to the process of putting down ideas in sentence and paragraph form. When should you begin drafting? Drafting takes time, so if you are not able to draft as you work on your research, be sure to set aside at least two, four, or even eight-hour blocks of time for several days in a row. If you try to draft a major segment of your paper before you stop writing, you will have the feeling of satisfaction that comes from getting part of the job done.

Drafting should be done long before the report is due. Writing a draft only a few days before the final report is due does not allow enough time for you to rethink your presentation of the research procedures, organization, or contents. Nor does it give you time to check for errors and then revise and polish the draft. When writers are rushed, they cannot be as critical as they should be and they will inevitably miss errors. The larger the project, the more time needed between the rough draft and the revising and polishing phases.

Getting Started

To make your drafting sessions the most productive,

1. Have a designated work area where you can spread out your notes and arrange them in the best order. By having your materials close at hand, you can work quickly and efficiently. If space is limited, put notes, photocopies, books, pamphlets, reports, outlines, and visuals in separate file folders, order them in sequence, and keep them together in a nearby box or file container.
2. Gather your supplies and writing tools: pen and pencils, new ribbons for typewriter or printer, paper (20 lb. weight for final copy), file folders, clips, binders, correction fluid, computer disks, rulers and drawing supplies or computer graphics packages, and a typewriter or computer and printer.

If you have everything organized, you will not need to leave the room to track down missing items. Interrupting your drafting at an inappropriate time breaks your concentration and further delays your producing a rough draft.

Before you begin writing, set up your basic page format: page length, margins, tabs, and — if you want — spacing. (Some writers who compose on word processors often prefer to use single spacing to draft on-screen and then they double space their copy for their final draft.) By drafting in the format required for the finished product, you will have the satisfaction of seeing your writing take physical shape; you will begin to develop a feel for what your final report will look like (see Chapter 13).

Each writer needs to develop his or her own drafting style. Many writers begin by working through their planning documents, such as their patterned notes, their tree diagrams, or their working outlines (see Chapter 4). They then use these guides to organize their writing. They move through their draft sentence by sentence, adding one idea to the previous one in a linear fashion. But you do not have to write in this linear way; no rule says that you need to begin at the beginning and work through to the end. Try to write what you can when you can. If that means drafting the last section first, fine. Regardless of the way you work, continually reread the evolving text, adjusting earlier words and sentences to conform with the text that has been added later.

AN INCREMENTAL PROCESS FOR DRAFTING RESEARCH REPORTS

As you plan and conduct your research, draft sections of your report as you work. Do not complete one section of your report before starting with the next. Instead, draft incrementally, moving no further than the rough draft stage of each section of the report before moving on to the next section. If you work this way, then when you have completed most of your research, you will have written a rough draft of most of your paper. By drafting a research report section by section, your completed draft emerges in increments. You avoid the problem of having to write up your paper after all of your research has been completed.

The processes involved in writing a research report are very different from the processes of writing an essay. Essays are limited in scope — they are usually only a few pages long and they typically cover a narrow topic. Essays can often be written in one sitting (although writers should always return a day later to revise and edit). But research reports reflect the results of conducting research over time — taking notes, reviewing literature, conducting experiments, or developing designs. An acceptable research report simply cannot be written in one session.

Professional research papers involve weeks or even months of planning and experimenting, as well as writing, about the research. Research reports in professional disciplines are not the same kind of writing assignments that you had in basic composition and writing classes. Instead, they are knowledge-gathering and problem-solving processes. The purpose of a research-writing assignment is not to teach students or employees how to write or to give them writing practice; the purpose is to conduct and report essential research. So write your research report incrementally, a bit here and a bit there. Let it develop over time. By writing some parts of your report early in the process, you can write and conduct research simultaneously.

Carpenters do not finish each room of a house before moving on to the next section; instead, they rough out the entire house, returning to finish off different parts of the house when appropriate. Similarly, try to rough out different sections of your report before trying to finish them. By moving to different parts of a paper before other parts are finished, you distance yourself from your draft and can become a more objective critic of your own writing.

The following advice will be useful to you no matter how you choose to adapt to a word processing program. In other words, it does not matter if you draft by hand and then key in the results later, or if you compose directly at the computer screen.

What to Do First

First, create a subdirectory of your word processing program to use as a container for your work in progress. Then create sub-subdirectories for individual parts of your paper and for the outline. If you work on a MacIntosh or if you work with Windows, try the folder concept rather than the directory concept for organizing computer files. Your main folder (with subfolders within) would look like Figure 11-1a for an original research report:

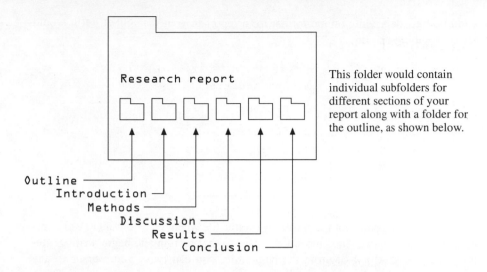

This folder would contain individual subfolders for different sections of your report along with a folder for the outline, as shown below.

F I G U R E 11-1a   The Main Folder for a Research Report

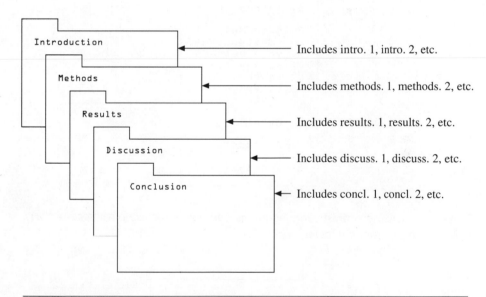

Includes intro. 1, intro. 2, etc.

Includes methods. 1, methods. 2, etc.

Includes results. 1, results. 2, etc.

Includes discuss. 1, discuss. 2, etc.

Includes concl. 1, concl. 2, etc.

F I G U R E 11-1b   Subfolders for the Research Report

As you work in each subfolder, create a file named and numbered for each part of your paper, for example, "outline.1." Each time you work on the outline, save it with a new name (e.g., "outline.2") and keep it in the outline folder. The outline file would differ, depending on the format for a report in your discipline, but it would look something like this:

```
1. Introduction

2. Methods

3. Results

4. Discussion

5. Conclusion
```

Open the most recent version of the outline file whenever you want to work on a section of your report. Then move the cursor to that section and begin writing. Remember: you need not begin at the beginning; you can move your cursor to any section. In the sample below, we indicate how a researcher who chooses to begin drafting by working on the methods section would proceed.

```
1. Introduction

2. Methods
   (Write down
   your methods
   at any time
   in the
   research
   process.)

3. Results

4. Discussion

5. Conclusion
```

Remember: when you finish working on the outline file (or any other section file), save it in the appropriate folder.

```
Outline of Report

(includes all outlines, files, saved as
"outline.1," "outline.2," etc.)
```

Also, you might want to save each section of your outline in a separate file in the appropriate section folder. In each sub-folder, you would have a complete record of your work — saved section by section as well as in one piece; in other words, if you rename each file every time you work on it and save it to the appropriate subdirectory or folder, then you can read previous files to check to see if you have expressed yourself more clearly in an earlier version.

How to Proceed

Consider the following procedure each time you sit down to work on your report. Load the outline file and give it a new name (so you will not erase the previous version of the file). Then, move your cursor to the section you want to work on and type in either rough ideas or finished paragraphs. Use the outline file as your scratch pad for the section you are working on. There you have access to the rest of your outline — with some sections complete and some incomplete or in various stages of completion. Then at the end of each writing session, use your word processor to block and copy the updated version of that section and save it to the file for that section.

To review, try working like this:

1. Work on drafting a section in the outline file, and rename it each time so that you have access to earlier versions.
2. As you feel relatively satisfied with the results of your drafting session, block the section and save it in the file corresponding to the section of the report you are working on. (Thus, you will have a separate copy of the section as well as a complete copy of the draft in progress.)
3. If you want to refine your section without the distraction of related sections, you can load just the section file and rework it. As you finish, remember to copy it to the appropriate section of the outline file when you finish with that section. (Thus, your outline file will always have the most current results of your work.)
4. Whenever you work in the outline file, feel free to revise sections other than the one you are working on. (Every time you revise a section, reread previous sections. As you reread those sections, look for awkward sentences and incomplete ideas and change them. When you resave the file, you will have updated not only the section you were focusing on, but you will have revised other sections as well. Remember to copy changes to the appropriate section files.)

To sum up, whenever you have the chance, jot down notes and, if possible, draft individual sections before moving on to the next step of your project. For example, after you have read the literature related to your topic, draft a literature review — even if you haven't yet clarified your research questions. Then, when you are ready to add your research question or thesis statement to the introduction, open a word processing file and add it to your emerging draft. Your draft will then grow in increments.

As you design the research plan and consider various research methodologies, try to do some of your thinking in writing. By jotting down your thoughts, you can clarify your thinking and ideas; you can then determine what you need to do next. Instead of stopping when you get stuck, use drafting to continue your momentum.

ORGANIZING YOUR REPORT

Let your content, purpose, and audience influence how you organize your information. Different kinds of research reports require different kinds of organization. These varying reports are discussed separately in Chapters 14, 15, 16, and 17, but some organizational concepts apply to almost all such writing.

Use an outline file, as suggested above, to build the text of your draft. You may want to take notes and to brainstorm directly in that file. Or you may prefer to use a separate file for gathering ideas and planning. Any time that you want to copy a section of text from individual files to the draft file, you will be able to do so.

If you are going to write a report that does not require a fixed organization, create an outline with your own headings corresponding to your topic. As long as you remember that a word processor is a fluid medium, you should not have the problem paper-and-pencil writers have when they let the outline control them, rather than guide them. Let your content and movement of ideas suggest the form rather than imposing the form artificially. When and how you organize information depends on you and the writing task.

DEVELOPING VISUALS FOR RESEARCH REPORTS

When writing research reports, the old adage "a picture is worth a thousand words" can be expanded to "a good visual saves a thousand words." Using visuals carefully helps you communicate your ideas effectively and efficiently.

Style manuals often group visuals into two major categories—tables and figures. Tables usually, but not always, present numerical data, while figures present data and information through more generalized representations. Tables summarize numerical values of the key concepts—the variables of the research question. Thus, most writers usually build tables around numbers, percentages, or statistical tests. For some research reports, raw numbers will be sufficient; for other research reports advanced statistical analyses—chi-square, correlation, t-test, analysis of variance, regression, or mathematical computations—may be required.

As you look across the disciplines, you will find many different visuals: tables, bar graphs, line graphs, pie charts, schematics, line art, equations, and photographs. Not only do visuals present the key information, but they can help structure and support the narrative. Experienced writers often develop their visuals for research reports before they begin drafting a specific section. Visuals help them as they draft their reports, since the images and the words together help the writer express ideas. When writing the narrative, skilled writers do not repeat and discuss all of the data in the visual; they focus on its meaning instead. They will, however, point out any unusual aspects of the data.

How do you decide which kind of visual to use? Whether you use tables or figures depends upon your research project, your assignment requirements, and your intended audience — your readers. Figures usually present information in a general way; line graphs show trends or patterns. Bar graphs and pie charts provide comparisons. Photographs provide a real image of a subject or scene, while line art provides artistic renditions of subjects. Schematics, equations, and decision trees use symbols to represent concepts, variables, or ideas.

You should keep in mind that the visual impact of your report depends to a great degree on the layout or appearance of your final copy. Carefully designed tables and figures, as well as effective use of such typographical elements as white space, bullets, titles, and subtitles, can make the difference between a mediocre and an impressive report.

Visuals can improve the layout or design of your research report by breaking up the narrative. Examine successful magazines, books, brochures, and other publications; you will find hundreds of visuals. Publishers long ago learned that visuals break up the grayness of the printed page and thus add visual appeal.

HOW TO DETERMINE WHETHER YOU NEED TO USE VISUALS

Whether or not you need to use visuals depends upon the discipline, your subject, and the type of research report you are writing. Generally, research papers in the humanities — fields such as literature, music, theater, foreign languages, and dance — contain fewer visuals than do research papers in the empirical social sciences, biological sciences, physical sciences, and engineering.

Some research topics lend themselves better to visuals than others do. For example, most engineering research reports require more visuals than philosophy research reports. A paper arguing the benefits of meditation might be developed without visuals, while a research paper comparing strategies for reducing radon in schools could lend itself to many visuals.

Visuals often form the heart of original research reports and problem-solving research reports, while they usually play a lesser role in literature review papers and thesis argument research papers. Overall, original research reports usually contain more tables and line graphs than do other visuals. Problem-solving and design research reports depend heavily on line art, equations, and schematics (See Chapter 17 for an example) to present key information. If literature research reports do contain visuals, they are usually simple tables, bar graphs, pie charts, or line art. Occasionally, thesis statement research reports contain simple visuals. Whatever the research paper, visuals

1. Summarize key information,
2. Improve report design, and
3. Enhance the message.

If you develop visuals carefully, you can reduce the length of your paper. When handled carefully, one or two visuals can present the essence of many pages of text in the research report. By summarizing the key information, supporting the narrative, and improving the overall design, visuals can enhance your message and help readers understand your points. Working together, visuals and narrative can help you communicate most effectively.

Which Visuals Should You Use?

While you are reviewing literature for your research report, locate research journals in your discipline and examine their use of visuals. Note especially the variety of visuals used, the kinds most frequently used, their placement within the text, and their style. Some publications use specific kinds more frequently than other publications do. Furthermore, style guide conventions for visuals vary widely across the disciplines. Some use Arabic numerals to number visuals, while others use letters or Roman numerals. Some style guides stipulate that legends — titles or captions — be placed above tables and below figures, but a few follow other practices. Still other style guides call for open and simple visuals, and a few call for using boxes around figures plus vertical and horizontal lines to separate the rows and columns in tables. In short, look carefully at the style used in the discipline of your research report and follow it unless your instructor tells you otherwise.

Adapting Visuals to Your Audience

Visuals should be suited to your audience — if readers cannot understand tables, figures, and graphs, their effectiveness will be lost. When considering what kinds of visuals to use, carefully consider your audience and ask yourself, "What kinds of visuals have my readers seen? What kinds of visuals can they read and understand?"

Remember too that your readers may not know the terms you use in your visuals. Or the abbreviations you use may mean something different to them. For example, *ppm* stands for parts per million when you are discussing chemical equations and pages per minute when you are discussing laser printers. Symbols and abbreviations often mean different things in different fields. When in doubt, explain terms with footnotes.

What Are the Key Components of Visuals?

Tables and figures differ in their fundamental components. This first section reviews the key components of tables and then the key components of figures.

Presenting data in formal tables requires that you follow some standard conventions. To begin, note the table elements in Figure 11-2. Note especially the location of the table number, title, spanner heads, rules (the parallel lines) and footnotes. The title (label of the table) goes above the data and describes the table contents.

Unlike tables, figures include several different kinds of visuals. In Figure 11-3 note the placement of the figure number and the legend; also note the simplicity of the visual. For bar graphs, note the values above the bars, and label the horizontal and

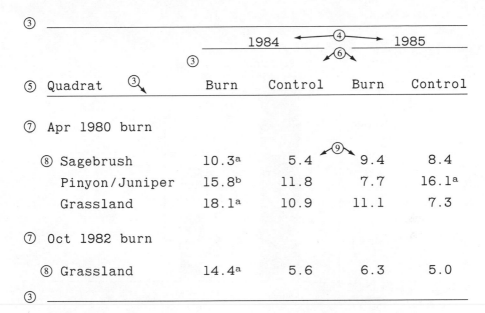

① Table 10

② Average Mule Deer Census on Burned and Seeded versus Unburned Control Quadrats

	1984		1985	
Quadrat	Burn	Control	Burn	Control
Apr 1980 burn				
Sagebrush	10.3[a]	5.4	9.4	8.4
Pinyon/Juniper	15.8[b]	11.8	7.7	16.1[a]
Grassland	18.1[a]	10.9	11.1	7.3
Oct 1982 burn				
Grassland	14.4[a]	5.6	6.3	5.0

⑩ Note: Each quadrat was censused 3 times each January.

⑪ [a]Greater ($p < 0.05$) than other treatment within year, Mann-Whitney U test.

[b]$p < 0.1$, Mann-Whitney U test.

Legend

① table number
② table title
③ rule
④ spanner head
⑤ stub head
⑥ column heads
⑦ stub subheading
⑧ stub
⑨ body
⑩ note, applying to entire table
⑪ note, applying to specific parts of table

FIGURE 11-2   The Main Components of a Table

Source: D. Zimmerman, "Written Communications" in A. Y. Cooperrider, R. J. Boyd, and H. R. Stuart, eds., _Inventory and Monitory of Wildlife Habitat_ (Denver, Colo.: U.S. Department of the Interior, Bureau of Land Management Service Center), 814.

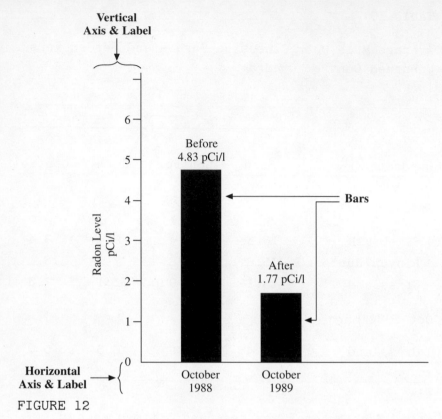

FIGURE 12

Average Radon Level in a Home Before and After Adding a Forced Air Ventilation System to the Crawl Space

---

F I G U R E   11-3   The Main Components of a Figure

---

vertical axes. For line graphs, limit the number of lines to four or five and make each line distinct from the others. For circle graphs, begin with the largest segment at noon, working clockwise around the circle and placing labels either in the segments or outside them if the segments are too narrow.

How Do You Prepare the Layout and Design?

In preparing all visuals elements, follow the style manual, style book, or other guide of your discipline. Beyond the style book guidelines, you can enhance the typographical design of your research report by using overviews or previews; using descriptive heads and subheads; and using bullet lists for key points.

A brief overview or preview of a section prepares your reader for what will follow. For example, study the introductions of the chapters of this book. Note that they list the major points to be covered in the subsequent narrative. In addition to overviews, consider using descriptive heads and subheads — either declarative statements or questions — to help your readers. Such descriptive heads help them to recall their previous knowledge on a subject and also help them to build a knowledge base for reading the subsequent sections of the report. Finally, bullet lists, as illustrated in the example below, highlight key elements. Such lists make the key points stand out and give readers a preview of what is to come.

```
    When producing overhead transparencies for presen-
tations, your copy should be


    • Big
    • Bold
    • Simple


By big, we mean the copy should be at least one inch
high on the screen for every 20 feet of viewing dis-
tance. For bold, we mean . . . .
```

Too often visuals contain too much information, are cluttered, and are not tied clearly to the research question. Readers become confused and have difficulties understanding the message. To avoid such problems, keep your visuals to one major idea, keep them simple, and tie them directly to your research question. By keeping your visuals to one major idea related to your research question, you will make your message clear.

Consider the follow example based on a research project investigating how students interacted with desktop publishing systems. The specific objective was to determine where students turned for help when learning PageMaker on an IBM system early in the semester. The specific question was:

How frequently did students seek help from selected information sources when learning to use a desk top publishing system early in the semester?

Now consider Table 11-1 in Figure 11-4 on the following page.

Table 11-1

Assessment of How Frequently Students Sought Help from Selected Sources Early in the Semester

Sources	Mean[a]	S.D.[b]	n[c]
Other students	2.19	1.28	31
The class instructor	2.17	1.23	29
The laboratory instructor	1.36	.71	31
Laboratory handouts or instruction sheets	3.36	1.34	28
The software manuals	3.96	1.14	25
The hardware manuals	4.30	1.06	23
Just trying or playing with software	2.00	.89	31
Just trying or playing with computer	2.00	.97	31
Just trying or playing with the mouse	1.90	1.00	30
Just trying or playing with the keyboard	1.97	.96	30
Just trying or playing with the monitor	2.93	1.39	29
Just trying or playing with the scanner	3.28	1.41	29

[a]Mean calculated by summing the ratings (1 to 5 scale where 1 = Very frequently to 5 = Hardly ever) of each individual's response in the sample ($n=29$ to 31) and dividing by the n answering that question.

[b]The standard deviation of the responses; see SPSS for its methods of calculating basic statistics.

[c]n = sample size (number of students responding to each question).

FIGURE 11-4   A Sample Table and Narrative

Proposed narrative for the table:

> Students sought help most often by using the systems from the laboratory instructor and laboratory handouts and instruction sheets, and they used the hardware and software manuals the least (Table 11-1).

How Do You Produce Tables?

To produce tables, some researchers prepare rough plans, others work directly on the word processor to develop finished tables, and still others take their files from statistical packages. Whichever way you work, you will need to develop the legend, heads, stubheads, and the data for the cells. Also, you will have to arrange them so the data reflect the research question.

When preparing tables, follow these guidelines unless your style guide indicates different conventions:

Number the tables with Arabic numbers,

Put table numbers and titles above the tables,

Limit divider rules,

Select clean, crisp type faces for copy,

Indicate units in columns,

Indicate blank cells with dashes or zeros, and

Align numbers on decimal points and commas.

To begin a table, draft the title, the spanner heads, and the columns and rows, and then add your data to the cells. When working on a typewriter or computer, use the five-space tab settings to make typing easier. Some software programs and electronic typewriters have tab settings that automatically align numbers on decimal points. If you have not previously used such functions, practice with them before typing your final visuals.

How Do You Prepare Figures?

First check the conventions of the style guide or publication that you are following when writing your paper. Remember too that the style manuals classify illustrations as either tables or figures. Anything that is not a table is considered a figure.

When preparing figures, follow these guidelines unless your style guide indicates different conventions:

Number figures with Arabic numbers,

Put figure numbers and titles below the figures,

Select clear, crisp type faces, for any copy, and

Label all components or parts simply and clearly; then follow the style manual or journal style for your research report.

If you lack artistic skills and must prepare visuals, consider using artists' supplies (such as presstype and similar artwork) or computer software programs. Check the art or graphic arts department of your college's bookstore or nearby art supply stores for a wide selection of presstype and art supplies. By using presstype and prepared graphics, you can prepare professional-looking visuals with minimal practice.

Alternatively, check your school's computer laboratories to see what graphic visual and drawing software programs are available. Common software programs include Harvard Graphics, WordPerfect Draw, Corel Draw, and MicroSoft Paint.

Many of these programs have excellent tutorials to help you learn the system, including introductory guides and functions. Learn the basics of using the software early in the term so you do not find yourself trying to learn a software program under deadline pressure. Too often, inexperienced users encounter major hurdles that cannot be overcome under deadline pressures of research papers. To further avoid problems, learn how to build a variety of basic figures that you might use in your research reports. In that way, you can quickly make the figures you will need for your projects.

Placing Visuals in the Text

After developing tables and figures, you need to place them properly in your text. Some style guides require that you incorporate your visuals into the narrative (the typed final copy) of your report, while others ask you to place all visuals at the back of your report. Whichever way you go, begin by preparing the visuals on separate pages (or files, if you are working on a computer). If you must incorporate the final version into your narrative, preparing the visuals on separate pages gives a good idea how much space they require. If you are using a word processor, you can force a page break before and after the visual.

In most professional settings, most publications require that the authors place the visuals at the back of their research reports. The publication's staff then places the tables and figures in the appropriate location in the production process. If you place visuals at the back of the report, indicate their location in the narrative by inserting a comment, such as

[Insert Table 1 about here]

Such notations usually go immediately after the paragraph in which either the table or figure is first mentioned. When using this approach, you need not spend lots of time juggling your narrative to insert the visuals in the final research report.

If your instructor requires that you insert visuals in your narrative, you can save yourself work by indicating the visual location (see above) when writing drafts. Then you can insert your visuals when you type the final manuscript.

PROGRESS REPORTS—KEEPING TRACK OF YOUR DRAFT

Progress reports are succinct documents in which you report your activities on your research paper for a stated time period. Filing these reports encourages you to draft in stages, to think about parts of your final report, to identify what you still have left to accomplish, to identify potential difficulties, and, if necessary, to seek guidance when you need help to overcome the problems.

Your instructor may ask you to file progress reports weekly, biweekly, monthly, or less often. You will need to ask when they are due. The formats progress reports take include memos, letters, or formal reports. In the student example below, Marie uses a standard memo format. Other formats include the standard business letter (Chapter 7 for the standard business letter format) or a formal report (Chapter 13).

Within the report, use a combination of narrative paragraphs and short lists to highlight your accomplishments. Use narratives to summarize succinctly the key elements, and use lists to highlight major accomplishments and items of special note. Remember that lists and highlighted items make it easier for your readers to find relevant information.

Marie's progress report details what she has accomplished on gathering information and designing a system to reduce radon in a tri-level home. Radon is a radioactive gas that comes from some soils; some researchers estimate that radon build-up in homes, schools, and work places may cause up to 30,000 cases of lung cancer annually.

Tips on Writing Progress Reports

As you work on your progress reports, keep the following suggestions in mind:

1. Keep your progress reports short—not more than two pages.
2. Use the designated format.
3. To draft your report, ask yourself four questions:
   What have I accomplished on my report (or since the last reporting period)?
   What do I need to accomplish in the next reporting period or to finish the report?
   Do I need help in resolving any of the difficulties that I encountered?
4. List your answers to these questions on paper and use your list as a planning tool from which you can draft your progress report.
5. Prepare visuals, if they will help you report your progress.
6. Draft your progress report using terms your readers will understand.
7. Set your report aside to cool.
8. Revise the report for completeness, accuracy, organization, style, grammar, mechanics, spelling, and related issues.

TO: Professor Ed Carpenter
      500 Aylesworth
      Colorado State University
FROM: Marie Edwards
      345 Strong Hall
RE: September Progress Report: A System
                                Design for
                                Reducing Radon
                                in a Tri-Level
                                Home
DATE: October 1, 1990

Thus far, I have collected the basic information, reviewed the needed literature, and interviewed five radon control specialists. I anticipate completing the system design by November 1 and my design report by November 22.

Progress to Date
1. Over the last four weeks I have reviewed the radon measures collected in your home last winter. Radon levels in your home, at an average of 6.6, exceed the EPA's safe level of picocuries per liter, but fall within an acceptable range. However, the EPA suggests continued monitoring and recommends that remedial measures be considered.
2. Through literature review and interviews with five radon control experts, I have identified six techniques that can reduce radon levels: (a) seal all cracks in the concrete walls and floor in your basement; (b) Install a plastic barrier between the framed wall in the basement and crawl space; (c) pressurize your crawl space by installing a small fan and air distribution system;

(d) install two sub-slab ventilation sinks
(fans that suck air from below the concrete
floor) below the basement floor; (e) add an
exterior ventilation system around the foundation of your basement; and (f) install an
air-to-air heat exchanger/ventilator system
to bring fresh air into your home and exhaust the stale, radon-ladened air.

Remaining Activities

During the next month, I will examine the
floor plan of your home, conduct an on-site in-
spection, examine any soils reports or soils
tests on your home, select the available radon
reduction techniques, develop a step-wise system for installation and testing, obtain cost
estimates of supplies and installation, prepare
the illustrations, and plan and write the research report.

Problems or Difficulties Encountered

None.

Once you have a draft, ask yourself the following questions:

1. Have I included all relevant activities that I have done during the reporting period?
2. Will the reader understand all items, lists, and visuals that I have included? If not, do I need to add any explanation?
3. Have I kept the report short?
4. Did I use an acceptable format?
5. Have I checked the report for clarity, conciseness, spelling, mechanics, grammar, style, and related issues?
6. Will I be able to complete the report by the deadline?
7. Do I have a copy for my files?

CONCLUSION

You should get to know yourself as a writer and develop a drafting style that suits your needs. We have suggested an incremental method that works for us and for most researchers we know. You will need to adapt that method to your own requirements.

What is important is that you develop a research-writing process that is distinctly different from your essay-writing process. Research takes time, and writing research reports is difficult and time-consuming for many students. To use your time effectively, and to allow yourself the opportunity to reflect over the ideas you have produced in previous drafting sessions, try the incremental drafting method discussed in this chapter. And do draft your text and your visuals interactively — using words to suggest images and images to direct your word choices.

Finally write a progress report — even if you do not have to. By assessing what you have, you develop a better sense of what you still need to do to complete your research report.

CHAPTER 12

Strategies for
Revising and Editing

Since terms like *revising* and *editing* have different meanings in different discourse communities, you should find out how writers in your field use these terms. In the following discussion, *revision* means the act of detecting, diagnosing, and solving large-scale problems such as focus, organization, or coherence; *editing* means the process of identifying and correcting sentence or paragraph-level flaws.

To help you learn how to revise and edit more effectively, this chapter covers the following topics:

differences between revising and editing,
guidelines for revision and editing

—revising for content,
—revising for organization,
—revising for coherence,
—revising visuals,
—editing for preciseness and clarity, and
—editing for errors.

WHY IS REVISION SOMETIMES CONSIDERED DIFFERENT FROM EDITING?

To inexperienced writers, revising and editing are synonymous. But inexperienced writers seldom make more than superficial changes in their text, whereas experienced writers make changes at a deeper level. Experienced writers usually see revising as much more global than editing. When experienced writers revise, they make major changes in content, style, or organization — changes that make a significant difference in the quality of their drafts. They literally re-see their texts, looking at their sentences and paragraphs with a critical eye after having examined a rough draft.

You will hear the terms *revision* and *editing* used interchangeably by some people and selectively by others. In journalism and publishing, for example, the term *editing* refers to the practice of detecting global problems with a piece of writing as well as isolating sentence structure, grammar, and editing errors. Newspaper reporters, magazine writers, and their respective editors often lump all editing activities together, but they differentiate between making corrections on the manuscript copy and the final copy which is set in type.

Professional technical editors who work for businesses, industries, and government agencies often classify revision and editing into several manageable activities. The specifics will vary between organizations. At the Jet Propulsion Laboratory, for example, Robert Van Buren and Mary Fran Buehler (1980) developed a "levels of edit" concept for technical publications. Of their nine levels of edit, the more relevant for preparing research reports are the format edit, which covers typographical and format issues; the mechanical style edit, which focuses on capitalization, abbreviations and similar conventions; the language edit, which covers spelling, grammar, punctuation and usage; and the substantive edit, which concentrates on the content and completeness of the manuscript (Van Buren and Buehler 1980).

The Chicago Manual of Style, one of the major style manuals in the publishing field, divides the editorial function into mechanical and substantive editing (Chicago Manual of Style 1982, 51). Mechanical editing focuses on consistency of spelling, grammar, and other style matters; substantive editing focuses on rewriting, reorganizing, and suggesting how to enhance the manuscript. Copyediting, according to *The Chicago Manual of Style*, entails concentrating on every detail in the typed manuscript (1982, 51). Editors use copyediting symbols for making changes as they prepare the manuscript for typesetting. To copyedit a manuscript, they use a specific set of symbols, as explained in Appendix A of this book. After the copy is typeset, they check — or proofread — the typeset galleys (columns of type).

As you can see, different discourse communities simply use the term "editing" in different ways. No one way is right or wrong, just a different method of approaching the task of improving a draft manuscript and converting it into a final, acceptable version of a manuscript.

Whatever you and your instructors or colleagues call this activity of preparing the final version of your research report, re-examine your entire report first for larger issues — content, organization, and format. Look too for inconsistencies, gaps, and other problems before you turn to the finishing touches. In other words, follow an in-depth approach to revision and editing whenever possible. Only after you are finished with the larger issues, however, should you concentrate on spelling, style, and grammar.

GUIDELINES FOR REVISION AND EDITING

One way to break down the revising and editing activities into manageable shape is to structure your revision and editing sessions sequentially:

1. Begin by looking at content.
2. Check the organization: consider the paragraphing as well as the use of headings, subheadings, and visuals.
3. Review coherence: maintain topic unity, including effective transitional phrases, and so on.
4. Consider precision and clarity of expression: examine word choice and sentence structure, sentence variety, and sentence length.
5. Edit for grammar, spelling, and typographical errors.
6. Double-check your draft against your style manual or style sheet as you format and type or print the final version of your report.

Revising the Content

First things first. With errors or omissions in content, your report doesn't stand a chance of being effective. Whether you have conducted original scientific research or more standard library research, you have a responsibility to your audience. You need to follow through on what you set out to do. Be sure that you have given your readers enough information to enable them to replicate the research. Ask yourself the following questions:

Have I told my readers why I conducted this research?

Have I made it clear how my research fits into other researchers' investigations?

Have I pointed out potential problems with my data-collection techniques?

Have I reported all the necessary details?

Have I been thorough in reporting the results?

Have I made any errors in reasoning? Logic?

Have I made any errors in my inferences?

Even if your research has relied more on secondary sources than on original investigation, you need to be similarly complete. If, for instance, you are making recommendations about what kinds of software to purchase for your office, read more than popular computing publications; also delve into the literature of other fields. For instance, if you are doing a report for a law firm on available software for attorneys, you should explore not only legal journals, but popular computing journals and even journals devoted to composition and rhetoric (since these journals sometimes carry essays on legal writing or reviews of software related to legal writing). Further, you should check to see if academic computer journals have carried any reports on legal software. In addition, you should either *try* the software you are recommending or *interview* or *observe* someone who has used the software. Published reviews are inadequate and unconvincing sources.

What you need to keep in mind about content, then, is that until you have collected all the necessary information and incorporated it into your report, you will not be able to do a final revision for matters such as those covered in the following sections of this chapter — organization, coherence, and clarity of expression.

Revising the Organization of Your Report

Good report writing is organized so that readers can follow the movement of the report, the flow of the argument, and the presentation of the information. *Organization* refers to the overall order of presentation and to the connectedness or logical links between the individual sections and the overall point. For example, cookbooks generally give an overall idea of the dish to be prepared before they present the step-by-step version of the recipe. The step-by-step directions (though a separate section of the recipe) must be consistent with the presentation of background information about it.

One way to check the organization of your report is to read through it slowly, writing summary glosses in the margin to remind you at a glance of the point of each paragraph. Then, by reading over your glosses and tracking your thoughts, you can spot places where you may lose your reader because your organization is not automatically clear to someone less familiar with your topic. You may need to make some coherence links clearer for the reader (see the list below). You might, for instance, need to add transitional phrases or transitional paragraphs, insert several paragraphs of elaboration to clarify the connections, or rearrange the organization.

Here is a list of transitional words and phrases to help readers with the organization of a report:

> First, . . .
> Second, . . .
> Third, . . .
>
> One way is to . . .
> Another way is to . . .
> Still another way is to . . .
>
> Moreover, . . .
> Furthermore, . . .
> Finally, . . .

Consider the following questions as you review your report for organizational problems:

1. Have I broken down my material into an appropriate organization? *If not, how can I reorganize the components of my report?*
2. Have I clarified my central idea or my main points? *If not, how can I revise my main points to make them clear?*
3. Have I used headings and subheadings to emphasize the organization of my report?
4. Does an analysis of my organization reveal any omissions? Any need to delete material? *If so, what should be cut? What should be added?*
5. Is it clear how the individual sections of my report (separate paragraphs, separate sections, heads and subheads) are connected to the main idea? *If not, how can I make those connections?*

Revising for Coherence

Coherence means, literally, sticking together. Sometimes, after carefully gathering information and writing it up, you will read through your draft and notice that your text is difficult to follow. If this happens, check to see whether you have written an organized, but ultimately incoherent paper. That is, you might have produced a report that includes all the right content in all the right places (Introduction, Methods, and so on) but fails because a reader cannot follow the connections on a sentence-by-sentence or a paragraph-by-paragraph level.

Writers typically use what are called coherence links to help readers follow complex reports including the following strategies: *consistency* in following an overall movement of ideas (chronological organization, cause-effect organization); use of *transitions* between sections (either transitional words or orienting phrases); clearly written *topic sentences* that connect to the main point of the section or of the entire report; and effective use of *headings and subheadings*.

In a coherent report, your reader will be able to follow what you say and will be convinced that your argument is valid. Further, your reader will believe that you carried out your research effectively. If your report confuses your reader, you will not have succeeded either as a researcher or as a writer.

Consider the following questions when you revise for coherence problems:

1. Do I provide the reader with a road map of my report? (For instance, reports in many fields include a road map statement in the introductory section — a statement such as ''In this report I will first . . . ; next, I will . . . ; then I will . . . ; finally, I will . . .'')
2. Do I include transitional phrases or connecting sentences whenever I shift to different ideas?
3. Do I maintain topic consistency within paragraphs? That is, if I am focusing on a topic such as the damage to the environment, do I

remain focused on the damage rather than switching to what environmentalists can do to help remedy the problems?

4. Do I use transitional devices such as synonyms and pronoun references within paragraphs to let the reader know that I have not shifted
topics?

Revising Visuals

As you revise, look again at the effectiveness of your visuals (tables and figures), and then reconsider your typographical presentation. Begin by reconsidering
how well the tables and figures help answer the research question(s) that directed the
report. Is the information you present tied closely to the original question or hypothesis that directed your research? Have you carefully tied the elements of the research
question, thesis statement, or hypothesis to the information presented in the tables
and figures? If not, revise as needed to clarify your visual presentation.

Next consider the technical accuracy of the elements of your visuals by asking
such questions as

Have I included all of the visuals?

Are the titles appropriately labeled?

Are the heads and legends included?

Are the heads and legends appropriately labeled? Complete?

Are the visuals numbered correctly? Sequentially through the manuscript?

Are the correct data entered in the visuals?

Are the statistical and mathematical calculations correct?

Do the scales on figures present the information correctly?

Once you have the content of the visuals revised, then consider how well the visuals
work by reconsidering how well they will help the readers understand your content.
Begin such a revision by asking questions like

Do the visuals support the narrative?

Are the visuals complete?

Are the visuals simple?

Do the visuals focus on one point, concept, or idea?

Will the readers readily understand the visuals?

By using these questions to guide you as you reconsider your visuals, you will have
determined whether they clearly communicate your findings to your readers.

When looking at the format — the typographical aspect of your manuscript —
ask such questions as

Do I have sufficient levels of heads and subheads?

Do I have too many levels of heads and subheads?

Are the heads distinctly labeled so the readers can easily identify the major sections of the research report?

Do all of the major sections have heads that clearly delineate the respective sections?

Is the typeface and type size for the narrative appropriate for the readers?

Have I consistently used the appropriate typefaces for the different sections of the manuscript?

Revising for the visuals requires careful consideration of the visual impact of your presentation. As you work, keep in mind that the visual impact forms the first impression of your report; often this first impression determines how your readers will finally react to your report and to the research you are reporting.

Edit for Clarity and Conciseness

At this point, make one or more trips through your draft looking for ways to improve the clarity and conciseness. Remember: long, wordy sentences detract from your report's communicative effectiveness.

Although it is not a firm rule, it is usually true that if your sentences run beyond twenty words, readers will have trouble understanding you. Make sure, too, that your ideas flow smoothly from one sentence to the next and from one paragraph to the next.

When you trim your copy, cut it as much as you can without distorting its completeness or effectiveness. You will find that you can usually say the same thing in fewer words. Among the effective strategies for trimming sentences in your drafts are

Replace weak verbs with strong ones

Remove excess prepositional phrases

Remove excess clauses

Use concrete, specific terms

Minimize acronyms, jargon, and similar terms

Cut wordiness (Zimmerman and Clark 1987).

Here are some examples of these strategies:

1. *Replace weak verbs with strong ones.* Whenever possible, use the active voice. Consider these passive forms and then their recast active voice forms:

WEAK: The opening song was sung by the lead actor.
BETTER: The lead actor sang the opening song.

WEAK: A recession for 1995 was predicted by the bank's
economist.
BETTER: The bank's economist predicted a recession for 1995.

Frequently, you can identify passive voice constructions by looking for *is, was, were* and other *to be* verb forms, the prepositional phrase, *by X,* or by asking, "Who carried out the action?"

There are always exceptions. Sometimes, as Joseph Williams points out in *Style* (Williams 1991), passive voice is appropriate. Choose passive constructions when no need exists to identify the actor, to focus on what's happening, to avoid legal problems, to provide variety, and to build to a climax (Zimmerman and Clark 1987, 195).

2. *Replace abstract nouns and adjectives—words ending in* al, tion, ence, ment, *and* ure. You can frequently recast sentences and use stronger verbs that carry more meaning:

WEAK: The Police Department's sting operation is an inducement
of drug dealers into the apartment.
BETTER: For the Police Department's sting operation, officers
induced drug dealers into the apartment.

3. *Minimize "There are . . ." and other padded constructions.* Although not incorrect, excessive uses of "There are . . ." and similar constructions reflect wordy writing. Consider the following:

WEAK: There are three ways the actor can portray the villain.
BETTER: The actor can portray the villain in three ways.

Other similar padded constructions include "It was reported that . . ." and "These are . . ."

4. *Whenever possible, delete excess prepositional phrases.* You can reduce the number of prepositional phrases by deleting unnecessary ones, or recasting them into adjectives or adverbs:

WEAK: In the five chapters of this book that follow . . .
BETTER: In the following five chapters . . .

WEAK: The coonhound bayed at the moon in a mournful manner.
BETTER: The coonhound bayed mournfully at the moon.

WEAK: The actor's coat of a red color was torn as he left the stage.
BETTER: The actor tore his red coat as he left the stage.

5. *Whenever possible, remove or recast excessive clauses.* You can eliminate them, reduce them to prepositional phrases, or recast them as adjectives.

WEAK: This play, which we are watching, makes me sad.
BETTER: This play makes me sad.

WEAK: Actors that have no lines seldom steal the show.
BETTER: Actors with no lines seldom steal the show.

WEAK: John Jones, who is an applied mathematician, works for an insurance company.
BETTER: John Jones, an applied mathematician, works for an insurance company.

6. *Whenever possible, replace vague, general terms.* Vague, general terms tell nothing. Eliminate such terms or replace them with specific, concrete terms. Vague terms include *little, big, very, short, tall, a lot, too much, soon, shortly, large,* and *strong.*

WEAK: The boy led his big dog into the arena.
BETTER: The boy led his Great Dane into the arena.

7. *Whenever possible, minimize acronyms, jargon, and similar terms.* In many settings, writers become familiar with terminology and jargon that their readers may not understand. When editing your drafts, look for and eliminate such terms.

WEAK: Please complete your assignment ASAP.
BETTER: Please complete your report by noon, October 25th.

WEAK: He works as a deer biologist for the PGC.
BETTER: He works as a deer biologist for the Pennsylvania Game Commission.

8. *Whenever possible, cut wordiness.* When you edit, cut unnecessary words, phrases, sentences, and passages.

WEAK: Other schools have their library resources consolidated in one building.
BETTER: Other schools have all library resources in one building.

WEAK: To gain shelf space in the stacks, some libraries separate
large books and place oversized books together.

BETTER: To gain space in the stacks, some libraries shelve large
books together.

When you polish your drafts, take a lesson from professional writers and editors and use the copyediting symbols presented in Appendix A. By using such symbols you standardize your changes, speed the revision process, and make it easier to incorporate changes when you revise your text on screen.

Editing for Errors

Tools of the Trade.   Before you begin a final check for appearance details, you will need (1) a grammar handbook, (2) a style manual, and (3) a collegiate dictionary. These publications establish conventions and help you make sure that the details of your research reports are consistent with the established guidelines of your discipline. You should remember, however, that the requirements listed by one style guide will differ markedly from those in other style guides (Appendix B). Since each discourse community establishes its own conventions and norms, each style guide often reflects the language practices of that community alone.

Grammar handbooks focus on grammar and usage, punctuation, mechanics, spelling, sentence structure, and expression. Even though these handbooks are typically issued as general guidelines for good writing, keep in mind that each handbook editor selects the principles that seem most appropriate and current from his or her perspective, but each editor's views of language appropriateness will differ. To assure consistency within your paper, select one respected grammar handbook, such as the *Harbrace College Handbook*, and consult it regularly.

Style manuals provide guidance for preparing reports, articles, and papers for specific academic disciplines or publishers; they also provide details about punctuation, grammar, and usage. Keep in mind that different grammar handbooks, style manuals, and dictionaries agree on many points but disagree on others. Style manuals usually take precedence over the grammatical advice in grammar handbooks and dictionaries, but be sure to use the correct manual for each course or for each profession.

As you take a variety of courses or as you shift professions, remember that each may use a different style manual, grammar handbook, or even dictionary. For example, the *MLA Handbook* provides guidance for research reports in the humanities; the *Publication Manual of the American Psychological Association* provides guidance for many social sciences; and the *CBE Style Manual* provides guidance for publications covering the biological sciences. Although the general topics are often similar, the details differ for handling references, abbreviations, punctuation, numbers, illustrations, footnotes, typing, and format. Furthermore, many style manuals specify which collegiate dictionaries you should use when checking spelling.

Collegiate dictionaries usually contain preferred and alternate spellings for 150,000 to 200,000 words; they may also include sections on punctuation and mechanics, manuscript form, symbols, listings of junior and four year colleges, and a brief style manual.

Appendix C lists selected grammar handbooks, style manuals, and dictionaries for different academic fields. If you do not have a good collegiate dictionary, a standard grammar handbook, and a style manual for your major field, consider buying them. By having them readily available, you can check details as you draft your research reports.

How to Proceed.   At this point, focus on the finer details of preparing your manuscript. Even though you may spot and correct spelling, mechanics, and other errors as you check your drafts for content, organization, and other problems, set aside specific time to concentrate on grammar and spelling. Further, keep in mind that few people can check for more than two or three different kinds of errors at one time, so try making different trips through your draft.

To check for spelling and typographical errors, slowly read through your draft, looking at each word. Concentrate on what you are reading and mentally check the spelling of each word. If you have trouble spotting errors, try reading your draft aloud and thinking about each word as you read. If you still have trouble spotting spelling errors, try reading the paper backwards, bottom to top, and right to left. You can then focus on each word and carefully consider it without being tied to reading the sentences. But such an approach needs to be coupled with a regular reading. Focusing on individual words does not let you know if you have used the wrong word, or if you have used a word out of context.

If you continue to have trouble spotting spelling errors, try tape recording your draft as you read it aloud. Then play the recording back and check the recording against the draft. If you still have trouble catching spelling and typographical errors, ask a friend to read your draft aloud. New eyes and ears reviewing any manuscript help spot weak content areas as well as spelling and typographical errors.

If you write on a personal computer, carefully read your copy on the screen for spelling errors. Then invoke the spelling checker program, if your word processing program has such an option. Such software provides a quick way to screen your manuscript for typographical and spelling errors. *But be careful: spelling checkers do not catch all errors.* If you use the wrong word—"too" instead of "to" for example—a spelling program will not flag your error. Furthermore, most spelling checkers are limited to about 100,000 words, so many words used in specialized fields do not appear in the standard dictionaries included with your word processor. However, you can add the specialized words as a supplemental dictionary to many programs. When you do, make sure that you correctly spell the words you enter.

Finally, never trust your reading of the copy on the screen. Two problems can emerge. First, you may miss items on the screen. Second, although rarely, errors may not appear on the screen but may slip into a manuscript during the printing. So, whenever you print a hard copy, always read that hard copy before turning in your assignment.

If you are told to follow a specific style manual, check that manual to see what grammar rules it includes and what dictionary it recommends that you follow. When you review a draft and encounter problems, check your references for those specific rules. Among the more commonly occurring errors are verb-subject agreement, pronoun agreement, usages such as who/whom, which/that, comma splices and run-on sentences, misplaced modifiers, contractions, possessives, and hyphenation. If you know you tend to make a specific kind of error, look carefully for that error as you review your draft.

With the advent of computers, grammar checking programs, such as *Correct Grammar™* and *Grammatik III™*, can help writers check their manuscripts. The programs work by comparing your draft against the rules programmed into the software. If the draft does not agree with the rule, the program stops, flags the item as a potential problem, and lets you examine the potential error and make any needed corrections. When you use such programs, carefully examine the suggestion to see if you have indeed made an error.

CONCLUSION

In earlier chapters we encouraged you to revise as you draft. In this chapter we have stressed the importance of devoting a block of time in your writing process to revision and editing. As you draft, you may make many changes, but the primary emphasis of your writing sessions is on generating a section of text. When you finally say, "That's it—I've done all I can do," you have arrived at the revising or editing stage of the writing process. At this stage, you need to review your manuscript critically and objectively. So set aside a definite portion of time for revision and editing. Think of these activities as strategies that can help you improve your research report. If you have developed your own revising strategy, use it; if not, follow the suggestions in this chapter. The quality of your research reports will improve, and you will be pleased with the results.

CHAPTER **13**

Finishing Up

T his chapter covers the essential tasks most report writers must consider at the final stage of their project. Let these questions help you assess your remaining tasks: (1) Are you expected to include an abstract with your finished paper? (2) Do you need to put your footnotes into finished form? (3) Do you need a bibliography or a list of references? (4) What formatting concerns do you need to address before you type or print your finished report?

After you have taken stock of what you have to do, turn to the appropriate section of this chapter:

writing the abstract,

preparing citations and the bibliography/literature-cited section,

sample style guides,

revising and editing the reference list, and

formatting research reports.

WRITING THE ABSTRACT

Although the order in which you complete these tasks is not fixed, many writers prefer to complete the abstract before working on the list of references. Because the abstract summarizes the research report, you should consider writing it as soon as you finish your report, when the material is fresh in your mind. If you understand the purpose of an abstract and you follow some basic guidelines, you should find it easy to write.

What Is an Abstract?

An abstract summarizes or highlights the key points in the research report and gives the reader some idea of its overall contents. It should give readers an overview of the article and help them decide if they need to read the entire article. Abstracts must be written to stand alone. That is, they must contain all the essential information and not force readers to read any other part of the research report itself. In a generic sense, abstracts include the *title* of the research report, the *authors' names*, a *narrative summarizing* the report, and *key words* for cataloging, indexing and, subsequently, locating the report.

A Close Look at Different Kinds of Abstracts

A careful review of academic disciplines shows different kinds of abstracts. *Descriptive abstracts* tell about a research report in a general way, describe the issues or problems the writer has explored, and help readers decide whether they need to read the full research report. In contrast, carefully written *informative abstracts* give readers the specifics of the research report.

Different kinds of research reports lend themselves to writing different kinds of abstracts. Original research reports usually lend themselves best to informative abstracts. Such projects are narrowly focused, investigate a narrowly defined area of one subject, and have limited findings. Informative abstracts commonly occur in journals covering agriculture, biology, chemistry, medical sciences, sociology, psychology, and related empirical social sciences. In professional settings, informative abstracts provide effective overviews for test reports, experiments, and evaluations.

Often, research reports with a wider focus, such as literature reviews, thesis statements and position reports, and problem solving and design reports lend themselves to descriptive abstracts. Descriptive abstracts commonly occur in journal articles in art, engineering, the humanities, mathematics, architecture, and statistics.

The examples in the following illustrations show two effective, succinct abstracts. The first, an informative abstract, summarizes a research project that answers a narrow research question, while the second, an effective descriptive abstract, gives readers a succinct summary of the proposed design.

AN INFORMATIVE ABSTRACT

A Study of the Tensile Strength of Four White Glues on Pine Wood
Susan McOllough Zimmer

Contact cements contain methylene formaldehyde that emits hazardous fumes that may cause cancer. Therefore, the United States Government is encouraging research to find a substitute adhesive. White wood adhesives are a possible replacement because they are transparent and non-toxic. To be suitable replacements, the glues must have the same tensile strength as contact cements. This report focuses on research that asked, "What are the tensile strengths of four commercially available white glues?" Fours brands were applied to one-inch square blocks, let dry and cure according to manufacture's specifications, and then tested on a universal testing machine. The adhesive yielded strengths of 43–45 psi. Because of these low strengths, none of the four white glues is a suitable replacement for contact cement.

KEY WORDS: Replacement for contact cement, tensile strengths, white glues, white adhesives, wood adhesives.

A DESCRIPTIVE ABSTRACT

A Radon Mitigation Plan for a Colorado Residential Home
Marie Edwards

Radon, a naturally occurring gas and by-product of the breakdown of uranium, granite, shale, phosphate and pitchblende, may cause between 5,000 and 20,000 lung cancer deaths annually. This report documents a strategy to reduce the radon levels in a home that tested above the EPA's recommended 4 pCi/l (picocuries per liter). The tri-level home contains a 1500 square foot living area, an 800 square foot basement, and a 700 square foot crawl space. During the late fall, winter, and early spring, the residents heat the home with a natural gas forced-air furnace. The detail mitigation plan elaborates on five steps: (1) sealing all cracks in the basement floor, walls, and foundation; (2) isolating the crawl space air from the remainder of the house; (3) pressurizing the crawl space; (4) installing sub-slab ventilation units; and (5) installing an air-to-air exchanger for the furnace. The mitigation plan calls for implementing the steps one at a time over two years and testing the radon levels after each step. Thus, the residents need only implement as many of the steps as are needed to reduce the radon to an acceptable level.

KEY WORDS: Radon, mitigation, cracks, crawl space, basement, houses, sub-slab ventilation, air-to-air exchangers, picocuries per liter, radon mitigation, pressurizing crawl space.

Guidelines for Writing Abstracts

Most abstracts should include the following ingredients:

title
author's name
narrative
key words

The general layout includes the title of the research report, followed by the author's name, the narrative, and then the key words. Most style manuals suggest limiting the narrative to between 25 and 600 words; seldom is an abstract more than 10 percent of the report's length. For many research reports, a 50 to 100 word abstract should suffice.

When you draft the text of the abstract, do not include illustrations, tables, or figures; similarly, do not refer to parts of the main report and do not cite any literature. The abstract should stand on its own; readers may not have access to the original report. Abstracts often appear in abstracting journals and indexes and allow readers to determine whether a given research study is valuable background reading for their own needs.

Writing Informative Abstracts.   As you write an informative abstract, provide specifics that tell readers what happened. Read through the draft of your research report and ask yourself the following questions:

What was the purpose of the research?
How was the research carried out?
What were the key findings?

If you have organized your research report carefully, you have put your research question, objectives, or hypothesis near the close of your introduction. Simply summarize the rationale for the project and extract the research question from the narrative. In some cases, you can use it word for word from the original report.

Next, read the methodology section and ask yourself, "How did I collect the information (data) for my research project?" Talk out loud as you answer your question and summarize the key information. (Use a tape recorder if you want.)

Finally, read the conclusion and ask yourself, "What are the key findings?" Again, if you talk out loud as you answer the questions, you will summarize the essential points. Try to state the results in one, two, or three sentences.

If you have trouble capturing the key points for your abstract on paper, try telling a friend what you set out to do, how you did it, and what you found. Then, jot down the key ideas on paper. If you do not have a friend handy, pretend you are talking to someone and tape record what you say. Then play back the tape recording and write down the essential points. By talking aloud, most people instinctively abbreviate, summarize, and highlight the key points.

Next, select the key words for your abstract. Ask yourself what terms you would use to search an abstracting journal or index to find your research report. Your research question may provide the key words, but in some cases you might want to include words describing the methodology you used and your findings.

Writing Descriptive Abstracts. Descriptive abstracts can be more difficult to write than informative abstracts because the research reports on which they are based may cover more information and may have a more complex organization than an original research report. Three common kinds of descriptive abstracts are: (1) the literature review abstract; (2) the abstract for a thesis statement research report; and (3) the abstract for the problem-solving or design paper.

1. *Descriptive abstract for a literature review report.* To write a descriptive abstract for a literature review paper, ask yourself these questions:
   a. What was the overall purpose of your research report?
   b. What were the key points that you reported?
   Your answer(s) to the first question should come from your introductory section(s). The answers to the second question may be more difficult to ascertain. Review your major sections of the report and subheads of your paper. What were they? What did you include? What compelling evidence did you present? Let your answers guide your drafting of the narrative for research papers based on literature reviews.
2. *Descriptive abstract for a thesis statement research report.* To write an abstract for a thesis statement research paper, begin by restating the thesis statement or the position you have taken. Then ask yourself the following:
   a. How many points or key ideas did you present to support the thesis statement?
   b. What are these key ideas?
   Your answers should give you the essential points to make in your abstract. If you have trouble, review the major sections, subheads, and supporting information throughout the report to support your thesis statement or position. Using that information, draft the narrative for your abstract.
3. *Descriptive abstract for a problem-solving or design paper.* To get started on an abstract for a problem-solving and design research reports, ask:

a. What was the problem addressed?

b. What was the solution(s) or design proposed?

The answer to the first question should emerge early in the report, usually in the introduction. Succinctly describe the problem you faced. Depending on your report, you may have one or more solutions to summarize. In some cases, research reports may propose a series of solutions, often undertaken in a progressive manner. If so, summarize them in that order as you draft the narrative.

Revising Draft Abstracts

Let your abstract sit for an hour or more, or better yet, a day or two, before you return to reconsider it. Overall, consider three guidelines as you review your draft:

1. Does the abstract correctly reflect the content of your original research paper?
2. Will the abstract help readers decide whether or not they want to read your entire research report?
3. Does the abstract conform to the guidelines as to the kind of abstract — its length, format, and related style issues?

To answer the first question, review your report and then the abstract. Think about the content and make comparisons. Do they align properly? If not, then add, delete, or modify the content as needed.

To answer the second question, try to put yourself in your readers' positions and consider whether the abstract would help them determine whether or not they would want to read your entire research report. Test your abstract by having a friend read it and then tell you what the report will cover. If your friend's ideas differ from what you think your report covers, determine why. Also determine how you need to recast the content so it reflects your main points.

To answer the third question, review the abstract guidelines and then compare your abstract against those guidelines. Consider such specific questions as

1. Have you included the title?
2. Have you included the narrative?
3. Does your narrative conform to the specified length?
4. Have you included the key words?

If you answer no to questions 1, 2, or 4, recast the abstract to conform to the standards. If you answer no to question 4 and your narrative is too long, use the guidelines in Chapter 12 to cut your abstract by 20, 30, or 40 percent.

PREPARING THE CITATIONS AND THE BIBLIOGRAPHY/ LITERATURE-CITED SECTION

Some writers develop the citation and reference lists as they work, while others develop the footnotes, endnotes, or reference-cited section after they have written their entire paper. Whichever way you work, begin by having your bibliographic cards, photocopies, or other sources readily available.

If you are typing, you will have to completely type each set of footnotes before going to the next page. With word processing footnote programs, however, you can enter your footnote information after you finish writing your paper. You can develop your bibliography as you type your footnotes, making sure to add to the bibliography all sources that you refer to in your footnotes.

What to Include

At times, your list of references will include only works cited–references for which you have developed either footnotes or endnotes. At other times, you will want to include both a list of works cited and a bibliography — a more complete list of the literature on your topic. Including a bibliography is a courtesy to your readers, who may be interested in pursuing the topic further and will thus welcome some guidance in selecting sources. At still other times, you may want only a bibliography, one which includes the works that you have cited and also includes some standard sources that you have consulted. Checking to see what other authors in your field have done will help you learn the standard conventions. Better yet, ask your instructor or supervisor what he or she would prefer.

If you are using the endnote, bibliography, or literature-cited formats, start your list of sources on a new page with the appropriate heading. Be sure that the title conforms with the style manual you are following: endnotes, bibliography, literature cited, etc. Then enter the full information on each source, again, conforming to your style guide.

When you use information from other sources in your research reports, credit all sources, whether they are literature, conference presentations, speeches, class lectures, movies, videotapes, slide sets, media, or interviews.

How to Proceed

Remember that different disciplines have distinct conventions, so work from the preferred style guide or a standard journal in your field. When you look at publications following a specific style, keep in mind that individual editors may deviate from the style manual, but that they strive to be consistent within the publication.

Note especially such details as preferred capitalization, use of periods, commas, underlining, and use of numbers or symbols and foreign words. Also note that some styles call for sources to be entered in the order of their first mention in the research paper, while other styles call for them to be entered in alphabetical order.

If you are working on a word processing program with a sort option, and your style calls for alphabetized references, you can enter your sources in any manner and then invoke the sort option to alphabetize your list. With sorting options and a moderate-speed computer, some programs can alphabetize 400 references in less than a minute. Such software options can save hours of work, but be sure to learn to use the option before using it on your reference file. Also remember to make backup copies of your reference file before you try a sort program. In that way, should something go wrong, you still have an original from which you can make another copy to alphabetize the reference list.

How you credit your sources is a style issue that style manuals and some grammar handbooks explain in detail. Generally, the techniques of crediting sources fall into four major categories:

Journalistic style

Footnote style

Endnote style

Author-date systems

These systems tell your readers the source of any supporting information that you used. In the case of literature papers, you would cite such sources as criticism about the literature, interviews with critics, and interviews with the author. In history, you would cite primary sources such as diaries, letters, and documents. You would also cite secondary sources that you consulted, such as histories written about the period in which the diaries or original sources were found.

Journalistic Citation Style

Whenever you read a newspaper or magazine, or hear a news broadcast on radio or television, you encounter such credits. Reporters use direct and indirect quotes when they write about interviews or when they give accounts of speeches, news conferences, and other presentations. Besides giving the information, the reporters may give some background as to where they obtained it. For instance, for interviews and accounts of speeches and interviews, they usually give the date and location.

Thus, the reporter writes

President George Bush, speaking at a press conference yesterday, said ". . .

or,

In an interview today, he said that . . .

For literature and media, journalistic styles usually call for quotation marks around the title. Journalistic style does not require a complete citation. Thus, the reporter would write:

> In "The Game of Science," professors Garvin McCain and Erwin Segal, wrote that . . .

The reporter would not indicate the publishing company or the date of publication.

Footnote Style

As the traditional citation style for many humanities disciplines, footnotes call for a superscript — a raised Arabic number — at the end of the sentence, and then the full citation at the bottom of the page or at the end of the research report. Footnotes should be numbered consecutively throughout the narrative. In longer publications, authors may number footnotes consecutively throughout a chapter or major section and begin with new footnote numbers with the next chapter or section. Here is an example of the citation within the body of a research report:

> In <u>A Theory of Discourse</u>, James Kinneavy explores the composition discipline and proposes a theoretical foundation for other researchers to follow.[1] His work provides . . .

Individual style manuals and handbooks provide more specifics. Figuring out the proper spacing at the bottom of each page for footnotes is a time-consuming and often frustrating task. Two changes are relieving this burden. First, several styles now call for listing all footnotes on one or more pages near the end of the research report. Thus, you need not be concerned about the spacing at the bottom of each page. Second, advanced word processing software now includes options that automatically place footnotes on the page where they occur.

Endnote Style

Endnotes use either a number set as a superscript, *Jones,*[1] a number enclosed in a parentheses, *Jones (1)*, or a number enclosed in brackets, *Jones [1]*, at the end of sentences. Then list all full citations at the end of the research report and arrange them either by the order of their mention within the narrative, or alphabetically by authors' last names, depending on the custom followed by your discipline. Here is an example of a sentence with an endnote citation within the narrative:

> From protocol analyses, Hayes and Flower consider writing to be a problem-solving activity that includes several distinct activities (1). Those activities include . . .

At the end of the article, you would then include the endnotes with the full details to the citations.

Author/Date Citation Style

For the author/date system, which is commonly used in many scientific and technical fields, you give the last name(s) of the writer(s) and the year of the publication. The information provided in the sentence determines whether you put parentheses around the name(s) and the date or merely around the date. Here is an example of author/date citation with the date in parentheses:

> Cooper and Holzman (1983) question the use of protocols as a technique
> to learn more about the writing process.

Because the authors are mentioned in the sentence, you put only the date in parentheses. Now consider the alternative that places the full citation within the parentheses:

> The mail questionnaire warrants careful consideration as a tool to assess
> the quality of computer manuals (Bethke 1983).

When the name and date are included within the parentheses, they may be separated by a comma or not, depending upon the style manual being followed. When multiple sources are cited within one set of parentheses, the individual citations may be separated by either commas or semicolons, depending upon the style you are following. At the end of the research report, you then arrange all citations alphabetically by the author's last name.

SAMPLE STYLE GUIDES: MLA AND APA BIBLIOGRAPHIC STYLES

The Modern Language Association (MLA) style allows citations for either endnotes or footnotes, while the American Psychological Association (APA) illustrates citations for the author/date system. As you study the examples, look carefully at the details.

MLA Footnote and Endnote Style

The following examples illustrate how to handle footnotes and endnotes for the first and second reference to a source. Keep in mind that nearly half of the *MLA Handbook* details specifics on documentation. Thus, the following illustrates the more commonly used general sources. Within the discussion on documentation, the *MLA Handbook* lists the appropriate abbreviations to use in citations.

Journal Articles

[1] Alice E. Moorehead, "Designing Ethnographic Research in Technical Communication: Case Study Theory into Application," Journal of Technical Writing and Communication 17 (1987): 325.
[2] Moorehead 326–28.
[3] Marilyn Cooper and Michael Holzman, "Talking about Protocols," College Composition and Communication 34 (1983): 284.

Books

[4] James L. Kinneavy, A Theory of Discourse (Englewood Cliffs: Prentice-Hall, 1971; New York: Norton, 1980).
[5] Kinneavy, pp. 281–90.
[6] Toby Fulwiler, ed., The Journal Book (Portsmouth: Boynton, 1987).

Newspapers and Magazines

[7] Paul Gray, "Russia's Prophet in Exile: Aleksandr Solzhenitsyn," Time 24 July 1989: 56.
[8] Nathan M. Adams, "The Ship That Outsailed Time," Reader's Digest June 1989: 117.
[9] Mike Pearson, "Ross' Voice Is Better With Time, Fine Like Wine," Rocky Mountain News 17 August 1989, Entertainment Sec.: 59, cols. 3–4.

Theses and Dissertations

[10] Jodi Wolf, "The Technical Communicator's Role: The Impact of Professionalism and Boundary Spanning," MA thesis, Colorado State U, 1989, 25.

Electronic Media

[11] Parenthood, dir. Ron Howard, with Steve Martin, Mary Steenburgen, and Jason Robards, Universal, 1989.

Lectures

[11] Charles Smith, "Critique as a Parser," Information Design, JT661, Colorado State U, 19 April 1989.

Personal Communication

[12] Carol Darr, personal interview, 31 May 1989.

MLA Bibliographic Style
The type of source being referenced is identified in brackets.

> Adams, Nathan M. "The Ship that Outsailed Time." Reader's Digest June 1989:117.   [magazine article]
>
> Cooper, Marilyn, and Michael Holzman, "Talking about Protocols." College Composition and Communication 34 (1983): 284–93.   [journal article]
>
> Darr, Carol. Personal interview. 31 May 1989.   [interview]
>
> Fulwiler, Toby, ed. The Journal Book. Portsmouth: Boynton, 1987.   [book]
>
> Gray, Paul. "Russia's Prophet in Exile: Aleksandr Solzhenitsyn." Time 24 July 1989: 56–60.   [magazine article]
>
> Kinneavy, James A. A Theory of Discourse. Englewood Cliffs: Prentice-Hall, 1971; New York: Norton, 1980.   [book]
>
> Moorehead, Alice, E. "Designing Ethnographic Research in Technical Communication: Case Study Theory into Application." Journal of Technical Writing and Communication 17 (1987): 325.   [journal article]
>
> Pearson, Mike. "Ross' Voice Is Better with Time, Fine like Wine." Rocky Mountain News 17 August 1989, Entertainment Sec.: 59, cols. 3–4.   [newspaper article]
>
> Smith, Charles. "Critique as a Parser." Information Design, JT661, Colorado State U, 19 April 1989.   [lecture]
>
> Wolf, Jodi. "The Technical Communicator's Role: The Impact of Professionalism and Boundary Spanning." MA thesis. Colorado State U, 1989.   [unpublished thesis]

American Psychological Association Style

The APA style follows the author-date citation style of many scientific disciplines, but the details vary among scientific fields. The following examples illustrate how to prepare full citations for the "Literature Cited" section at the end of the research report. Unlike the MLA style, the APA style does not use quotation marks around article titles and uses abbreviations for only parts of books or other publications, i.e., *chap.* for chapter, *ed.* for edition, *p.* (*pp.*) for page(s), *no.* for number, and others. The APA style capitalizes only the first word of the title. Note that the APA style should be used only for those items *cited* in the research report in contrast to bibliographic items, which compose a lengthy list of all works used for reseach on a topic.

Journal Articles

> Bethke, F. J. (1983). Measuring the usability of software manuals. Technical Communication, 30(2), 13–16.

McDowell, E., & Baney, L. (1983). A survey of communication skills needed and communication methods used in the dissemination of development information. Journal of Technology Transfer, 8(1), 59–67.

Lutz, J, Jarrat, S., Harkin, P., & Debs, M. B. (1987). Practical rhetoric: The art of composing. The Technical Writing Teacher, 14, 300–318.

Books

Ballatine, B. (1968). Nobody loves a cockroach. Boston: Little, Brown.

McCain, G., & Segal, E. M. (1982). *The game of science*. Monterey: Brooks/Cole.

Newspapers and Magazines

Study links well-to-do lifestyle, background with higher IQs. (1989, August 17). Fort Collins Coloradoan, p. 1.

Linden, E. (1989, June 12). An old idea makes a comeback. Time, p. 71.

Conference Proceedings

Knapp, J. T. (1988). Empirical studies: Readers' retrievability aids, writers' anxiety, and listeners' priorities. Proceedings of the 34th International Technical Communication Conference (pp. RET-45–RET-47). Washington, DC: Society for Technical Communication.

Technical Reports

Pinelli, T. E., Glassman, M., Oliu, W., & Barclay, R. O. (1989). Technical communications in aeronautics: Results of an exploratory study. NASA Technical memorandum 101534, Parts 1 & 2. Hampton, VA: Langley Research Center, National Aeronautics and Space Administration.

Theses and Dissertations

Wolf, J. (1989). The technical communicator's role: The impact of professionalism and boundary spanning. Unpublished master's thesis, Colorado State University, Fort Collins.

Electronic Media

Zimmerman, D. E. (1980). Making decisions for managing fuels. [A slide set.] National Fuel Inventory and Appraisal Project, U.S. Forest Service. U.S. Department of Agriculture. Fort Collins, CO (23 minutes, 132 slides).

Personal Communication.   Personal communications, i.e. interviews, telephone conversations, memos, letters, speeches, and other non-recoverable sources, are not used in the reference list. Instead, you cite them within the narrative. For example: C. Darr (personal communication, May 31, 1989) or (C. Darr, personal communication, May 31, 1989).

REVISING AND EDITING THE REFERENCE LIST

When you revise and edit your reference lists, consider

Completeness of information,
Appropriateness of style,
Consistency of presentation, and
Careful attention to details.

Revising and polishing your citations within the narrative and your reference list entails close attention to details as you check and recheck the style manual guidelines. As with any revising and editing, focus first on the larger issues, and then concentrate on the details.

Follow an Appropriate Style

Again, you must look carefully at each guideline in the style that you are following. Look for periods, colons, italics (underline typed copy to represent italics), capitalization, abbreviations, spacing, and points.

To illustrate, look again at the details of the following citation according to APA style. Note the order of names, periods, dates. Observe the use of the comma, the ampersand, and the parentheses:

McDowell, E., & Baney, L. (1983). A survey of communication skills
    needed and communication methods used in the dissemination of
    development information. Journal of Technology Transfer, 8(1),
    59–67.

The details mount quickly. Each citation can contain a dozen or more potential errors, depending upon the citation and style you are following. So look closely, watch the details, and double-check your work.

Check for Consistency of Presentation

To achieve consistency, look at one or two details at a time as you review the paper. If the style calls for your reference list, citations, or bibliography to be presented in alphabetical order by last names, check carefully to make sure the last names follow sequentially. Then look carefully at the name order. Does the style call for the last name to be followed by the first and second initials? First name? Is it the same way for the second and third authors' names on multiple citations? Check carefully where dates are positioned in the citation. Are they in the same place?

Once you have the list, check to make sure that it is complete. Why? Three errors frequently occur in some research papers: (1) not including all the citations, (2) including extra citations, and (3) overlooking inaccurate citations. Read through the entire draft looking for citations. As you find each one, check it against your reference list to make sure that you have included it and that you have accurately entered all of the needed information. Consider marking it with a red check so you are sure you reviewed it. Every time you find a new citation in the narrative of your research report, check it off. Work methodically through the narrative, page by page, checking the citations off your reference list and adding any references that you missed.

Once you have marked all the items that you have found in the narrative, check your reference list for any extra sources. If you find extra ones, delete them. If you have failed to cite them in the narrative, and you should have, add the citations in the appropriate places.

Next check the specific citations to ensure that they conform to the style manual you are following. Check one style issue at a time for all citations in your list. In that way, you keep the style issue clearly in mind as you work.

Begin by checking how authors' names are listed. Does the last name come first or last? Are first names used, or only initials? If you have second authors, how are the first name, initials, and last name ordered? What kinds of punctuation separate one author from the second or third? Then consider the next component of the citations — either the title or the date, depending upon the style. Look carefully at the details and make your references conform to the appropriate style. Note especially the ordering of elements, the use of different punctuation, and the use of abbreviations. Complete all style issues, and then set the copy aside.

When working on word processing systems, print a copy of the references and set it aside. Then check the hard copy. Why? Some writers report difficulties trying to correct all details on the screen, so they print a hard copy, make the needed corrections on it, enter them on their file, and then reprint it.

FORMATTING RESEARCH REPORTS

Consider the physical arrangement of your words — the body copy — as the manuscript's format. When you plan your manuscript's format, you want to achieve a crisp, clean arrangement that gives a good first impression, makes reading your report easy, and leaves plenty of room for editing and comments.

When preparing your final research report, use standard 8.5 x 11 inch, 20-pound bond weight, white typing paper. Avoid the erasable bond papers because the typed words may smudge and the surface coating may clog your instructors' pens. When laying out your pages, use at least a 1 to 1.5 inch margin on all sides — top, right and left sides, and bottom.

STANDARD PAGE FORMAT

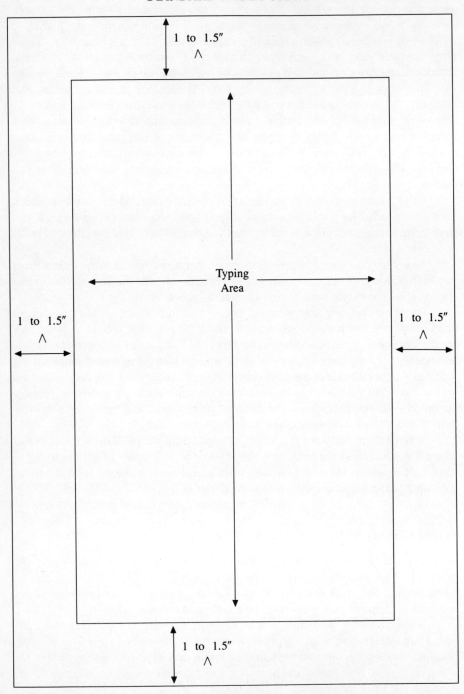

Check for one more thing — completeness. Take time to make sure that you have included everything for the research report assignment. To start, check your manuscript against the following list:

Title page
Abstract
Table of contents
List of illustrations, if required
Body of the report
    All chapters
    All sections
References cited or bibliography
Appendixes
Illustrations
Any additional required materials

To check the manuscript for completeness, review the table of contents and check each part of the report and mark it off on the table of contents. All the parts there? If not, have you deleted some parts? Have you added new parts? If needed, revise the outline accordingly.

Final Formatting Issues

Manuscript format is a style issue, and style manuals and grammar handbooks do differ in particulars. Likewise, some instructors may have a preferred manuscript format. Use the following guidelines for formatting your reports, unless you are required to follow a specific style manual, or unless your instructor has given you an alternative.

Typing and Printing.   Your copy should come out bold, black, and crisp. The best looking copy (type), comes from laser printers, electric and electronic typewriters, and letter-quality printers. For typewriters and daisy wheel printers, use carbon ribbons. If you use a typewriter or printer that uses cloth ribbons, put in a fresh ribbon that produces a solid, black image.

A problem emerges with dot matrix printers. Some instructors find reading the light, gray copy produced by some dot matrix printers difficult to read. On the other hand, some dot matrix printers produce black, crisp, easy-to-read, near letter-quality copy. If you plan to use dot-matrix printers, check with your instructor.

Now consider the typeface itself. With the advent of electric and electronic typewriters, daisy-wheel printers, and laser printers, you often have access to a wide variety of typefaces and type sizes for printing your research reports. For the best results, use a standard 10 or 12 pitch type face, such as Elite, Prestige, or Courier. If the printer specifies a type size, use at least a 10 or 12 point typeface such as Courier. Avoid typing or printing the body of your report in italic, bold face, script, fancy typefaces, or 15 pitch fonts, because many people find such copy hard to read.

Use Double-spacing.   When typing, indent paragraphs five spaces from the left margin and use ragged right margins. When preparing manuscripts on some word processing systems, be sure to turn justification off. Avoid justified right margins, as they make copy hard to read.

When using electric and electronic typewriters and computer printers, make sure you use the correct settings with the different type faces. For units that have both 10 or 12 pitch options, avoid setting the unit on 12 pitch and using a 10 pitch wheel or typeface that creates compressed or overlapping typing such as this:

```
Weeds grow fast in early summer.
```

    (10 pitch wheel set on 12 pitch spacing.)

```
Weeds grow fast in early summer.
```

    (10 pitch wheel set on 10 pitch spacing.)

Such copy appears strange, detracts from the overall appearance of your paper, and makes for difficult reading.

If you use 1.5 inch margins, top and bottom, you will have about 24 lines of double spaced typing on a page. If you use 1.25 inch margins, top and bottom, you will have about 25 lines of copy, while 1 inch margins, top and bottom, provide about 26 lines of copy. Keep in mind that the line count includes all lines — even the page numbers as a line.

Format Specific Pages with Care.   As with other style issues, the format of pages often differs. Pages 199 and 200 provide two approaches to title pages, and page 201 provides guidance on subsequent pages.

For research reports calling for separate title pages, drop down about one-third of the way to begin your title (see page 199). Center the title and capitalize only the first letters of words according to the grammar handbook or style manual that you are following. Place your by-line or credit line below the title. Next place the course number, title, instructor's name, and date on separate lines. Double space between all lines.

Some styles, such as the Modern Language Association, call for a one inch margin at the top of the page followed by your name, your professor or supervisor's name, course title, and date in the upper left-hand corner (see page 200). You then double-space once, center the title on the page, and then double-space twice before beginning your body copy.

A SEPARATE TITLE PAGE

A

Radon Mitigation Plan

for a Residential Home

Marie Edwards

Advanced Composition

Section 3

Professor John Carpenter

November 15, 1989

A COMBINATION TITLE/BODY COPY PAGE

1″

Marie Edwards

Advanced Composition Sec. 3

Professor Carpenter

November 15, 1989

A Radon Mitigaton Plan for a

Residential Home

1″   1″

A naturally occurring by-product
from the breakdown of certain rocks and
minerals may be threatening the health
of many Americans. Radon gas, found in
soils containing uranium, granite,
shale, phosphate and pitchblende, seeps
through the soil and into buildings
through dirt floors, cracks in concrete
floors and walls, floor drains, sumps,
joints and other small openings
(Environmental Protection Agency,
1986). Many experts claim that this
odorless, tasteless, and colorless gas
is a major indoor pollution problem
that increases the risk of lung cancer.
The gas itself does not cause
cancer; rather, its ''daughter'' or
''progeny'' cause the problem. The

1″

A BODY COPY PAGE

1″

Edwards   1
Radon Mitigaton Design

Radon—A Potential Health Threat
A naturally occurring by-product
from the breakdown of certain rocks and
minerals may be threatening the health
of many Americans. Radon gas, found in
soils containing uranium, granite,
shale, phosphate and pitchblende, seeps
through the soil and into buildings
through dirt floors, cracks in concrete
1″   floors and walls, floor drains, sumps,   1″
joints and other small openings
(Environmental Protection Agency,
1986). Many experts claim that this
odorless, tasteless, and colorless gas
is a major indoor pollution problem
that increases the risk of lung cancer.
The gas itself does not cause
cancer; rather, its ''daughters'' or
''progeny'' cause the problem. The
progeny are radioactive by-products
that become trapped in the lungs of
anyone who breathes air containing
radon. As the progeny undergo further
breakdown, they release small bursts of
energy that can damage lung tissue and
lead to cancer (Environmental
Protection Agency, 1986). Some

1″

Most styles for body copy call for an identification or "slug lines" in the upper right-hand or left-hand corners of each page followed by either double spacing or quadruple spacing (MLA style) before you begin the body copy. At a minimum, the slug lines should include your name, an abbreviated report title, and the page number. Some word processing programs will enable you to automatically place page numbers and identification lines (headers) on each page. Study the software manuals carefully and test how the program runs before trying to print your entire research report. You may discover that you have to vary the settings.

Many style manuals call for placing the page numbers in the upper right-hand corner of the page, while others call for centered page numbers at the top or bottom of the page. As with other details, placement of page numbers is a matter of style.

Style manuals differ in their treatment of handling illustrations (tables and figures) in the text (see Appendix B). The *MLA Handbook* calls for illustrations to be incorporated in the body copy (i.e., placed as close as possible to the part of the report that first mentions the illustration [Gibaldi and Achtert 1988:82]). Other style manuals simply call for an insertion note such as

(Insert Table 1 about here)

The illustrations (tables and figures) then go at the end of the report. Such an approach simplifies typing, but readers must then flip to the end of the report to read the tables.

Bind Reports According to Your Guidelines.   Because instructors' preferences vary, some instructors or supervisors will ask you to staple your assignments in the upper right-hand corner; others will ask that you clip the pages together; others will ask you to submit them in file folders or larger envelopes; and still others will ask that you bind your reports. So ask your instructor or supervisor about their preferences on packaging the reports.

CONCLUSION

This chapter has covered the basics of writing an abstract, details on footnoting and developing a bibliography, and guidelines for formatting the finished paper. These finishing touches take a considerable amount of time. If you think about all of the work that has gone into your report, you will probably muster the commitment needed to finish the job right. Besides, the satisfaction and pride of finally seeing an attractive project will make the last steps worthwhile.

Here's a final list of questions to use when you think you are done:

A Checklist for Finishing Reports
1. Did you use the appropriate style?
2. Did you use the correct style for quotations and paraphrasing?

3. Did you use the correct citation system for your course?
4. Did you use the correct headings, if required?
5. Does your paper meet the specifications for length or word count?
6. Does your paper meet the format specifications?
   a. Title page layout
   b. Body page layout
7. Have you included all front matter, if required?
   a. Title page
   b. Table of contents
   c. List of figures
   d. Acknowledgments
8. Have you included all back matter, if required?
   a. List of references cited or bibliography
   b. All citations that you used within the body of your paper
   c. Appendix
   d. Other items: figures, tables, etc.
9. Have you included all tables, figures, or illustrations, if required? If used, did you credit the sources?
10. Have you included all pages? (Double check. It is easy to drop a page and not notice it.)

PART THREE

APPROACHES TO WRITING RESEARCH REPORTS

CHAPTER 14

Writing Literature Review Research Reports

$\mathbf{I}$n various courses in the humanities, the social sciences, and the physical and biological sciences, as well as in engineering and technological fields, instructors often require that students review a selected body of literature and report what they have learned. Literature review research papers may be either a section of larger, multi-section research papers or stand-alone papers, intended as syntheses of key issues in a given field. Such papers may be one of the most common kinds of reports that you will have to write.

Some instructors will assign a specific topic and audience for this kind of report, while other instructors ask students to find their own topic and specify the audience for their report. To write a review of literature, follow this general process: once you have identified a topic, begin with a general research question; then review preliminary literature, revising your research question as needed before beginning to draft your report. Be sure to analyze the usefulness of your sources and to organize them in an effective way.

This chapter

provides a brief explanation of the literature review research report,

suggests strategies for preparing to write literature review research reports, presents specific organizational strategies,

provides guidance for writing and revising the research report, and

includes two examples.

WHAT IS A LITERATURE REVIEW RESEARCH REPORT?

A literature review report is a synthesis of information on a topic presented in an organized formal narrative. Instructors may ask you to write a literature review research paper in order (1) to familiarize you with an academic discipline or discourse community, (2) to build your literature searching skills, (3) to improve your writing skills, (4) to refine your analytical skills, (5) to develop your critical thinking, and (6) to expose you to new subjects. As a professional, you may write literature review reports to document what other professionals have learned, developed, or investigated on a topic of interest to your employer.

To accomplish these objectives, supervisors and instructors often ask that you comply with specific guidelines. Some will specify a minimum number of pages, while others will specify a minimum number of literature sources. Some instructors will accept encyclopedias and general references as sources, while other instructors will accept only more specialized sources — the research journals and special reports in each discipline.

PREPARING TO WRITE LITERATURE REVIEW RESEARCH REPORTS

As with other research reports, you can learn lessons from experts to enhance your skills. As amateurs turn to expert golfers, tennis players, chess masters, or other experts, you can learn from expert writers who have written effective literature review reports. So consider finding and examining samples of literature reviews in your field.

You really can't begin thinking about organizing and mentally drafting your research report until you have studied the literature on your topic. But you *can* take careful notes on each source as you work. And you can develop a bibliography file — or even an annotated bibliography — early in your research-writing process. If you work this way, then when you are ready to draft your report you will be able to move from notes to rough draft with ease. Doing preliminary note-taking can help you synthesize ideas as you write your rough draft.

When you begin planning how to organize your research paper, be sure to distinguish between organization and format. Organization is the logical arrangement or structuring of ideas; format is the use of layout, heads, subheads, and other typography to help readers understand your organization.

The key to building logical presentations centers on knowing your topic and determining a natural organization that suits your ideas. Knowledge of a variety of organizational strategies, patterns, or schemes for structuring writing will help you identify an appropriate organizational pattern. As you draft, you can either adapt your material to an established pattern that seems to fit your material, or you can develop an original organization suitable to your content.

A LOOK AT SELECTED ORGANIZATIONAL PATTERNS

The more common organizational patterns include the following:

1. General to particular
2. Particular to general
3. Spatial arrangement or geographical pattern
4. Functional or process oriented
5. Order of importance
6. Chronological/historical/time order/sequence
7. Elimination of possible solutions
8. Simple to complex
9. Pro and con
10. Cause and effect
11. Combinations thereof.

Consider the expanded discussion of each organizational pattern and the examples that illustrate it.

General to Particular

This pattern moves from the overall to the specifics. A literature review research report on pollution in major cities could first present sources on air pollution, its components, and its causes. The review of sources on pollution in general would be followed by articles and books about its specific components — ozone, carbon dioxide, carbon monoxide, particulates, lead, and so forth. The coverage of sources focusing on general causes could refer to automobiles, trucks, businesses, industries, and then move to specific kinds of autos — older versus newer models, gasoline versus diesel engines, sizes of engines, and so forth.

Particular to General

Here the pattern begins with specifics and moves to more general descriptions. A literature review research paper on factors that contribute to endangering a species could first review sources focusing on specific, endangered species and the reasons for their being endangered. With that basis, the report could turn to sources that cover common causes of their being endangered: habitat destruction, pesticides and herbicides, illegal hunting, and disturbance by people.

Geographical or Spatial

The physical arrangement or layout of the topic guides your discussion in this situation. For example, if you were writing a literature review of oil spills along the East Coast, you could present sources on oil spill accounts beginning in Maine and moving down the East Coast to Florida. (News articles covering the economy and unemployment often use this geographical method of organization referring to the Northeast, the West, the South, and so forth.) When you use geographical or spatial organization, consider adding a map or line drawing to help readers follow your discussion.

Functional or Process

Often used to describe how something works or how an activity is carried out, a functional pattern explains a sequence of key activities. If you were doing a literature review on the American Heart Association's Slim for Life Program, you could organize your sources according to their focus on various components of the program: (1) having participants assess their current eating habits, (2) establishing a weight reduction goal, (3) understanding the rewards system/point system, (4) increasing exercise, (5) controlling eating stimuli, (6) slowing the eating pace, and so forth.

Functional patterns work especially well to describe how a machine works, the biochemical systems of a plant or animal function, or how a business or government organization solves problems.

Order of Importance

For this approach, the narrative moves from the most important to the least important factors. For example, a literature review research paper on the risk factors of heart disease might cover sources that stress various risks: genetic history of heart disease in a family, overweight and obesity, body shape, smoking habits, exercise habits, eating habits, stress factors, drinking alcoholic beverages, blood pressure, cholesterol levels, and so on. Risk factors would be ranked from highest to the lowest, and sources discussing those factors covered in decreasing order of importance.

Chronological/Historical/Time Order/Sequencing

Such a once-upon-a-time story sequence usually starts at Point A, often the beginning, and moves through point Z, usually the end or a closing point. For example, suppose you were writing a literature review of the major technological advances of computers. You could organize the paper around the major events of the technology (the forerunners of computers, building the first computer, and so on, up to a specified date). As an alternative, you might organize the paper by development periods: before 1940, 1940 to 1949, 1950 to 1959, and so on.

But you need not start at the beginning and move forward. You can start at any point and move forward or backward. For instance, to look at the impact of agricultural research and the marketing of fresh produce through supermarkets, you could begin by focusing on articles about the diverse fresh fruits and vegetables in today's supermarkets, and then move backward in five to ten year increments to articles reporting the kinds of produce, seasons available, and points of origin.

Elimination of Possible Solutions

For research papers focusing on solving a particular problem, this organizational pattern considers each possible solution and discounts those unlikely or least likely to solve the problem and finally offers the most likely solution. For example, if you were reviewing the literature on approaches to software development, you might first present the do-it-yourself approach; then you could move to the cooperative approach involving a content area specialist and a programmer; finally, you could discuss the team approach to software development. An alternative approach, used in articles for many trade magazines, is to present the problem and review the most likely solution first, recapping or reviewing other plausible solutions later in the article.

Simple to Complex

This organizational pattern considers simple situations and moves on to more complex ones. For example, a literature review research paper on pest control might first summarize articles on simple pest controls for the home garden, such as catching and squashing the insects, then move to integrated pest management for the truck farm that combines biological and chemical control techniques.

Pro and Con

This organizational pattern requires a careful look at the positive and negative points surrounding a topic. For example, a community has six trains that run its main street between 7 AM and 5 PM daily; it forms a committee to look at the pros and cons of banning trains from running through town. The organization of the review could center around published sources covering the pros of banning the trains: the reduction of auto traffic jams, noise levels, and the movement of hazardous wastes through town; elimination of the problem of ambulances and fire engines being blocked by trains; lower air pollution levels because of the lack of trains and autos waiting for the trains to pass; and so on. On the con side, the paper could discuss sources that emphasize potential law suits from the railroad itself, the surrounding communities (where the trains might be rerouted), negative publicity, increased transportation costs, reduction in taxes from railroads to support schools, the costs of rebuilding the streets, and more. Each pro and con would be discussed in depth.

Cause and Effect

Here you look at the effect (the end result) and ask what factors contributed to it. For example, if you were doing a literature review of the causes of auto accidents, you could review the literature by first discussing sources that report causes of accidents, such as driving while under the influence of alcohol, driving while under the influence of drugs, lack of attentiveness when driving, environmental factors (rain, snow, excessive heat), mechanical failures, lack of defensive driving skills, and so on.

To organize the causes, you would consider reviewing sources that treat the most likely or the greatest causative agent first, the next second, and so forth. For example, when United Flight 232 crashed in Sioux City, Iowa in July 1989, investigators initially identified the major problems as an explosion of engine number two in the tail, a loss of the hydraulic system for flight controls, and loss of parts of the plane. Of the people who died in the crash, medical investigators identified the major causes of death as the impact upon crashing and the fire following the crash. For the people who survived the crash, the factors contributing to their survival included their seating positions; the quick evacuation of the plane; and the medical emergency preparedness of the Sioux City police, fire departments, national guard, and medical community; and the advance warning of a pending crash. A literature review of that situation might be organized according to the respective emphases of each source.

Combinations of Organizational Strategies

Sometimes, combining two or more organizational strategies enhances organization and helps you present your information more effectively. For example, *Time* magazine combined geographical and time factors to explain major stock market actions around the world in the crash of October 1987. You might organize your literature review of the crash according to the geographical area in which your source was published and the date of publication. In other words, you could review sources published on the day of the crash in three different locations and then move to coverage in these same publications a month later.

To learn additional ways of organizing reports, take a few minutes to see what organizational strategies other writers follow when writing reports and articles. If they do not seem to follow any of these strategies, try to analyze their basic organizational strategy and consider it too.

In many cases several organizational strategies might work for your topic, but strive to select the single one that best makes your points. In selecting the strategy, consider your content, research question, your readers, and the sources you have gathered. All four should influence your selection of how you organize your information.

Once you have your basic plan and information and are ready to begin writing, set aside a block of time — an hour or two at the least — to draft your literature review. Be sure to adapt your drafting strategy to the nature of the literature review paper. For example, consider labeling the categories into which you have grouped your literature summaries. Then create headings for each category–either with a word processor or on paper — and begin drafting in any one section. If some of your summaries of the literature appear skimpy, you can write yourself a note like "add more information" and then keep drafting, knowing that you will add material to that section later. In other words, what is important at the drafting stage is to "crank out a draft." Thus, if you think some sections are easier than others, write them first. Write what you can when you can.

Once your draft is completed, put it aside for some time — a few hours, overnight, or better yet a few days. Forget about it and let your mind rest.

When you return to your draft, approach it with a clear mind and reconsider your purpose, content, and audience. Try as best you can to put yourself in your readers' minds as they read your report for the first time. Remember that one reason some of your readers will be reading your report is to determine whether they would like to consult the original source you are summarizing. So be sure that you have accurately represented each author's ideas. Rethink and restructure your draft, if needed. Keep in mind that revising begins by rethinking the larger issues about your draft and then working your way down to the finer details. Let the checklists in Chapters 7, 8, and 9 guide you as you fine-tune your draft and polish its appearance. For now, consider the points made in the following checklist.

Checklist for Revising Literature Review Drafts

1. What is the purpose of your draft?
   a. Is the purpose clear to your readers?
   b. Does the content support the purpose? In other words, have you reviewed appropriate sources?
2. Is the paper complete?
   a. Have you included the key sources on your topic?
   b. If you have said that you will cover three, four, or five major kinds of sources, have you included all of them?
   c. Have you included all illustrations, if used?
3. Does the organization achieve its purpose?
   a. Does the organization help make the purpose clear?
   b. Does the organization help readers see the major trends in the literature?
   c. Would an alternative organization enhance the report?
4. Have you taken your readers into account?
   a. Will they understand your terms?
   b. Do you need to include definitions in the narrative?
5. Have you accurately represented the ideas in the sources you are reporting?
   a. Do you present enough detail?
   b. Do you present adequate summaries?
   c. Do you include supporting data? Is it needed?

LITERATURE REVIEW RESEARCH PAPER: SAMPLE #1

This first example represents a full literature review paper that explores the feasibility of using an existing technology in a new way to solve an old problem—estimating wildlife populations. The author follows the *Journal of Wildlife Management's* style.

When reading this first literature review paper for a course in wildlife management techniques—a specific, scientific discourse community—note how succinctly the author presents information; he knows that readers of such papers have had a background in statistics and have taken courses in zoology, mammalogy, chemistry, physics, and statistics.

Note especially how the author

uses a general to particular patterns of organization,

begins by introducing the general problem,

focuses first on the method of using radioisotopes for estimating wildlife populations and the associated issues and problems,

narrows the discussion to estimating furbearer populations in general and using radioisotopes in particular,

provides a succinct closing,

reports the information with little interpretation, and

cuts carefully to the key points or elements reported in the literature he cites.

The Use of Radioactive Isotopes for
Marking Aquatic Furbearers
in Capture/Recapture
Population Estimates

Presented to
Dr. R. J. Robel
The Division of Biology
Kansas State University
For the Course
"Wildlife Management Techniques"

D. E. Burkhead
November 30, 1988

2

Introduction

This paper reviews the problems associated with estimating aquatic furbearer populations using capture/recapture techniques and using radioactive isotopes as a tool for developing population models. The review focuses on North American furbearers found in inland waters, primarily the river otter (<u>Lutra canadensis</u>), the North American beaver (<u>Castor canadensis</u>) and the muskrat (<u>Ondatra zibethicus</u>). Marine mammals have been excluded because their life histories do not lend themselves to radioisotope labeling.

The author provides an overview of the paper in a general sense.

Next the author limits the focus of his research report to specific animals in one geographic region.

Overview of Capture/Recapture Techniques

Since they were developed in the 1930s and 1940s, capture/recapture techniques have enabled biologists to estimate animal populations (White et al. 1982). The validity of data based on these techniques depends on adherence to the assumptions underlying the

Here the author begins exploring the scientific issues of estimating populations and the underlying assumptions.

JWM

3

model used. In general, the
stronger the assumptions, the more
"powerful" the model (Seber 1982).

      White et al. (1982) list three
assumptions for all capture/recap-
ture studies: (1) The population in
question is closed (Some open
models do not require strict
adherence to this assumption, but
still require geographic closure);
(2) Marks are not lost during the
study; (3) No marks are missed and
all marks are correctly identified
during each sampling period. In addition, capture/recapture techniques require that all animals
have equal or known capture proba-
bilities (Davis and Winstead 1980).

      To meet the closure assump-
tion, researchers conduct studies
over a short time period to minimize immigration, emigration, mor-
tality and natality. When using
conventional capture/recapture
techniques during a short time,
researchers often have difficulty
obtaining the large samples needed
for statistical validity. For

Note here the succinct summary of the earlier literature.

Here the author reminds readers of the basic statistical assumptions.

Next the author explains the needed criteria for conducting such studies.

JWM

4

example, river otters occur in low densities and have low recapture rates, and thus, conventional techniques produce poor population estimates (Shirley et al. 1988).

Many methods have been tried for marking aquatic furbearers. Miller (1964) reports that researchers have used web-punching, tail branding, tail rivets, and ear tags to mark beaver. Except for ear tags, these methods require that animals be recaptured to examine them for marks. The techniques are also subject to loss and misidentification because of obliteration or difficulties distinguishing them from bite marks.

At this point, the author begins focusing on specific techniques that have been used with aquatic furbearers.

Further, many factors influence capture probability including environmental variables, such as weather, and biological variables, such as age, sex, home range size, and behavioral responses (Seber 1982). Some population estimation models have corrections for these factors, but such models sacrifice precision (Seber 1982).

Moving on, the author suggests confounding factors that might alter population estimates—i.e. problems with the techniques.

5

Uses of Radioactive Isotopes in Ecology

Radioisotopes have a wide variety of biological applications. Peterle (1980) reports their use in pesticide research, hydrobiology, fish culture, entomology, animal physiology, energetics, and ecology. Some species that have been labeled for individual recognition with radioactive isotopes include grouse, ducks, fish, roads, reptiles, rodents, dogs (<u>Canis familiaris</u>), badgers (<u>Taxidea taxus</u>), rabbits, fox, bobcats (<u>Lynx rufus</u>), and humans (Hooper et al. 1971, Wolff and Holleman 1978, Kruuk et al. 1980, Peterle 1980, Knaus et al. 1983, Shirley et al. 1988).

Many systems are available for radiological studies. In 1980 the basic assay equipment could be purchased for under $2,000, but the additional cost of optional equipment, such as multichannel analyzers, increases the price to over $25,000 (Peterle 1980). Additional costs

6

occur with the expense of training or hiring qualified personnel to operate the equipment and obtain the required permits. Thus, cost/benefit analysis should be an integral part of planning the methodology, when considering an experiment of this nature.

Many different radioactive isotopes have been used in biological studies. The isotope selected is based on the data needed. For example ^{131}I and ^{99}Tc have been used in clinical diagnosis of disease and investigations of glandular function (Peterle 1980). Capture/recapture studies require (1) An isotope chosen with a long physical and biological half-life to ensure detection during the study; (2) High energy gamma rays produced by a larger percentage of the disintegrations per minute for easy detection using gamma scintillation techniques; (3) No behavioral changes of the animal induced; and (4) An evaluation of potential health hazards (Conner 1982). ^{65}Zn

Now the author begins limiting the scope by focusing on specific isotopes, their uses and limitations.

7

fulfills these requirements. It has
a physical half-life of 245 days, a
biological half-life of 933 days;
high energy gamma rays are produced
by 47% of the disintegrations per
minute (USHEW 1970 and Conner
1982); and it has not been found to
change behaviors (Conner 1982).

    The use of radioactive iso-
topes to mark individuals for cap-
ture/recapture studies is limited
primarily to those compounds that
are excreted as metabolic by-products. Some studies (Gentry et al.
1971, Wolff and Holleman 1978) have
attempted to mark individuals with
doses large enough to be detected
with field equipment ($\geq$ 3$\times$ background count). Wolff and Holleman
(1978) used ^{65}Zn injected intramuscularly in doses 1.67$\times$ (100
μCi) and 5$\times$ (300 μCi), the maximum
allowable total body burden for hu-
mans, to trace genetic relationships of Taiga voles (<u>Microtus
xanthognathus</u>) and white mice (<u>Mus
musculus</u>). Maximum allowable total
body burden of ^{65}Zn for humans is

*Here the author re-
ports specific
applications.*

8

60 μCi (USHEW 1970, p. 206). Not
only do doses of this size present
health hazards, but labeling the
entire organism requires the recapture of the individual to identify
the "mark." Knaus et al. (1983)
detected ^{65}Zn in feces of river otters using as dose of 23 μCi (3.8
μCi/kg of body weight.) and found
no increase in detectability by
doubling the dose.

The limiting factor of radio-
markers for capture/recapture studies is the time the marker remains
identifiable in the feces (Knaus et
al. 1983). Since the duration of
detectability does not depend on
dosage (Knaus et al. 1983), the administration technique appears to
be more critical. Nellis et al.
(1967) found that ^{65}Zn administered
orally to fox, opossum, or bobcat
was detectable in feces for about
one month, while intramuscular in-
jections were detectable for about
one year in the feces.

Next he explores the limitations of the different techniques.

JWM

9

Applications to Aquatic Furbearers   Note the subhead.

Aquatic furbearers present
unique problems in determining pop-
ulation size. They are not readily   Now the author returns to aquatic fur-
accessible to the researcher be-   bearers and
concentrates on using
cause they live in the water, and   isotopes to mark
them.
they are active at night. Further-
more, except for muskrat, they are   Note how the author
carefully spells out
difficult to capture in large   the problems and difficulties with isotopes
enough numbers to ensure statisti-   when used with
aquatic furbearers.
cal validity. All leave feces at
toilet stations or construct scent
stations (Boutin and Birkenholz
1987, Melquist and Donkert 1987,
Novak 1987), which are available to
the researcher for "recapture."
Shirley et al. (1988) successfully used ^{65}Zn to label feces,
so they could estimate river otter   Now the author
moves into discussing
populations. By injection of a 1 ml   the technique with a
specific species —
solution of ^{65}ZnCl$_2$in 0.5M hydrogen   otter.
chloride intramuscularly, the re-
searchers were able to identify
scats from "marked" individuals.
Using an airboat, they searched the
marsh for latrine sites, collected
fecal samples, took them to the

10

laboratory and analyzed them with an auto-gamma scintillation spectrometer. The researchers found that capturing and handling the otters only once was advantageous, because trapping was time consuming and produced few recaptures. One probable bias was that the personnel conducting radio telemetry studies of individual animals in the same population were the same personnel who search the marsh for scats. This resulted in a negative bias, because they knew of latrine sites and that increased recaptures.

Muskrats have been censused using traditional capture/recapture techniques, house counts, and pushup counts (Boutin and Birkenholz 1987). Capture/recapture techniques are time consuming and costly, while house and pushup counts cannot be used in areas where bank denning predominates. The researchers also stressed the need for accurate and reliable population estimates for effectively

Now the author explores using isotopes to estimate muskrat populations.

Note that the writer has used a term (pushup counts) that a general reader would not be expected to know but that readers familiar with wildlife management terminology might well know.

JWM

11

managing harvest populations. Conner (1982) stated that since Zn intake is less in omnivores or
herbivores than in carnivores, the
biological half-life would be increased. This, coupled with their
habit of using latrine sites that
are easily located, warrants further investigation into the suit-
ability of using radioactive traces
for capture/recapture studies.

   Unlike river otter and muskrats, beaver do not use latrine
sites, but they do deposit castoreum at scent stations (Novak
1987). Thus, beaver have the potential to be marked with radioactive
isotopes. Castoreum is composed of
aromatic carboxylic acids, phenols
and aromatic ketones (Maurer and
Ohloff 1976). A carbon isotope
would be easily incorporated into
castoreum; however, ^{14}C has been
found to cause behavioral abnor-
malities (Buchanon et al. 1953).
Further research into the structure
of castoreum and possible isotopes
to mark it is needed before beaver

Note the transition to
discussing another
species.

JWM

12

could be censused using radioisotopes. Further, beaver exhibit differences in scent mount visitation
rates by sex and age (Novak 1987).
However, visitation frequencies appear constant and could be incorporated into the model calculations.

Conclusion

When estimating population
size in aquatic furbearers, the assumptions of capture/recapture
models using conventional techniques are difficult to ensure. Radioisotope labeling of feces or
other deposits will allow researchers to adhere more closely to
the assumptions of the estimator
being used.

After discussing the techniques and related issues, the author succinctly wraps up the report.

JWM

13

Literature Cited

Bouten, S., and D. E. Birkenholz. 1987. Muskrat and round-tailed muskrat. Pages 314–325 in M. Novak, J. A. Baker, M. E. Obbard, and B. Malloch, eds. Wildlife furbearer management and conservation in North America. The Ontario Trappers Association. Ontario.

Buchanon, D. S., A. Nakao, and G. Edwards. 1953. Carbon isotope effects on biological systems. Science 117:541–545.

Chew, R. M. 1971. The excretion of ^{65}Zn and ^{54}Mn as indices of energy metabolism of <u>Permoyscus polionotus</u>. J. Mammal. 52:337–350.

Conner, M. C. 1982. Determination of bobcat (<u>Lynx rufus</u>) and raccoon (<u>Procyon lotor</u>) population abundance by radio-isotope tagging. M.S. thesis. Univ. of Florida. Gainesville, 55 pp.

Note the subhead.

The author conforms this section to the *Journal of Wildlife Management* style.

Note the capitalization and lack of underlining in publication titles — the JWM style.

Citation of a research journal.

JWM

Note the abbreviations used in the JWM style.

14

Davis, D. E., and R. L. Winstead. 1980. Estimating numbers of wildlife populations. Pages 221-245 in Schmnitz, S. D. ed. Wildlife management techniques manual. Fourth edition. The Wildlife Society. Washington, DC.

Gentry, J. B., H. M. Smith, and R. J. Beyers. 1971. Use of radioactively tagged bait to study movement patterns in small populations. Ann. Zool. Fenn. 8:17-21.

Hooper, F. F., H. A. Podoliak, and S. F. Snieszko. 1961. Use of radioisotopes in hyrobiology and fish culture. Trans. Amer. Fish. Soc. 90:49-57.

Knaus, R. M., N. Kinler and R. G. Linscombe. 1983. Estimating river otter populations: the feasibility of Zn-65 to label feces. Wildl. Soc. Bull. 11:375-377.

Here the author cites a chapter within a book.

Note the order of initials and last names in multiple authored articles and books.

15

Kruuk, H., M. Gorman and T. Par-
     rish. 1980. The use of ^{65}Zn
     for estimating populations of
     carnivores. Oikos 34:206-208.

Maurer, B., and G. Oholoff. 1976.
     Investigations of the nitro-
     gen-containing compounds in
     castoreum. Hevl. Chim. Acta
     59:1169-1185. (In German with
     English summary.) From Novak,
     M. 1987. Beaver. Pages
     282-313. In M. Novak, J. A.
     Baker, M.E. Obbard and B. Mal-
     loch. eds. Wild furbearers and
     conservation in North America.
     The Ontario Trappers Associa-
     tion. Ontario.

Miller, D. R. 1964. Colored plastic
     ear markers for beavers. J.
     Wildl. Manag. 18:859-861.

Nellis, D. W., J. H. Jenkins, and
     A. D. Marshall. 1967. Radioac-
     tive zinc as a feces tag in
     rabbits, foxes and bobcats.
     Proc. 21st Conf. SE. Assoc. of
     Game and Fish Comiss. pp.
     205-207.

JWM

16

Novak, M. 1987. Beaver. Pages
        282-313. In M. Novak, J. A.,
        Baker, M.E. Obbard and B. Mal-
        loch. eds. Wild furbearers and
        conservation in North America.
        The Ontario Trappers Associa-
        tion. Ontario.

Peterle, T. J. 1980. Radioisotopes
        and their use in wildlife.
        Pages 521-530. In S. D. Schem-
        nizt ed. Wildlife management
        techniques manual. The Wild-
        life Society. Bethesda, MD.

Richmond, C. R., J. E. Furchner,
        G. A. Trafton, and W. H. Lang-
        ham. 1962. Comparative metabo-
        lism of radionuclides in
        mammals-I: Uptake and reten-
        tion of orally administered
        ^{65}Zn by four mammalian spe-
        cies. Health Physics
        8:481-489.

Seber, G. A. 1982. The estimation
        of animal abundance. MacMillan
        Publishing Co., Inc. New York.
        645pp.

17

Shirley, M. G., R. G. Linscombe, N.W. Kinkler, R. M. Knaus, and V. L. Wright. 1988. Population estimates or river otters in a Louisiana coastal marshland. J. Wildl. Manag. 52:512-515.

USHEW. 1970. Radiological health handbook. Rev. ed. USHEW Public Health Service. Rockville, MD. 458pp.

White, G. C., D. R. Anderson, K. P. Burnham, and D. L. Otis. 1982. Capture-recapture removal methods for sampling closed populations. U.S. Dept. Energy, Office of Health and Env. Res., Nat. Env. Res. Park. Los Alamos, NM. 235pp.

Wolff, J. O., and D. F. Holleman. 1978. Use of radioisotopes to establish genetic relationships in free-ranging small mammals. J. Mammal. 59:859-860.

Here the author cites a government publication. Note the details.

JWM

THE LITERATURE REVIEW PAPER: SAMPLE #2

This second example of a literature review paper consists of one section of a master's degree thesis in which the author reviews one of several bodies of literature relevant to his project. He follows the American Psychological Association style. Note especially how the author:

begins with a general overview of the full topic to be discussed,

outlines the literature review section by identifying the three bodies of literature that he will explore,

focuses on the first body of literature and summarizes the key perspectives from that literature, and

uses an elaborated narrative of discussing the literature cited and exploring its meanings.

The Relationship of Students' Learning
Style Types to Approaches to Writing

Musser B. Moore

Master of Science Degree

Colorado State University

Fort Collins, CO

October 1990

APA

Relationship

2

Literature Review

    This study's objectives and
research hypotheses derive from
three main bodies of research
literature:

      product vs. process approaches
        to teaching writing,
      writing strategies, and
      learning styles.

A perspective on teaching writing:
  process vs. product approaches.

    To better understand how
students approach learning to
write, I briefly summarize here
several perspectives on teaching
writing.

    Since the 1940s the ways
people have approached writing and
the teaching of writing have
changed. Goldstein (1984) suggests
that these changes originate from
three major sources: modern
rhetoric, empirical research on
writing, and composition pedagogy.

Note how the author
provides the informa-
tion and then elabo-
rates on the points
and builds a flowing
narrative.

Relationship

3

She described modern rhetoricians
as those who view functional writing as a process where readers and
writers together use language to
create meaning. Classical rhetoricians, according to Goldstein,
would maintain that technical writing should simply state facts.

Goldstein shows that recent
empirical research on the cognitive
processes that occur during reading
and writing has influenced how
technical writing is taught. Now
some instructors place more emphasis on the mental process of
writing and less on the final communication product (Flower, 1979).

Burhans (1983) distinguishes
between current-traditional and
contemporary approaches to teaching
writing. According to Burhans, current-traditional approaches emphasize the written product and tend
to stress the importance of grammar, spelling, and other features.

Relationship

4

Contemporary approaches focus more on the writing process, and tend to view writing as a recursive process of discovery, learning, and problem solving. However, Burhans' research on college writing courses reveals that, despite the emergence of the contemporary approach to pedagogy over the past 25 to 30 years, most college level writing courses still reflect a product-based approach.

Not all authors, however, believe that current teaching strategies match the challenges of business's and industry's needs for technical communication. Hunt and Wilkerson (1985) maintain that much teaching of technical writing is still based on literary skills taught by people with little or no practical experience in real technical writing.

Berlin (1982) agrees that a process-oriented approach to teaching writing is more valuable and practical for most students than a

Here the author provides a transition from one subject to the next.

Note especially here the lengthy discussion given to the Berlin citation and article.

Relationship

5

product-oriented approach. He names
the more contemporary approach to
teaching writing as new rhetoric
and differentiates it from other
pedagogic theories by the nature of
knowledge. New rhetoricians maintain that knowledge is dynamic and
created through the elements of the
communication process: writer, audience, reality, language. More
traditional or classical approaches
treat knowledge as static and concentrate on the mechanics of ex-
pressing that knowledge (Berlin,
1982).

Winkler (1983) differentiates
between the product and process approach to writing on the basis of
the theoretical models comprising
the approaches. She suggests that the
traditional product approach emphasizes structural models, or stylistic formats, for teaching
writing. As such, students may
learn the kinds of information they
need to produce a given piece of

Again, the author be-
gins a lengthy citation
to one article or
reference.

APA

Relationship

6

writing, but they receive little
guidance on how to obtain that information. She suggests one useful
writing strategy includes using inventional models. Inventional
models serve as analogies allowing
students to better understand how
to modify known structural models
for particular writing situations.
Winkler (1983) believes these inventional models invoke flexible,
recursive writing procedures with
which students can easily incorporate new insights or ideas into
their writing.

 According to Flower (1979),
students should learn to transform
writer-based prose into reader-
based prose for more effective
writing. She shows that most effective writers not only present information but model information for
the reader's needs.

 Programs emphasizing the cognitive basis of writing (Collins &
Gentmer, 1980; Grunig, Ramsay &

Relationship

7

Schneider, 1985; Flower, 1979;
Flower & Hayes, 1981), problem-
solving approaches (Flower, 1985;
Coe and Gutierrez, 1981), and
schema theories (Kent, 1987; Sypher
& Applegate, 1984) illustrate the
contemporary direction of writing
instruction. . . .

Moore's literature review then recaps writing strategies, learning theory, and learning styles before detailing the purpose of his research and providing the research questions.

APA

References

For his references, the author conforms to the American Psychological Association (APA) style.

Berlin, J. A. (1982). Contemporary
    composition: The major ped-
    agogic theories. College En-
    glish, 44, 765-77.
Burhans, C. S. (1983). The teaching
    of writing and the knowledge
    gap. College English, 45(7),
    639-656.

Relationship

8

Coe, R. M., & Gutierrez, K. (1981). Using problem-solving pro-cedures and process analysis to help students with writing problems. College Composition and Communication, 22(3), 262-271.

Note the sequence of names and order of initials.

Note the italics for the title and volume numbers and the use of commas.

Collins, A., & Gentner, D. (1980). A framework for cognitive theory of writing. In L.W. Gree & E.R. Steinberg (Eds.), Cognitive Processes in Writing. Hillsdale, NJ: Lawrence Earlbaum Associates.

Flower, L. (1979). Writer-based prose: A cognitive basis for problems in writing. College English, 41(1), 19-37.

Note how the APA style requires paren-theses around the date and the period follow-ing the date.

Flower, L. & Hayes, J. R. (1981). A cognitive process theory of writing. College Composition and Communication, 37(1), 16-55.

Goldstein, J. R. (1984). Trends in teaching technical writing. Technical Communication, 15(2) 25-34.

Relationship

9

Grunig, J. E., Ramsey, S., &
    Schneider, L. A. (1985). An
    axiomatic theory of cognition
    and writing. Journal of Tech-
    nical Writing and Communica-
    tion, 15(2), 95-130.
Hunt, P., & Wilkerson, S. (1985).
    Technical communication: The
    academic dilemma. Journal of
    Technical Writing and Communi-
    cations, 10(4), 323-327.
Kent, T. (1987). Schema theory and
    technical communication. Jour-
    nal of Technical Writing and
    Communication, 17(3), 243-252.
Syper, H. E., & Applegate, J. A.
    (1984). Organizing communica-
    tion behavior: The role of
    schemas and constructs. In R.
    N. Bostron (Ed.). Communica-
    tion Yearbook 8. Beverly
    Hills, CA: Sage.

APA

Note here how APA
handles chapters
within books and city,
state, and publisher.

Relationship

10

Winkler, V. M. (1983). The role of
models in scientific and technical writing. In P. V. Anderson, R. J. Brockman, & C. R.
Miller (Eds.), <u>New essays in
technical and scientific communication: Research, theory,
practice</u>. Baywood's technical
communication series 2. Farm-
ingdale, NY: Baywood.

CHAPTER 15

Writing Original Research Reports

In many academic fields, you will be asked to do original research and to report that research in a paper that conforms to the conventions of your discipline. Your research might involve collecting original information by observing people, animals, and plants, by experimenting with physical objects or their actions, or by interviewing people. This chapter provides basic guidance for developing original research reports. In the process, it

provides a brief explanation of the original research report,

teaches you to examine your research question carefully as you prepare to write your report,

suggests that you select appropriate information-gathering strategies,

provides guidance for writing the research report, and

includes samples of two original research reports.

THE ORIGINAL RESEARCH REPORT

The original research report is often considered as the standard in a range of disciplines including agriculture, chemistry, biological sciences, medicine, nursing, psychology, sociology, communications, and related disciplines. Articles using this basic approach appear in many of the academic research journals of these fields. Technical reports follow a similar organizational approach. If you are in graduate school, you will probably discover that many theses and doctoral dissertations use this basic approach, too.

Most original research reports include the following functional sections:

1. *Introduction*—establishes the rationale and provides the research question or hypothesis.
2. *Methodology*—explains how the information was collected and analyzed.
3. *Results*—reports the primary findings or results of the research.
4. *Discussion*—explores the implications of the results and their potential meaning.
5. *Conclusions*—provides a succinct summary of the key findings and their meaning.

The names of each section vary from academic field to field. Some fields combine sections, while other fields present the information in a different order; nevertheless, the function of each part remains much the same. Original research papers usually

build on the work of other investigations,

investigate a narrowly defined question,

focus on an investigation at one point in time,

present the findings succinctly and clearly, and

pose additional questions to be investigated.

EXPLORING THE RESEARCH QUESTION

While the research question for literature review research reports allows for wide-ranging approaches, the research question directing an original research question calls for a narrowly defined question that directs the researcher's investigation.

For a literature review research paper, you might ask, "Do computers enhance students' college educations?" Such a question might produce widely varying research reports that would illustrate diverse dimensions of how students use computers in college. But such a broad question cannot be used for an original research report.

Suppose you were interested in the influence of the computer on writing. You might ask, "Does using computers enhance students' writing?" This question is too broad, for it requires a careful look at the entire question and its multiple ramifications. What do you mean by "computers"? Are you talking about the hardware? The software? If you are talking about the software, what kind of software are you considering? Word processing programs? Spelling checking programs? Grammar checking programs?

What do you mean by "enhance"? How could you define "enhance" so that you might measure it? What do you mean by "writing"? Do you mean drafting the original manuscript? The entire process for producing the final written product? The number of spelling errors? The kind and number of grammatical errors? The organization and logical development of the ideas? And, more importantly, doesn't the way the teacher uses the computer figure into all of this?

You might decide to consider a more narrowly defined question, such as, "Does using a word processor with a spelling checker increase students' abilities to find spelling errors?" Such a question gives direction to an investigation and suggests that two groups of students should be tested at the beginning of the term to assess their abilities to spot spelling errors. Then one group, the treatment group, would use the spelling checker software during the term, while the other group, the control, would not use the software. At the end of ten weeks, both groups would be tested again to determine their abilities to spot spelling errors. You could then compare the changes in each group's ability to spot spelling errors over the ten-week period. If the treatment group could spot significantly more spelling errors than the control group, then it might be possible to infer that spelling checkers enhance spelling abilities.

Once you have your data collected, you have come a long way toward generating the final draft of your research report. You may find it easier to work on separate parts of the report, one at a time, or you may find it easier to write the entire report in a couple of sittings. Whatever way you work, the following discussion provides useful suggestions for composing and revising your draft research report.

SELECTING AN INFORMATION-GATHERING STRATEGY FOR RESEARCH REPORTS

The writers of the sample reports at the end of this chapter used only a few of the multitude of information-gathering techniques you can choose to collect original research data for addressing your questions. In science, research methods are sometimes divided into descriptive studies, associative studies, and experimental studies. Descriptive studies merely tell about or describe what was observed. Associative or correlational studies relate one factor (variable) to another. Finally, experimental studies provide the opportunity to make inferences of causality; for example, does X cause Y?

In the first sample report, Susan's project was an experiment (page 252); the second, Joan's study, on the other hand, describes the writing practices of professionals and could be called a descriptive study (page 263). Joan talks only about the writer's revising and editing practices and carefully avoids saying that computers make professionals better writers. Susan's experiment enables her to present an inference: one glue has a higher tensile strength than others. She has reached this conclusion through the experimental approach she used to collect her information. Joan's descriptive study involved collecting her data by interviewing professionals about their editing and revising practices, while Susan's experiment consisted of collecting her data by testing (by making observations of the tensile strengths of glue).

In contrast, a correlation study would explore the relationships between two or more factors, such as the one between students' working part time to fund their college expenses and their overall grade point average. If you wanted to know the relationship between these two factors, you could survey a random sample of seniors to find out if students who work twenty or more hours a week have significantly higher grade point averages than students who do no part-time work during the terms. There are limits to this type of study. At best, you could only correlate or associate working twenty or more hours a week with the higher grade point average. You could not say that working twenty or more hours a week causes students to make higher grades.

THE ORIGINAL RESEARCH REPORT

The main body of most original research reports follows a functional organization:

Introduction
Methods
Results
Discussion
Conclusion

The title page, abstract, and appendix round out the report. Keep in mind that different academic disciplines may label the different sections with different names, but the sections often have a similar function, as discussed under each area.

Introduction

The heart of planning the introduction centers on developing the rationale that leads to the research question. That usually requires citing the appropriate literature, defining the major variables you are considering, and building a strong case for investigating the research question.

Consider the introductions in the samples at the end of this chapter. Susan begins by pointing out the government's call for replacing contact cements and by explaining why contact cements need to be replaced. Then she explores the alternative glues that might be considered as replacements. Next she suggests that white wood adhesives are a likely replacement and gives her rationale for making that decision. Finally, she explains that the strengths of wood glues need to be investigated and presents her research question.

In her introduction, Joan first argues that composing on a computer is faster and explains why; she cites authors who claim that using the standard VDT screen presents some problems and gives the findings of several studies. She then adds that inexperienced writers use computers differently than experienced writers do, and she points out that most studies focus on novice writers rather than experienced ones. Next she presents her research question as an objective statement: ''I will study how four professional writers edit and revise both on-line text and hard copy.''

Like Joan, you might use the introduction from your original proposal as the basis for your research report's introduction. If you developed a solid proposal and refined the research question, all you would need to do is edit your original introduction. However, if your research question changed while you continued reviewing the literature, you might find it necessary to revise, recast, and rework the introduction. Also, if your literature review revealed that different writers used different terms or defined the same terms differently for the variables you are investigating, then you might need to name and define your variables carefully.

As you close your introduction, build the rationale that leads to your research question. Keep in mind that the rationale needs to be clearly stated and should cover a narrowly defined area. If it is not focused, you will have difficulty writing up your results and supporting your findings.

Methods

In the methods section, you need to explain, often in some detail, how you collected your original information, being sure to give enough details so that someone can replicate or repeat your project. Depending on the kind of research project you undertake, this section can include many different subdivisions.

In her methods section, Susan explained the number of samples she used, the size, and the kind of wood. She then detailed the process she used for conducting the tests and for performing her basic calculations. Joan, on the other hand, (1) explained that she studied four professionals who compose on computers daily, (2) identified the kinds of materials they wrote, and (3) explained her interviewing strategy.

At times, research projects take place in special settings that may influence the results. For example, many research projects that focus on natural science, agricultural, and natural resource topics would need a discussion of the geographical location, weather conditions, study period, and related factors.

If the research setting is important, describe it. If you used a special piece of equipment or apparatus to collect information, describe that, too. Report how many objects, people, animals, plants, or other things you observed (or measured), and explain how you selected them. If you used a random sample (see p. 109), report the specific type of random sample you used. If you used a purposeful sample (see p. 109), report the characteristics of the units you sampled. Further, remember to report your sample size — the number of units you sampled or studied. Also, be sure to report your plan for collecting data. Did you interview people only once? Did you observe the animals over a three-week period? Did you have treatment and control groups? Did you measure them only once, twice, or more often?

Finally, explain how you analyzed the data. Did you use specific kinds of statistical tests? Did you use computer software programs? If so, acknowledge them.

If your technique was unique or you had to adapt or develop an existing analysis technique, then report that in enough detail so your readers can understand what you did.

Results

The results section presents your findings and should clearly report, "Here's what I found." Often you can best write the results section by first developing visuals — tables, figures, or illustrations that succinctly show your findings. Figures and tables are especially relevant when presenting real numbers or empirical data rather than incorporating data into a lengthy discussion. In fact, research on data presentation suggests that bar graphs are easier to understand than tables, and tables are more easily understood than data presented in a narrative (Powers et al. 1961).

Only when your data are brief should you describe them in the narrative rather than present them in a visual. Keep in mind that most readers can take away from any reading only a few key points; thus, do not labor on and on describing detail after detail of data in your narrative (see pages 256–257).

When you select a visual form for your data presentation, remember that your readers need to be able to read and interpret that kind of illustration. Thus, when you write about the data in the visuals, first discuss the most important or key findings of your study. Begin to generalize as Susan did when she pointed out the strength of the glues she tested.

For her opening paragraph, Joan painted a general picture of the writers she studied, noted how long they worked daily, and summarized their writing style (see page 269). In the second paragraph, she summarized her findings and referred her readers to a table — a practice you should try to follow in your reports.

Make your visuals report the key information and relate directly to your research question. After discussing your key findings, talk about the aberrations or the unusual findings, if any, in the data. Finally, keep your narrative succinct.

Discussion

In the discussion section, talk about the implications or meaning of your results. What do your findings mean? How do your findings compare to the findings of other researchers who have investigated the topic? For example, Joan began her discussion with "professional writers experience some of the same difficulties reported in earlier studies of student writers and clerk-typists" and then she cited the previous literature.

In contrast, Susan was following a different journal's style. She combined both the results and discussion sections. Thus, she first reported her findings and later discussed the implications, "Because of the low tensile strengths, these adhesives are not a satisfactory replacement for contact cements."

As part of the discussion section, you might suggest a follow-up investigation for another writer, including the specific points that might be explored and how they might undertake their projects.

Conclusions

When you write the conclusion section, ask yourself, "What are the two or three major findings of the study?" If you have trouble, pretend that you are talking to a friend and you have only two minutes to tell her what you found in your study. Such an approach will help you summarize your findings cogently.

WRITING THE ORIGINAL RESEARCH REPORT

Remember to draft research reports incrementally, writing what you can when you can. By doing so, you can assemble the pieces of your research report gradually, and you need not let a problem with one part stop you from working on another part. The real advantage of incremental writing is that it helps you break down a large project into a series of small tasks. Small tasks are much easier to handle than large ones. For example, if you have a thirty-page paper to write, it may sound almost overwhelming. But writing a three-page introduction sounds like a manageable task.

To further aid an incremental approach to writing, capitalize on proposals, progress reports, and other materials that you have written during your research. If you have written a proposal, revise it, as needed, for your introduction and methods sections. If you have written progress reports, revise them, if appropriate, for other parts of your report. Why should you consider revising existing documents? Largely because you have written them separately and they may need to be re-worked when they are intertwined. If you compose on a personal computer, you need only revise and edit your existing documents.

REVISING YOUR DRAFTS

As with other writing tasks described in this book, once you complete the draft of your original research report, set it aside for a day or two, or a week or more, if possible. Then return to the draft with a critical eye to reconsider and rethink it. Approach your task with a questioning mind, reread and reexamine each section, and question the accuracy, completeness, interpretation, and presentation of your entire draft. To guide your efforts, use the questions in the checklist on pages 250–251.

Check the overall accuracy of your content and presentation, and try to enhance the organization within sections. When you make changes, make changes that strengthen the presentation. Keep in mind that you cannot change how you collected your information or your data, nor can you change your results. You might, however, find that you need to collect additional information, or that you need to recalculate your statistics or mathematics. You might also find that further checking will lead you to new insights and interpretations of the results.

In most cases, restrict the changes in your introduction, methods, and results sections to clarifying your points and correcting any inaccuracies. In contrast to the other sections, however, you may want to carefully reconsider your discussion section. After setting your draft aside, try to put yourself in another person's position when that person looks at your paper for the first time. Would another person interpret your findings differently? If so, why? If not, why not? Can you offer alternative explanations for your results? Make sure your interpretations align with the data you present in the results section.

Check your conclusion section to make sure that you have not introduced any new information, new points, or interpretations. If you have, move them to the results or discussion sections and include the new information where appropriate.

Finally, keep in mind that once you have the content, organization, and presentation established, you will then need to work on details of polishing the appearance.

Checklist for Revising Drafts of Research Reports

1. Read the introduction section and ask
   a. Have I clearly defined all terms and variables?
   b. Does the literature review provide support and rationale for the research question?
   c. Is the research question clearly stated?
2. Read the methods section and ask
   a. Have I described all techniques that I used to collect information?
   b. Have I provided enough detail so readers can clearly understand my measurement or information gathering techniques?
3. Read the results section and ask
   a. Does the narrative and the tables or figures, if used, answer the research question?
   b. Do I have the needed tables and figures?
   c. Are the calculations, mathematics, and statistics in the tables and figures correct? Have I double-checked my calculations?
   d. Does the narrative highlight or summarize the important findings or generalize the results from the tables or figures?
   e. Does the narrative repeat too much of the detailed information from the tables or figures?
   f. Does the narrative discuss any aberrations or unusual aspects of the data?
4. Read the discussion section and ask
   a. Does the narrative explain the importance, significance, or meaningfulness of the results?
   b. Does the narrative discussing the findings relate directly to the research question? If not, why not?
   c. Do the data in the results section support the narrative or discussion?
   d. Does the narrative cite other studies or compare the findings with the findings of other projects?
   e. Does the narrative include any suggestions for future research or a follow-up study?

5. Read the conclusion section and ask
   a. Does the conclusion highlight the findings with one, two, three, or more key points?
   b. Does the conclusion include any new information, interpretations, or points? If so, reconsider them.
6. Reread each section and ask
   a. Would an alternative organization within this section enhance the presentation?
   b. Is the narrative focused and to the point?
   c. Are there points that I should delete?
   d. Are there points that I should add?

ORIGINAL RESEARCH REPORTS, EXAMPLE #1

The first report is an original study of the tensile strengths of four commercially available glues. The purpose of the study is to determine if commercially available white wood adhesives can replace contact cement as an adhesive in household use. As you read the first example, note how the author

uses an informative abstract to overview the report,

defines the key concepts and reviews relevant literature in the introduction,

provides a narrowly defined research question,

details the experimental procedure of testing the different wood glues,

combines the results and discussion into one section, and

provides a succinct summary to close the article.

A Study of the Tensile Strengths
of Four White Glues on White Pine Wood

Susan McOllough Zimmer

April 18, 1988
Colorado State University
Fort Collins, CO 80523

2

Abstract

A Study of the Tensile Strength of
Four White Glues on Pine Wood
Susan McOllough Zimmer

Contact cements contain methylene
formaldehyde that emits hazardous
fumes that may cause cancer. Therefore the United States Government
is encouraging research to find a
substitute adhesive. White wood
adhesives are a possible replacement because they are transparent
and nontoxic. To be suitable replacements, the glues must have the
same tensile strength as contact
cements. Therefore, this report
focuses on research that asks,
"What are the tensile strengths of
four commercially available white
glues?" Four brands were applied
to one-inch square blocks, let dry
and cure according to manufacturer's
specifications, and then tested
on a universal testing machine.
The adhesive yielded strengths of
43-45 psi. Because of these low

Here the author pro-
vides an informative
abstract.

Note the brief back-
ground on the is-
sue/problem/research
topic.

Here is the research
question that guides
the research project.

And a succinct sum-
mary of the results
wraps up the abstract.

3

strengths, none of the four white
glues is a suitable replacement for
contact cement.

KEY WORDS: Replacement for contact
cement, tensile strengths, white
glues, white adhesives, wood
adhesives.

The author provides
key words under
which the research re-
port might be
catalogued.

4

Introduction

The United States Government
expressed the need for more water-
borne adhesives to replace contact
cements (Veebhester 1987). Contact
cements contain formaldehyde, which
in turn contains methylene chloride. This substance, a proven car-
cinogen in mice, can be hazardous
to humans (Smithers et al. 1985).
Contact cements are used in counter
tops, particle board, hard board
and veneers (Smithers et al. 1985).
Because of the cement's wide usage,
the government imposed time limits
on workers' exposure to the cement
and methylene chloride fumes (Veebhester 1987). Recently, concern
spread to contact cement's usage in
building products and fumes emitted
in homes and offices; this prompted
research to determine a safer wood
adhesive (Veebhester 1987).

To begin the author
reviews key literature
and immediately
moves into the prob-
lem statement.

Aliphated wood glues have tensile strengths of 30-42 psi, but
are not ideal because of little
flexibility and yellowish dis-
coloration when dry (Taub 1988).

Additional research is
reviewed here to give
a better understanding
of the problem.

5

Resin glues provide only 28-35 psi
strengths and are an opaque brown
color when dry. Most importantly,
they contain formaldehyde that is
irritating to skin and toxic if in-
gested or inhaled (Taub 1988).

 White wood adhesives are a
likely substitute for contact cements because they are transparent
when dry, are water based, and do
not contain toxic chemicals or emit
hazardous fumes (Burns et al.
1986). The four wood adhesives
tested here are such glues. To determine if commercially available
white wood adhesives can replace
contact cement, the following questions needs to be answered: Is
there a significant difference in
the tensile strengths of glues A,
B, C, and D? What are the tensile
strengths of glues A, B, C, and D?

The author sketches the problem suc-cinctly and then pre-sents the research question that will drive the investigation.

Methodology

 The following procedure used
12 samples of white pine, 1 in × 1
in × 1.5 in (width by length by
height). To conduct the tests, I

6

1. Cleaned gluing surfaces (1 in ×
   1 in) of dust and dirt.

2. Glued specimens in accordance
   with manufacturer's specifications, and allowed the specified
   setup time.

3. Glued specimens with the grain
   of the wood parallel in each
   piece.

4. Placed the specimen in the grips
   of the tensile testing machine.
   Centered the sample in grips.

5. Applied load at rate of 100
   pounds per minute.

6. Recorded maximum load carried by
   sample at failure.

7. Replicated the tests three
   times.

8. Averaged the results for each
   adhesive.

$$X_1 + X_2 + X_3/3 = \overline{X}$$

   Where X_1, X_2, and X_3 are the results for each trial of one
   adhesive.

Here the researcher
presents the details of
the experiment/
research project; it is
designed to determine
the relative strengths
of the different glues.

Results and Discussion

Generally, these adhesives are
4.0 psi stronger than aliphated

7

glues and 6.0 psi stronger than resin glues. The adhesives tested yield ultimate tensile strengths averaging between 34 and 45 psi. Brand B had the strongest average strength, while Brand D was the weakest. Brands A and C were of nearly equal strengths (Table 1).

Table 1. Tensile test results and averages of individual samples

Glue	Trial (PSI)			Average
	1	2	3	
A	37.2	41.3	40.8	39.8
B	45.8	44.3	46.3	45.5
C	38.7	43.4	37.5	39.9
D	35.5	33.1	34.2	34.2
	Grand Average			39.8

Here the author signals that a table provides a summary of the data and then indicates where the table should be inserted in the text if the report were to be typeset for publication.

Another difference in the adhesives was the fracture points. Brands A, B & C fractured where the glue contacted the wood, Figure A. Brand D fractured between the layers of glue, Figure B. This may

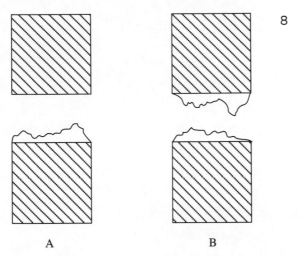

8

A   B

Figure A represents the fracture points for Brands A, B, and C, while Figure B represents the fracture points for Brand D.

The major point here is that Brand D glue is inferior to the others tested.

suggest that the chemical structure of Brand D is inferior to that of the stronger adhesives.

Because of the low tensile strengths, these adhesives are not a satisfactory replacement for contact cements. The idea substitute should be similar to white adhesives in that it is transparent when dry and hazard free (Smither et al. 1985). However, the replacement should have greater tensile strength, 50 to 60 psi, to ensure solid bonding in structural mate-

9

rials such as counter tops, particle, and hard board (Smither et al.
1985).

Temperature was an uncon-
trolled variable in this experiment
and thus may have decreased the resulting tensile strengths. Both the
adhesives and wood samples were below the specified temperature, 60°,
when tested. Manufacturer's specifications indicated that the glues
should be 60° or above when applied
for best results.

Here the author ac-
knowledges a poten-
tial limitation of the
research that may
have influenced the
results.

Conclusion

White glues—Brands A, B, C,
and D cannot replace contact cements because of their low tensile
strengths—between 34 and 45 psi.
Greater tensile strength is required to replace contact cements
in building and structural materials. The United States Government
must continue its research to determine a replacement for the hazardous contact cement.

Note the tight presen-
tation and recap of
the findings as well as
the call for additional
research.

10

References

Breber, K. I., and M. H. Schneider. 1985. Wood-Polymer Combinations: The Chemical Modification of Wood by Aldoxysilane Coupling Agent. Wood Science 19: 67-73.

Burns, R., and R. Snider. 1986. Solutions to common gluing problems. Wood Products 21: 117-20.

Smithers, J., and E. Postier. 1985. Log sorting, edge gluing used in small log systems. World of Wood 116: 24-27.

Taub, S. E. 1988. Which glue for which job? Consumer Reports 1: 46-51.

Veebhester, E. G. 1987. Government's role in expanding adhesive manufacturing. Wood Products 9: 112-14.

ORIGINAL RESEARCH REPORTS, EXAMPLE #2

Using a case study method, the author of the following research report investigates the composing strategies of four professional writers who compose with a word processor. As you read, notice how the writer

provides a succinct abstract that details the key elements of the study,

builds a detailed literature review that identifies the key concepts and establishes the rationale for the research question,

explains how she collected the information,

outlines her basic findings, and

discusses what her findings mean and their implications.

Editing and Revising Strategies

of Four Professional Writers

Who Compose on Computers

Joan Zito

April 18, 1988

Colorado State University

Editing and Revising Strategies

2

Abstract

Editing and Revising Strategies of
Four Professional Writers Who
Compose on Computers
Joan Zito

Earlier reports show that writers
who compose on a computer experience reading, editing, and revising
difficulties because of the terminal's limited text display. I asked
four experienced writers about
their editing and revising strategies. Because of the decreased
reading speed and limited display
of video display terminals, most of
the writers interviewed prefer to
edit and revise from hard copy.
Three writers used integrated
spelling checkers.

KEY WORDS: Editing, revising, video
display terminals

Note how the author handles this descriptive abstract.

Rationale is provided here.

Research question follows here. Note also that it contains or suggests the methods used.

The last sentence provides the key findings.

Editing and Revising Strategies

3

Introduction

Many writers and researchers agree
that composing text on a computer
is faster than using a typewriter
or writing longhand (Beck &
Stribravy, 1986; Dauite, 1986; Fluegelman & Hewes, 1983; Zinsser,
1983). Writers say they can quickly
compose ideas because they know
they can easily return to correct
spelling errors, delete sentences,
and rearrange paragraphs. They need
not retype whole pages because of
minor errors.

> The author begins with a broad overview of the literature.

Composing on a computer may be
easier, but revising can be slow
and difficult (Fluegelman & Hewes,
1983; Lutz, 1984; Zinsser, 1983).
Krull & Rubens (1985) estimate that
the standard video display terminal
(VDT) shows about 24 lines of text
and 1100 characters on the screen
at one time. In contrast, an 8.5 x
11 inch sheet of paper with normal
margins and a 36-pica line contains
almost 62 lines and 3800 characters.

> Next the author moves into a specific review of the litera-ture related to her study.

Editing and Revising Strategies

4

Fluegelman & Hewes (1983) and
Zinsser (1983) say the limited text
display of a VDT makes it difficult
to perceive continuity when reorganizing text. College students
have difficulty locating information, detecting errors, and reading
their texts (Haas & Hayes, 1986).
Clerk-typists proofread on-line
text slower than they proofread
hard copy (Gould & Grischkowsky,
1984).

Introductory composition students, graduate students, and
clerk-typists have been subjects in
most on-line editing and revising
studies (Beck & Stribravy, 1980,
1986; Collier, 1983; Dauite, 1986).
Sommers (1980) and Flower, Hayes,
Carey, Schriver, & Stratman (1986)
report that novice writers revise
text differently than experienced
writers. Novice writers spend little time rereading and primarily
correct spelling and punctuation
errors. Experienced writers reread

The literature review
then focuses on topics
related directly to the
study.

Editing and Revising Strategies

5

extensively and change content,
structure, and voice.

    Lutz (1984) studied experi-
enced writers working at a computer
terminal and with pen and paper.
They spent less time planning, and
edited and revised more at the computer than when using paper and
pencil. When proofreading and re-
structuring material, they felt impaired by the limited text display
of the VDT.

    The aforementioned studies re-
veal that writers experience difficulties with the computer
terminal's limited display, but no
research reports on how professional writers deal with these
problems. Therefore, I will study
how four professional writers edit
and revise both on-line text and
hard copy.

Here the author provides the rationale for her study and then gives her specific research question or statement of purpose.

Methods

The subjects were four professionals who daily compose on a com-

Next the author describes the writing activities of the subjects that she interviewed. This gives a background or glimpse of the subjects.

Editing and Revising Strategies

6

puter. Two subjects are technical communicators who write manuals, réports, and promotional pamphlets. Another writer composes business documents and résumés and is nearing completion of a novel. The fourth writer, a scientist, has written and published eighteen research journal articles.

I interviewed the four experienced writers about their composing, revising, and editing habits. In this report, revising will mean rewriting and rearranging sentences, paragraphs, and ideas. Editing will mean correcting spelling, punctuation, and simple grammar errors.

Now the author explains how many writers she interviewed and the focus of her questions during the interviews.

I asked each writer how many years they had been using a computer, how much time they spent daily using a computer, and what type of equipment they used. I also asked about the number of lines of text on their computer terminals.

In this section, the author provides more specifics on the details and questions asked.

Because planning and generating sentences can influence revis-

Editing and Revising Strategies

7

ing and editing methods, I asked
about their composing practices. Do
they enter the ideas into the computer as fast as they are generated, without regard to order, or
in a linear fashion? Do they finish
writing about one idea before composing the next idea?

    After this background informa-
tion was collected, the writers
answered questions about their revising and editing habits. Do they
revise and edit on-line or from hard
copy? Do they revise and edit while
composing or after composing an
idea, paragraph, or page? Why did
they choose their particular methods?
I also asked the writers about their
use, if any, of integrated spelling, grammar, and style checkers.

Results

    The writers' experience in
composing text on a computer ranged
from 2.5 to 5 years. They worked at
a terminal from 2 to 5.5. hours

Here the author suc-
cinctly summarizes
her findings and then
begins expanding on
her findings.

Editing and Revising Strategies

8

daily. All used a standard 13 inch VDT with 20 to 24 lines of text display, and they composed in a linear pattern. They either planned their text in their mind, used an outline, or used a standard re-search report organization.

All writers revised only from hard copy (Table 1). They said they needed to see an entire manuscript page to perceive the continuity of their writing. They reported diffi-culty moving blocks of text if they could not first examine the hard copy. Further, they said using a hard copy let them see both the text to be moved and its intended position.

Note the crisp, clear presentation and the short sentences. The author does not engage in reflections about the results of the study — she holds such points for the discussion sec-tion that will follow.

Table 1

Percentage of Professional Writers Using Revising and Editing Methods ($n=4$)

	Hard Copy	On-line Copy	Hard Copy and On-line Copy
Revising	100%	0%	0%
Editing	25%	25%	50%

Note the simple format of the table with the centered titles, title above the data, and limited number of di-vider rules.

Note also the insertion of the sample size, $n=4$, in the title.

Editing and Revising Strategies

9

    The writers also said they pe-
riodically stopped to read and reread their writing as they entered
the text, to check its order and
flow. All said they could read hard
copy faster than they could read
text displayed on a VDT.

    Reading speed also influenced
the writers' editing methods. Most
of the writers said they edit from
hard copy because they can read hard
copy faster than they can read text
display on a VDT (Table 1). One
writer uses only hard copy for
editing. This writer reads aloud
the printed text looking for a specific error such as too many
"that"s. He then rereads the copy
looking for a second common error
that has been corrected by reviewers on his earlier documents.
This writer is the only one interviewed who also uses an integrated
grammar checker, GRAMMATIK 2 (Table
2). Also, he and two of the other
writers use an integrated spelling

Here the author notes
the divergent charac-
teristics of one of the
subjects.

Editing and Revising Strategies

10

checker (Table 2). Of the four writers interviewed, he has the least amount of writing experience.

Two writers said they try to correct errors on-line but use hard copy for serious copy editing. Only one writer uses a grammar checker.

Table 2
Percentage of Professional Writers Using Three Types of Integrated Checkers (n=4)

	Spelling	Grammar	Style	None
Number of Writers	75%	25%	0	25%

Only one writer edits entirely on-line. This writer does not have direct access to a printer. He composes text on a computer in his office, but must use a printer elsewhere in the building. He checks his text with an integrated spelling checker. This writer has five years experience and writes on

Then comes a discussion of the divergent characteristics of a second writer.

Editing and Revising Strategies

11

a computer between four and five
hours daily.

Discussion

Results of these interviews
show that professional writers experience some of the same difficulties reported in earlier studies
of student writers and clerk-typists (Beck & Stibravy, 1986; Haas &
Hayes, 1986; Gould & Grischkowsky,
1984). They said that reading text
from a VDT is slower than reading
printed text. Also, they said they
need to see an entire page or more
to perceive the continuity of their
writing. Therefore, most writers
edit and revise their writing from
hard copy.

The amount of experience writing on a computer does not influence the writers' revising strategies,
but it may influence their editing
methods. Only the least experienced
writer in this study uses an integrated grammar checker.

The author then places the study in the context of previous research.

Editing and Revising Strategies

12

Computer manufacturers are attempting to accommodate people who write manuscripts and prepare documents on a computer. Some companies now sell 14-inch VDTs. They still display only 20 to 24 lines, but the characters are larger and the image is sharper than on a 13-inch terminal. Such terminals may help increase reading speed. Also, some newer VDTs can display an entire page or two of text at one time. These terminals are primarily used for formatting layout, as the characters are too small to read for extensive editing and revising.

Earlier reports show that composing text on a computer is faster than writing in longhand or at a typewriter. Also, for some writers, integrated checkers help locate simple errors. Yet, because of the decreased reading speed and limited text display of the VDT, the four writers in this study prefer to edit and revise from hard copy.

The final paragraph of the discussion serves as the conclusion to the study.

Editing and Revising Strategies

13

                    References

Beck, C. E., & Stibravy, J. A.
    (1986). The effect of word
    processors on writing quality.
    Technical Communication,
    33(2), 84-87.
Collier, R. M. (1983). The word
    processor and revision strate-
    gies. College Composition and
    Communication, 34(2), 149-155.
Dauite, C. (1986). Physical and
    cognitive factors in revising:
    Insights from studies with
    computers. Research in the
    Teaching of English, 20(2),
    141-159.
Flower, L., Hayes, J., Carey, L.,
    Schriver, K., & Stratman, J.
    (1986). Detection, diagnosis,
    and the strategies of revi-
    sion. College Composition and
    Communication, 37(1), 16-54.
Fluegelman, A., & Hewes, J. (1983).
    Writing in the Computer Age.
    Garden City, NY: Anchor Press/
    Doubleday.

The author follows the American Psychological Association style for the individual citations.

Editing and Revising Strategies

14

Gould, J., & Frischkowsky, N.
  (1984). Doing the same work
  with hard copy and with cath-
  ode-ray tube (CRT) computer
  terminals. Human Factors,
  26(3), 323-337.

Hass, C., & Hayes, J. (1986). What
  did I just say? Reading problems in writing with the machine. Research in the
  Teaching of English, 20(1),
  22-34.

Krull, R., & Rubens, P. (1985). Application of research on document design to on-line
  displays. Technical Communication, 32(4), 29-33.

Lutz, J. (1985). A study of revising and editing at the terminal. IEEE Transactions on
  Professional Communication,
  27(2), 73-77.

Editing and Revising Strategies

15

Sommers, N. (1980). Revision strat-
    egies of student writers and
    experienced adult writers.
    College Composition and Commu-
    nication, 31(4), 378-387.
Zinsser, W. (1983). Writing with a
    Word Processor. New York: Har-
    per & Row.

CHAPTER 16

Thesis Statement and Position Research Papers

For thesis statement research papers (sometimes called position research papers), a writer makes an assertion and then substantiates it. The writer provides evidence to convince readers that his or her position is the appropriate one. In many ways, such research reports are extended essays, in which writers argue their cases by providing supporting evidence gathered from multiple sources. This chapter does the following:

provides a brief explanation of thesis statement and position papers,

suggests ways you can research thesis statement and position papers,

provides guidance for writing and revising a thesis statement paper, and

includes sample papers.

THESIS STATEMENT AND POSITION RESEARCH PAPERS

In its most basic sense, a thesis or position paper allows you to argue your case, sell your idea, or try to persuade your readers of your position. Such efforts are common in our day-to-day world: the lawyer argues her case in front of the jury;

Company X tells us its product is better than its competitor's; a political party says its candidate is better than candidate B; politicians argue that burning the American flag is bad; and the fine-arts critic argues that a play, movie, or novel is worth reading or seeing. Abortion, smoking, legal drinking age, handgun control, wearing bicycle helmets, and hundreds of other topics are debated daily.

The approach to winning your argument centers on making the most compelling argument to support your position. To do so, you take a stand and then gather information to support your stand. To persuade your readers, you need to provide enough information to support your stand, and then you need to present that information in the most convincing order.

Begin considering a topic for a thesis or position research report by developing an initial position and then gathering additional information to support that position. As you delve into the evidence, you may discover that it does not support your position. If that happens, you need to reconsider your position, revise your thesis statement, and argue for your revised position. The key to a successful paper centers on presenting a logically defensible position and supporting that position with substantial evidence.

RESEARCHING AND DRAFTING THESIS STATEMENT AND POSITION RESEARCH REPORTS

Of the multitude of information gathering strategies that you can use for thesis statement research papers, the most common are literature reviewing, interviewing, and letter writing (see Chapters 6, 7, and 9). Depending on the topic, you also might find observing and surveying people helpful.

To determine your thesis statement (or position), first research your topic and seek information that helps make your points. Consider Greg Shouse's paper. Greg first described acid rain and explained its damage. Then he proposed his solution. He presented facts: 30 million tons of chemicals causing acid rain are released each year, primarily by U.S. electrical generating plants. He next explained the impact of acid rain on the soil and plants and illustrated his points with examples from the Camel Hump Mountains of Northern Vermont, noted damage to agricultural crops, explained impact on fish and other aquatic life, and documented the loss of fish and other fauna in Adirondack lakes. Then came his evidence on the impact of acid rain on humans, with quotes from a national expert reporting the results of health studies. To close his argument, he outlined how to solve the problem.

When you build the rationale to support your position, divide your information needs into categories and then seek information based on those categories. You can divide your needs for evidence by categories:

Data (facts)

Explanations

Examples

Quotes

You can use such information separately or use multiple techniques to illustrate the point you are making. Thus, you might make a point by providing hard data on information, illustrate the point with a real-world example, and then quote experts and others, if appropriate. If you can support your point in several ways, you improve the chance that your readers will see your point.

To illustrate, suppose you posed this thesis statement:

Cigarette smoking should be banned in the work place because of the problems it creates for non-smokers.

What kinds of evidence or points to support your position could you seek? Begin by asking,

What kinds of problems might secondary cigarette smoke create?

Then speculate on the problems by asking questions that concentrate on a part of the problem. Next speculate on possible evidence:

What kinds of health problems emerge? How many people suffer from secondary-smoke-induced diseases annually? How many die? Does secondary smoke impact nonsmokers' health in other ways? If so, what ways?

allergies?
increased colds and flu?
other diseases?

To provide evidence, you might look for statistics that report the number of people who die or suffer from smoke-induced diseases; or you could give examples of people who suffer from a particular disease; quote experts on the problem; or quote victims themselves. Using people-based examples emphasizes the data. Can the people continue working? If not, does the company or its insurance agent provide disability insurance? How has the disease changed their lives on a personal level? Are they frustrated? What kinds of problems do they face?

If you can find examples, you will be able to paint a picture by giving some background, and then discuss the kind and range of problems people face, their struggles, and their frustrations. Examples help readers understand the problems in human terms. Further, by combining facts, examples, and quotes, you reinforce your point with multiple evidence, thus making your point more meaningful to readers than data by itself.

With a sufficient variety of information available, you may be able to categorize your data from both factual and emotional perspectives. Sometimes you may find that factual data carries your argument better; in other cases, emotional appeals may be more effective; and in still other cases combining both may help make the point. Television coverage of diverse social dangers often uses combinations of such an approach. For example, in the late 1980s, television news programs began covering the problem of children being severely injured or drowning in backyard swimming pools. Broadcasters first provided statistics reporting the number of injuries and drowning cases, and then interviewed the parents of children who were injured or drowned, while showing the sobbing parents in the background.

Likewise, television documentaries focused on the dangers of motorboat propellers injuring and killing swimmers. In one particularly graphic piece, the announcer interviewed a sobbing, crying teenager who had been injured at 14 years of age and then showed still photographs of the scars she carries for life. The reporter quoted her as saying winter was the best time of the year for her because "heavy clothing covered her scars."

But emotional appeals may not be the strongest way to support your thesis statement for some readers; they may become numb to emotional appeals. Further, repeated emotional appeals may not make your case as effectively as straightforward presentations of the facts. No clear guidelines exist, other than putting yourself in the reader's position, and asking, "How will my readers react to an emotional appeal?"

Shifting Your Position

As you investigate a topic, you may not find enough evidence to support your thesis statement (position). What do you do? You can (1) selectively use only the information that supports your position, (2) attack the quality of the evidence against your thesis statement and its interpretations, or (3) change your thesis statement (position) and present new evidence supporting your new perspective.

If you opt for the first strategy, use the information that best supports your position and illustrate it in different ways to reinforce your position. If the data will not support your position, then consider examples with emotional appeals to make your point. A series of graphic examples may carry your argument more clearly than limited data.

If you opt for the second strategy, explore the quality of the opposing information and data collection methods and their data interpretations. If statistics were used, explore how the data were collected and analyzed. If a sample was drawn, determine whether the sampling scheme was a random sample or non-random approach. Ask: How many subjects or units were sampled? Were enough units or people sampled to make valid inferences about the data? How were the data analyzed? How was the study designed or data gathered? What alternative explanations and interpretations can be made using the same data? Question the data, using your understanding of how it was gathered. Keep in mind that major debates emerge about data gathering techniques and strategies across the disciplines. A full discussion of such points is beyond the scope of the book.

If you opt for the third strategy — changing your thesis statement (position) — consider acknowledging both sides of the issue, discounting the alternative statement, and then presenting your new thesis statement and the supporting evidence.

Keep in mind that people *do* change their positions and interpretations on major issues after studying the issues and the supporting evidence. In doing so, they often acknowledge their previous position and then explain the rationale and evidence that led them to their new position.

ORGANIZING THE THESIS STATEMENT AND POSITION RESEARCH REPORT

When organizing your information, you can use one of several organizational strategies. Among the strategies are

ascending order strategy,

descending order strategy, or

open strategy.

The strategy you select depends on the thesis statement, your evidence supporting your stance, your audience, and your paper's requirements. Keep in mind that a variety of organizational strategies may win your readers to your way of viewing the topic or issue (see pages 208–213). As you plan your research paper, consider the different strategies and determine which one appears to fit your approach the most effectively.

Ascending Order Strategy

The ascending order strategy holds that you first develop a succinct rationale for the thesis statement and then present a series of clearly defined points that support your thesis. Present your thesis statement first, and then give your supporting points in an ascending order of importance, build to a climax, and present your strongest argument last. As you state each point, present supporting evidence by giving data, examples, explanations, and quotations. To help your readers, consider giving them an overview of the points to come, and then developing each point in detail. Thus, after your thesis statement, write a paragraph that tells your readers that you will consider X number of points to support your thesis and then explain them in detail.

For example, suppose your thesis statement argues that writing is a problem-solving activity. You might write,

"By considering three bodies of evidence, we will see how writing is a problem-solving activity."

From here you could then progress to the first major point by writing something like,

"First, a mounting body of literature clearly shows that expert writers use similar mental strategies to those used by expert chess players, mathematicians, and other specialists. . . ."

From here, you would expand the narrative and cite the different researchers and their findings.

Alternatively, you can succinctly discuss each point and then expand your discussions. For example,

> Evidence supporting writing as a problem-solving activity comes from (1) a mounting body of studies finding that expert writers use mental strategies similar to those of other experts, (2) case studies of expert and novice writers, and (3) in-depth interviews of expert and novice writers.

Such an overview tells readers that three major points will follow. You would continue by recapping each point and developing it with substantial supporting evidence.

Descending Order Strategy

An alternative approach would be to present your thesis statement and then sequence your key points in the order of descending importance. Specifically, you would present the thesis statement and then the strongest point or piece of evidence, followed by your next strongest point, and so forth. In the introduction, give either an overview that suggests you will cover X number of points to support your thesis or succinctly recap the X points as illustrated above.

Open Strategy

For an open strategy let your content and audience guide your approach. Such an approach requires more complex organizational skills because you must think about your thesis statement, think about your supporting evidence, and then build your narrative based on your overall assessment. In his paper (see p. 286), Greg Shouse argues that the acid rain problem is real and must be confronted immediately. Then he provides a solution. He supports his argument by providing evidence from both Europe and North America illustrating the magnitude of the problem. A careful examination of his research paper clearly shows that he presents strong, diverse evidence that acid rain is a serious problem in the United States and Canada. Shouse then proposes the solution: passing legislation to limit the sources of pollution.

Which of the above strategies should you choose for your paper? Always select a strategy that is suitable for your assignment and your topic.

WRITING AND REVISING THESIS STATEMENT AND POSITION RESEARCH PAPERS

If you have been able to isolate an organizational strategy before you begin to draft your report, you might be able to develop a rough outline based on your chosen organization. For example, if you plan to write a paper about critical theory in literature, you might use descending order as your organizational pattern. For example, your thesis statement might be that although there are various theories of literary criticism, some are more important for students to master than others. Using descending order, you might argue that the most important strategy is formalist criticism; the next most important are historical criticism followed by reader-response criticism. The least important strategy, you could argue, is deconstruction theory. As you draft, you could use this organizational strategy as a rough outline to guide you as you consider each of the theories in your paper.

The key to rethinking and revising your draft is to reconsider the project from its very foundation. Use a questioning approach that begins by asking, ''Is this the best organization? Could an alternative way produce a better research paper?'' Let the questions in the following checklist start you asking questions about your draft. Then ask other questions as you think about your content, purpose, and audience.

Always consider your readers' positions as you review your research paper. Why? One of the greatest failures when arguing a point is not considering your arguments from other people's viewpoints. So, put yourself in your readers' shoes and view your draft from their perspective. Let the checklist questions about readers' viewpoints serve as your starting point, and then ask additional questions that concentrate on the content of your research paper and your organization. Simply ask, ''Will my research paper convince readers that my viewpoint is the one they should adopt?'' If the answer is ''no,'' then rework your draft until you think that you have convinced readers to accept and adopt your position.

A Checklist for Revising Draft Thesis Statement Papers

1. What is the thesis statement of your draft?
2. What are the key points that provide evidence to support your thesis statement?
3. Is your draft complete?
   a. Have you included all of the points?
   b. Have you included too many points?
   c. Have you discussed all the points that you promised to discuss?
4. Does the organization argue your points effectively?
   a. Should you reconsider your organizational strategy?
   b. Would reorganizing your evidence make your points more effectively?
5. Have you adequately considered your readers?
   a. Will they understand your terms?
   b. Have you defined, explained, or illustrated new terms?
6. Have you provided adequate support for your points?
   a. Do you present enough evidence?
   b. Do you present adequate documentation or citations?
   c. Do you include supporting data? Is it needed?
   d. Would using alternative evidence (explanations or quotations) make the points more effectively? If so, do you have them readily available? Will you need to dig out additional evidence?

AN EXAMPLE OF A THESIS RESEARCH PAPER

Written for a general audience, the following research paper takes a stand and supports it with diverse evidence. The paper familiarizes readers with the topic of acid rain and presents evidence as to why it is a major problem. The author successfully argues that acid rain is a serious problem, and that the United States must begin dealing with the problem. As you read the example, note how the author does the following:

begins with a general orientation and builds the case for his arguments,

presents his argument about people's awareness of acid rain and the need to deal with its causes,

provides explanations of this complex subject,

presents a varity of solutions,

presents his call to action and rationale as to why action must be taken, and

gives a series of steps for the call to action.

Acid Rain:
The Silent Crisis in America
Presented for
Professor Michael Beehler
English 326

Greg Shouse
June 1, 1988

When the first settlers arrived in America, they met a virgin land, full of opportunities and apparent unlimited resources. They could not have imagined that this new land would be subjected to over-exploitation. They, however, would be disappointed to learn that this is the case. It has always been part of human nature to benefit oneself at the expense of others. Humankind acts hastily, often not realizing that the consequences of its actions may harm later generations.

Note the narrative beginning that presents general information about the subject that is being developed.

Consider today's oil situation; humankind carelessly used this resource as if it could not be expended. Only when humankind

The author then moves into a problem related to the topic of his paper.

realized that it was limited did governments regulate its use. These irresponsible characteristics are likewise present in all areas of environmental exploitation. Many people feel that water reserves are currently being threatened, yet humankind goes on using them carelessly, never thinking of the consequences if mankind runs out of water. Only when the situation becomes threatening does humankind step back and realize its mistakes. One would think that we would have learned from our past mistakes, yet people are ignorant of the acid rain problem. As we squabble over whether or not to spend money to reduce the causes of acid rain, more and more of our lakes, timber, and other natural resources are being threatened. So what are we waiting for?

The author then presents the problem with which he will deal with in this paper.

The evidence is abundant, and we need only look to West Germany, where over half of the forests have been lost to acid rain—a silent killer. Germany has now taken steps to save its remaining resources. Likewise, America should take pre-

He then illustrates the problem with evidence and calls for solutions to the problem.

ventive measures now, rather than wait to see if anything will happen. However, experts in the United States argue for more research before committing our country to costly clean-up programs. The nation is torn between mixed emotions as the dispute rages between the economic and environment interests. Meanwhile, our Canadian neighbors are screaming for increased regulation because they receive much of the pollution that the U.S. creates.

The author presents the impact of the problem in Canada.

"Acid precipitation" describes atmospheric precipitation that is highly acidic. This precipitation is a byproduct of burning fossil fuels in general and coal in particular. When burned, coal produces sulfur dioxide (SO_2), as its primary byproduct. Nitrogen dioxide (NO_2) is another byproduct of coal burning and automobile exhausts. Both chemicals are carried into the atmosphere, where they mix with other chemicals to produce acid rain. Carbon dioxide (CO_2), a compound naturally present in the atmosphere, forms carbonic acid.

To help the reader understand the problem, the author defines the term.

Note also the use of chemical equations to clarify or identify the compounds in question.

Unpolluted moisture has a pH
of 7; however, when combined with
sufficient carbonic acid, the moisture becomes more acidic, with a pH
of 5.6. These measurements represent the acidity or alkalinity of
substances. pH, a scientific symbol, is a measure of the hydrogen
ion concentration on a scale of 1
to 14. A pH in the 1 to 7 range
classifies a substance as being
acidic. Conversely, a pH in the
range of 7 to 14 classifies substances as basic or alkaline. Neu-
tral water has a pH of 7, while
acid precipitation is anything less
than 5.6. The pH scale is on a log-
arithmic function. This means a
tenfold difference between one pH
number and the next. For example, a
change from a 5.6 pH to 4.6 pH
reading indicates a tenfold
increase in acidity; likewise,
moving from a 5.6 to a 3.6 reading
means a 100× increase in acidity
(Acid Rain: Its State by State Im-   Note here the citation
pacts ii).   style.

Acid deposition can be either
wet or dry. The former, acid rain,
often appears as rain, fog, hail or

snow. The latter takes forms as either a particulate or a gas (Acid Rain: Its State by State Impacts ii). In the Northeastern United States, SO_2 causes two-thirds of the acid, while NO_2 causes the remaining one-third (Gilleland 3). SO_2 emissions have nearly tripled since 1950 (Acid Rain: <u>It's State by State Impacts</u> i).

Currently, an estimated 30 million tons of sulfur dioxide are released in the U.S. annually. Seventy-five percent of this occurs east of the Mississippi River, of which 92 percent are emissions from Ohio River Valley electrical generation plants (<u>Collins</u>). These emissions are sent high into the atmosphere, where they are carried downwind for possibly thousands of miles. In fact, sulfur dioxide often remains in the air for four days. During this time, it mixes with natural chemicals in the air and changes into acid sulfate and acid nitrate, i.e, sulfuric and nitric acids (Gould 6). The acids are then brought back to earth much like ash fallout from a volcanic

> In this section, the author clarifies the extent of the problem by citing the specific amount of sulfur dioxide that is released each year.

> Here the author explains the chemical behavior or process of sulfur dioxide.

eruption.

When acid enters the soil, calcium either buffers or neutralizes it, depending upon the soil alkalinity. But incessant pounding by acidic precipitates exhausts the buffering ability of the soil, and its acidity increases. As acids accumulate in the top layer of the soil, the acids progressively remove nutrients, such as calcium and magnesium, that are vital to plant growth. This calcium imbalance activates the release of aluminum that damages plants' root systems, and limits plants' abilities to absorb water and nutrients. The resulting weakened condition makes plants and trees more vulnerable to disease (Acid Rain: Its State by State Impacts iv). A prime example of this is in the Camel Hump Mountains of northern Vermont, where core samples taken from red spruce trees revealed a tripling of aluminum concentrations since 1950. More than half of these same trees have died since the 1960s (<u>Acid Rain: Its State by State Impacts</u> iv).

Research also indicates that

The continuing of technical explanation functions as evidence of the problem's importance.

acid precipitation damages agricultural crops. A study by the
Brookhaven National Laboratory indicates that acid precipitation
does reduce yields of certain
crops. For example, under a simu-
lated precipitation of pH 4.1, the
soybean yields dropped by over 10%
(<u>Acid Rain: Its State by State Im-
pacts</u> iv). The acid interferes with
the required exchange of gases
within the plant and leaches essential nutrients, such as potassium,
calcium, and magnesium, from the
soil. Further, acid rains may also
reduce the effectiveness of some
pesticides (<u>Acid Rain: Its State by
State Impacts</u> iv).

> The author demon-
> strates his familiarity
> with research in the
> field, thus providing
> his own argument
> with credibility and
> authority.

Acid precipitation likewise
damages fish and other aquatic
life, depending on the alkalinity
of the water. The more alkaline the
water, the better it can buffer the
acidity of the rain (<u>Acid Rain: Its
State by State Impacts</u> iii). However, most lakes and streams cannot
withstand the incessant exposure of
high acid levels. As the water becomes more acidic, a low pH inter-
rupts the salt balance that

> In this section, the
> author explains how
> acid rain damages the
> soil and plants.

freshwater organisms must sustain in their body tissues and blood plasma. As the pH falls below 5.5, bottom-dwelling organisms, such as bacterial decomposers, begin to die (<u>Acid Rain: Its State by State Impacts</u> iii). These bacteria break up leaves and other organic materials on the bottom of lakes and streams and deoxygenate the water. Third, as other small organisms and plankton begin to disappear, frogs, insects, and other food sources for fish disappear too. Fourth, as calcium levels are reduced within the fish, their ability to produce eggs becomes impaired. In addition, the aluminum leached from the soil washes into lakes and streams where it accumulates on the delicate gill tissues of fish, clogs their respiratory systems, and causes them to suffocate (Gould 67). Since freshwater aquatic organisms are adapted to a pH of 5.6, even a slight decrease in pH harms them. When lake or stream waters fall below a pH of 5.5, aquatic life begins to die. If the pH falls below 5.0, the lake is invariably acid dead.

Again, the author uses the technical explanation to bolster his argument. A reader who understands what happens may begin to believe that something needs to be done.

A study done on 1000 lakes and
ponds in the Adirondack mountains
of the northeastern United States
and southeastern Canada found that
nearly 25% have been acidified to
the point where they can no longer
support trout or other game fish.
According to 1985 joint U.S. and
Canadian estimates, the current
rate of sulfur emissions will double by 1990 (Gould 21).

Here the author pre-
sents research related
to this aspect of the
problem.

In 1932 Silver Lake, a high-
altitude lake in the mountains of
Hamilton county, New York, had a pH
of 6.6 with excellent fishing for
brook trout (Gould 17). By 1969,
the numbers of fish had declined to
virtually zero despite yearly
aerial stockings of over 7000 fin-
gerlings. By 1975, Silver Lake had
a pH of 4.92, and a final netting
did not produce a single fish
(Gould 17).

More examples of the
impact of acid rain
strengthen the writer's
argument.

Acid rain can harm humans too.
According to National Air Coalition
chairman Richard Ayers,

The author has saved
his more compelling
argument for last — an
effective strategy.

A recent Harvard University
study estimated that the combined effects of particulate
and sulfate pollution causes

perhaps 5% of all deaths in the average polluted urban area. An earlier MIT analysis provided a best estimate that sulfates are a factor in 50,000 premature deaths annually in northeastern North America. ("It's point, counterpoint as acid rain debate heats up." 15)

Also note the lengthy direct quote—a practice more common in the humanities than the social, biological and physical sciences. Note that this paper was written for a composition class.

Other studies indicated that sulfur inhalation makes breathing harder for those suffering from asthma, heart-lung disease, bronchitis, and emphysema. The very young are particularly susceptible because they respire faster, thus retaining larger volumes of pollutants (Acid Rain: Its State by State Impacts V). According to Dr. Phillip Landrigan of the Mt Sinai School of Medicine, "acid rain is probably third after active smoking and passive smoking as a cause of lung disease" ("Acid test" 101).

The author then adds even more evidence to make his point stronger.

Also, fish contaminated by high levels of acid contain abnormally high aluminum and mercury concentrations and are dangerous for human consumption. Acid rain

And the author adds even more evidence.

can also corrode pipes and con-
duits, thus releasing lead, copper,
and cadmium into household water
(<u>Acid Rain: Its State by State Im-
pact</u> v).

In 1970, the U.S. Congress
passed the Clean Air Act to deal
with pollution. Two provisions of
the act dealt with the regulation
of sulfur emissions. The first provision called for an ambient air
standard to control pollution in
and around urban areas. Companies
dealt with this by building taller
stacks that sent the emissions
higher into the atmosphere and carried them further from the source.
As a result of this statute, more
than 40 percent of the emission
stacks (n=200) are 500 feet tall
(Collins). These second provision
limits sulfur to 1.7 pounds/1 million BTUs (British Thermal Units)
of coal burned for plants built after 1970.

> Now the author turns to talking about the ways to deal with acid rain. He focuses on reviewing the legislation related to the problem.

With the elevation of the
smokestacks came the international
controversy as the stacks pumped
emissions over the border into Canada. Eastern Canada is especially

> Here the author begins to bridge the problem and the solutions to the international issue of acid rain.

susceptible to the effects of acid
rain because granite rock lies under the region. This granite has an
acidic pH of 4 to 6 and is therefore a poor buffer (Collins). Thus,
acidity of the soils and waters
builds up quickly and speeds the
effects of acid rain. An estimated
48,000 lakes are currently threatened in Ontario, while 1,600 are
acid dead. Furthermore, 13 salmon-
bearing rivers in Nova Scotia are
dead (Rose 19).

　　　Therefore, Canada wants the
U.S. to curb its emissions because
acid rain threatens the Canadian
environment and economy. For example, 15 percent of Canada's GNP
comes from forestry, while its second largest industry is tourism.
One of the most popular tourist at-
tractions, fishing, is threatened
by acid raining down into Canada's
lakes.

　　　Canada has proposed a 50 percent cut in SO_2 emissions in both
countries, but the Reagan administration is unwilling to comply
and says that more research is
needed before any cleanup money is

He then notes the po-
litical issue and pres-
sures being exerted
by Canada.

spent. Unfortunately, the U.S. is
failing to abide by previous laws
signed by both countries. For example, Principle 21 of the 1972
Stockholm Declaration asserts,
"states [countries] have the responsibility to ensure that activities within their jurisdiction
or control do not cause damage to
the environment of other states or
areas beyond the limits of national
jurisdiction" (Schmandt 62).

This scenario could likewise
be applied to Europe, where emissions from the industrialized nations of central Europe are dumped
onto Norway and Sweden. The damages
are truly alarming. In Norway,
seven major southern rivers are 29
times as acidic as northern ones;
the acid levels have killed all
salmon in the southern rivers.
Likewise, a study of 5,000 lakes in
southern Norway found that trout
populations were extinct in 22% of
the lakes below 660 feet, and extinct in 68% of the lakes above
2620 feet (Gould 16).

Although many critics believe
that the problem must first be

The author then pre-
sents potential prob-
lems for Europe.

solved at the domestic level, the
acid rain dilemma pits state
against state. For example, in the
northeastern U.S., states favor
more stringent emission controls
because they receive the pollution
from the industries in the Midwest
and Great Lakes states. These
states, however, favor less stringent emission controls.

Here the author notes some attempts that have been tried to solve the problems.

Though several proposals have
been introduced to solve the problem, all agree that sulfur emission
must be cut back. Alternative energy sources, such as solar, wind,
hydroelectric, and nuclear power,
may solve the problem. However,
coal is a cheap resource for the
U.S. and our supply will last for
centuries. Therefore, three major
options have been proposed. The
first option is to burn coal with
less than 1 percent sulfur by
weight, rather than the current
high-sulfur coal with greater than
3 percent sulfur. However, this
would require alternating all
power-generating facilities to burn
low-sulfur coal. Although this
would benefit western mining inter-

Here the author points out where politicians agree.

He then explores the controversies around the various solutions.

ests with their low-sulfur coal,
the midwestern mining companies
that produce high-sulfur coal would
be devastated. The United Mine
Workers of America predicts the
loss of 83,000 jobs in high-sulfur
mining companies with a switch to
low-sulfur coal (Gould 24). The
second option focuses on removing   The author continues
the sulfur from the coal before it   pointing out the var-
                                       ious issues surround-
is burned. Although research on ef-   ing the proposed
ficient coal-burning techniques is   solution.
underway, the installation of cur-
rent systems would be costly. A
third option concentrates on using
control devices, such as scrubbers, to remove the sulfur during
or after coal burning. But installing scrubbers on an existing 300
megawatt utility facility would
cost between $60 and $90 million
(Gould 7).

Obviously we have a major
problem. Should we pay out of our
own pockets to make the Canadians
happy and preserve our environment?
Or should we turn our backs, like
Germany did, and hope the problem
goes away? Fortunately, our lack of
action angers legislators, like

Gerry Sikorski (D. Minn.). At a
hearing before the House Energy
Subcommittee on Health and the
Environment in July 1987, Mr.
Sikoroski introduced HR 2666 as an
amendment to the Clean Air Act. The
amendment gives electric utilities
until 1993 to reduce SO_2 emissions
by 5 million tons, and major sta-
tionary sources until 1997 to reduce an additional 5 million tons
in sulfur emissions ("It's point,
counterpoint . . ." 13). Further
provisions suggest that states be
given until 1997 to reduce NO_2
emissions by 2 million tons from
electric utilities and industrial
boilers. States can choose how this
is carried out. The amendment also
proposes a federal subsidy to keep
residential electrical rates from
increasing more than 10 percent
from the program ("It's point,
counterpoint . . ." 13).

Note here the legisla-
tion that is reviewed.

> Sikorski argues that we must
> act now. While we have
> stalled, some 3,000 of Amer-
> ica's lakes and 23,000 miles
> of America's streams have been
> lost to acid rain. Millions of

And now the author
provides a call to
action.

acres of America's forests and
croplands are at risk. . . .
Witnesses say there is no
problem called acid rain; or
if there is, we're not the
cause . . . What you're proposing costs jobs, causes unfair
problems for rate payers, or
whatever. They cry cost, cost,
cost of cleanup and ignore the
cost, cost, cost of no
cleanup. (Rose 19)

European nations face the same
dilemma: the costs versus the benefits. They too cannot find a cheap,
easy solution to the problem. However, studies adamantly emphasize
that the benefits of cleaning up
the problem are much greater than
the costs. For example, one source
predicts that although some industrialized countries spend 1 to 2
percent of the GNP on pollution
control, the remaining pollution
damages 3 to 5 percent of the total
GNP (Wetstone 138).

> He also points out the dilemma involved by acting now.

Unfortunately, the Reagan Administration calls for further research and less action. For
example, in December 1986, Reagan

met with Canadian Prime Minister
Brian Mulroney and agreed to spend
$2.5 billion by 1991 on new tech-
nologies to reduce acid rain, but
the Reagan Administration never
followed through on the agreement
(Rose 19). In March 1987, Reagan
proposed that he would recommend to
Congress $500 million a year for
fiscal 1988 and 1989 to promote
clean technologies. At a news conference the next day, he opposed
any legislation for stiffer emission controls (Rose 19). Canada,
meanwhile, wants agreements that
specify restrictions over a designated time period, but the U.S.
continues to back away from such
proposals. In fact, President
Reagan is quite upset with the Canadians; he feels that foreign governments should not interfere with
US domestic policies. In a meeting
with Canadian officials on January
24, 1988, Reagan rejected a Canadian treaty that suggested specified cuts in sulfur dioxide
emissions by a fixed deadline (Ember 15).

    The acid rain dilemma must be

Note the subproblems
related to acting now.

tackled now, because it will only
get worse with time. Further, we do
not need additional research; we
need only look to the problems in
Europe: Acid rain has destroyed
half of Germany's forests, while
the Germans sat back and waited until it was too late to solve the
problem. Americans should learn
from Germany's mistakes rather than
waiting until massive destruction
of our forests.

The author stresses
that now is the time
to act.

    In addition, we must consider
that Canada is an ally, a friend,
and a major trading partner. According to 1986 figures, Canada is
the largest importer of American
goods. So not only is it an ethical
issue, but an economic one too.
Americans cannot afford to hurt our
relations with our friend and
neighbor to the north.

And then he argues
why the time is right.

    Steps must be taken to solve
the problem of acid rain. First, we
must pass legislation to limit all
sulfur emissions. Second, cleanup
costs should rest on the nation as
a whole. Third, we should turn to
alternative, non-polluting energy
sources, such as hydroelectric,

Finally, the author
provides steps to
take.

solar, and wind energy. Fourth, we should consider how the Canadians feel about the issue.

The history of humankind is fraught with error. We should learn from our mistakes and those of others, and then avoid repeating them. If we fail to address the acid rain problem, we will see our environment disappear before our eyes because of our stupidity and lack of common sense. We can no longer live in the present, but we must look to the future. We must act now, before it is too late to correct the acid rain problem.

Note the conclusion and the long-range implications of not acting now.

Works Consulted

Acid Rain: Its State by State Impacts. National Wildlife Federation. U.S. Department of Commerce, National Technical Information Service, April 1984.

Collins, Don. Lecture on acid rain. Biology 105. Montana State University, 1 April, 1988.

Dempster, J. P., and Manning, W. J. "Herbaceous Plants on Different Soils Exposed to Acid Rain." <u>Environmental Pollution</u> (November 1987): 295-310.

Ember, Lois, "U.S., Canada Still Far Apart on Acid Rain Account." <u>Chemical and Engineering News</u> (8 February, 1988): 15.

Gilleland, Diane, and Swisher, James. <u>Acid Rain Control: The Costs of Compliance</u>. Carbondale: Southern Illinois University Press, 1985.

Gould, Roy. <u>Going Sour: Science and Politics of Acid Rain</u>. Boston: Birkhauser, 1985.

"It's Point, Counterpoint as Acid Rain Debates Heats Up." <u>Electrical World</u> (August 1987): 13-17.

Johnson, Arthur J. "Acid deposition: Trends, Relationships, and Effects." <u>Environment</u> (May 1986): 6-11.

Linthurst, Rick A. <u>Direct and Indirect Effects of Acidic Deposition on Vegetation</u>. Boston: Butterworth, 1984.

Munn, R. E. "An Integrated Ap-
     proach to Assessing Acid Depo-
     sition." Environment (May
     1986): 12-13.
"Napap Releases Interim Assess-
     ment: New Acid Rain Report
     Elicits Much Criticism."
     Journal of Forestry (November
     1987): 4.
National Research Council (U.S.).
     Acid Deposition Long Term
     Trends. Committee on Monitor-
     ing and Assessment of Trends
     in Acid Deposition, Environ-
     mental Studies Board, Commis-
     sion on Physical Sciences,
     Mathematics, and Resource.
     Washington, D.C.: National Re-
     search Council, National Acad-
     emy Press, 1986.
Prinz, Bernhard. "Major Hypotheses
     and Factors of Forest Damage
     in Europe." Environment (No-
     vember 1987): 11-15, 32-36.
Schmandt, Jurgen. Acid Rain and
     Friendly Neighbors: The Policy
     Dispute between Canada and the
     United States. Durham: Duke
     University Press, 1989.

Somers, Emanuel. "Environmental
      Hazards Show No Respect for
      National Boundaries." Envi-
      ronment (June 1987): 7-9,
      31-33.
"The acid test." Commonwealth, 27
      February 1987: 100-101.
United States Senate. Committee on
      the Environment and Public
      Works. Acid Deposition and Re-
      lated Air Pollution Issues.
      Hearing before the Committee
      on Environment and Public
      Works, United States Senate,
      Ninety-ninth Congress, Second
      Session, 26 June 1986. Wash-
      ington, D.C.: G.P.O., 1986.
Westone, Gregory S., and Rosen-
      cranz, Armin. Acid Rain in Eu-
      rope and North America.
      Environmental Law Institute,
      1983.

CHAPTER 17

Problem-Solving and Design Research Reports

Problem-solving and design research reports answer a question or solve problem. Professors in different classes and employers in different fields frequently require either a problem-solving or a design report. Although some disciplines draw some distinctions between these kinds of reports, you can consider them virtually identical.

This chapter does the following:

provides a brief explanation of problem-solving and design research reports,

suggests a problem-solving procedure you may be able to follow,

provides guidance for writing and revising problem-solving and design reports, and

presents an example of a design paper.

WHAT ARE THE CHARACTERISTICS OF PROBLEM-SOLVING OR DESIGN RESEARCH REPORTS?

In their research reports, engineering majors describe the robots they have designed, the cars they have modified to run on methane, the containers they have built to protect eggs dropped off a two or three story building. Mathematicians and statisticians develop reports on solutions to problems they have investigated. Architecture and landscape designers prepare various solutions to design problems in their fields. Professionals in business, agriculture, and natural resources design management plans. Nurses, social workers, and educators develop action programs to solve community issues.

The general approach to the problem-solving or design paper requires that a writer understand the problem, investigate it, and then propose a solution or a design that addresses the particular problem. The design report often requires that the researcher design an original solution, whereas the problem-solving paper allows the writer to propose using either an original or an existing solution.

A PROBLEM-SOLVING PROCEDURE

Some problem-solving research requires writers to propose and explore issues before designing or proposing solutions. To help them think through their problems, some professionals follow standard problem-solving strategies. One such strategy was regularly used by researchers Verner Sumoi and Thomas Haig, now retired, of the University of Wisconsin Space Science and Engineering Research Center, for more than two decades. It includes seven steps:

1. Clearly identify the problem
2. Establish criteria for solving the problem
3. Gather your information
4. Develop solutions to the problem
5. Compare your solutions against criteria
6. Select one of the proposed solutions
7. Write your report.

To illustrate the process, let's consider an everyday problem such as determining what kind of computer to purchase. If you choose to follow the Haig-Sumoi method, here is how you might proceed:

Step 1. Clearly State your Problem

Before you can state your problem specifically, you need to know the computer applications common to your field. You might need to interview juniors, seniors, and graduate students, as well as professors who understand the computer and software needs that your major requires. Once you know your specific needs, you can write a problem statement that clearly states your needs, including the hardware and software issues.

Step 2. State the Criteria for the Solution

Once you know the problem, state the limitations and requirements needed to guide your computer selection. You might consider developing a list of criteria such as the following:

1. The projected life span of the unit. (For example, "the basic unit should be able to be expanded over the next five years, if needed, for different functions.")
2. The software requirements.
3. The basic memory requirements and configurations.
4. The printing requirements. (For example, do you need a dot matrix, letter quality, or laser printer?)
5. The monitor and keyboard requirements.
6. The funds available to purchase the equipment.
7. The necessary expansion capabilities of the computer.
8. The modem or networking requirements for the computer.
9. The compatibility requirements.
10. Available discounts for the computer, components, and system.

When you consider your criteria, adopt the ones that fit your needs and can handle the tasks you face.

Step 3. Gather the Needed Information

To explore your problem, plan to use three major information-gathering strategies: (1) literature reviewing, (2) interviewing others, and (3) testing. First, check *Readers' Guide* or *InfoTrac* for articles on buying computers and check the library's card catalog and online computer catalog for books on buying personal computers. Identify the key books and articles and examine them to learn what general guidance they give you for buying computers. Next, interview students or colleagues who have purchased computers. With that information, you can reconsider your question and refine it, if needed. You may find it necessary to specify the software programs you will need and their hardware requirements. Finally, try to test the computer and the software — or, at least, read articles that describe others' experiences using the products. You could search for information about the different brands and/or models of computers, printers, and software you might consider purchasing. You might write to the computer and software manufacturers and request information on their products.

Meanwhile, you can search *InfoTrac* and *Readers' Guide* for articles reviewing different kinds of computers and software. Then you can visit computer stores and ask if you can try out the various brands.

Step 4. Develop or Design Solutions to the Problem

Based on the kinds of information you obtain, you could then search for information about those computers, read the information, and try to develop a solution that will serve your needs.

Step 5. Compare your Solutions or your Design Against Criteria

To compare your criteria against your solutions, build a table with the criteria listed down the left hand side and the solutions across the top, as illustrated in Table 17-1. Such a table gives you a clear, visual impression and simplifies your comparisons.

Step 6. Select or Design Solution

Based on your comparison of the alternatives, select the computer to buy. Remember that some criteria automatically rule out potential solutions. If no solution emerges, you must recast your question and begin your search again.

TABLE 17-1   A Comparison of Computers and Criteria

	Brand A	Brand B	Brand C
Comparison Criteria			
1. Number of expansion slots			
2. Software capabilities			
a. Word processing			
b. Graphics			
c. D-Base			
d. Desktop publishing			
3. Memory requirements			
RAM			
Hard disk			
Floppies			
4. Student discount*			
(etc.)			

*Continue adding or replacing the criteria based on your needs

Step 7. Write your Report

Your report should reflect your efforts and give your readers a clear idea of what you did, how you did it, and what you decided. When you organize your report, make your proposed solution clear to your readers. Most reports will concentrate on the problem's solution rather than on giving a historical account of the problem-solving and information-gathering process. When you do report your methods, be succinct.

As a general guideline, plan to spend about half of your time gathering information and at least one-third of your time writing up your results. Don't underestimate the time required to gather the needed information and to write your report.

WRITING AND REVISING PROBLEM-SOLVING AND DESIGN RESEARCH REPORTS

The information-gathering strategy used for this kind of report entails searching diverse sources to develop an in-depth understanding of the problem and the strategies and techniques that others have used to solve similar problems. A researcher may review literature, write to companies and organizations for information, interview experts, and conduct observational research.

The research design paper included at the end of this chapter emerged from investigating the available radon reduction techniques and selecting the ones to design a system to reduce radon to a safe level in the Carpenters' home. Such an approach often entails developing a good understanding of the problem and potential solutions and then proposing the best possible solution to the problem.

The design approach may be used for diverse applications including the following: (1) for designing equipment, products, processes, and buildings, such as those developed in fields such as engineering, manufacturing, and architecture; (2) to develop educational and social support programs in education, social work, and religion; (3) for health treatment programs in medicine, nursing, psychological counseling, and veterinary medicine; (4) for information campaigns in advertising and public relations; (5) in management programs such as those offered in industry and government agencies; (6) in resource management programs, such as those available in forestry, wildlife, and water resources; and (7) in crop and plant production regimes in agriculture.

When you are faced with a research paper in which you must identify the problem, seek information, and then pose a solution, you can use the full range of information-gathering strategies: literature searching in libraries, writing letters of request to corporations, interviewing people, conducting surveys, and observing. Reviewing literature proves to be extremely useful for many problems, as does making observations.

When you search for information to help solve problems, remember that the best solutions may come from using multiple information-gathering strategies.

Engineers and social scientists alike suggest addressing a problem from different per-spectives and using a combination of problem-solving strategies to find a solution.

Work from a Plan

When you begin thinking about writing your problem-solving report, develop a plan to guide you as you work. That plan may only be a list of rough ideas, a page of pattern notes or tree diagrams, a working rough outline, or possibly a more formal outline. Even if it is not elaborate, a planning document will help direct your efforts and will clear the way for you to make the most efficient use of your composing time. See Chapters 11, 12, and 13 for a process approach to writing research reports. By developing a plan before you begin to compose a draft, you force yourself to begin thinking about your content, audience, purpose, and organization early in your writ-ing process.

Consider Organizational Strategies

Overall, you will need to discuss the problem and its solution. For each section of your report, you can use a variety of organizational strategies. In discussing the problem, you might explore its results and then identify the causes. From here you could propose a solution (design) using process, function, spatial, or geographical organizational strategies. In the radon mitigation report (see p. 316), Marie Edwards first discusses radon and its sources and then proposes a five-step process to reduce the level of radon. Remember, the organizational strategies you select must fit your content, audience, and purpose.

A brief discussion of your problem may suffice in many cases, as the solution or design will constitute most of your research report. In some academic fields, you may opt to exclude any discussion of your methodology, while other fields may require it. When in doubt, review examples of problem-solving or design papers in your field, or ask your colleagues or professors for guidance.

As with writing other research reports, write what you can when you can. For some students, that means writing increments or parts of the research at different times. For other students, that means writing in one, two, or three marathon compos-ing sections.

If your report will have illustrations (figures or tables), consider roughing them out first and then writing your narrative around them. Such an approach allows you to integrate your narrative and visuals more effectively; frequently you can even reduce your narrative. As you work, remember not to repeat everything in your narrative that appears in the illustrations or tables. Instead, discuss only the more important or critical elements and any abbreviations that require explanation.

Take Time to Revise

As with writing other reports, setting a draft aside to cool enhances your ability to take a detached, critical look at your work. When you begin to reread your draft, try to reconsider the entire problem, your content, your audience, and your purpose. Take on a questioning attitude and use the following checklist to guide your re-thinking and revising of your draft.

For any design or problem solving report, the accuracy of your content becomes critical. A slip at this stage will cause you to lose credibility with your readers, so check and recheck the accuracy of your content. If possible, have another student review your paper for accuracy. Work hard to polish your draft into a top-notch research paper. To help you, let the following checklist guide your efforts.

A Checklist for Revising Drafts of Problem-Solving and Design Reports

1. Is the problem clearly stated?
2. Does the proposed design address the stated problem?
3. Have you provided enough evidence to show that the proposed design will work?
4. Have you clearly identified any limitations or restrictions to the design or proposed solution? Are they clear to readers?
5. Have you adequately considered your readers?
   a. Will your readers understand your terms?
   b. Have you defined any terms they might not understand?
6. Does the organization help readers understand your solution or design?
7. Have you provided adequate details and supporting evidence?
8. Have you checked the accuracy of the content, data, and illustrations?
9. Is the report complete?

A PROBLEM-SOLVING DESIGN RESEARCH REPORT

The following example illustrates a research report that identifies a problem — high radon levels in a Colorado home — and then proposes a solution for that problem. As you read it, note how Marie Edwards, the author,

identifies the general problem,

explains the potential magnitude of the problem,

narrows the problem to one Colorado home,

details the problem-identification procedures, and

suggests a series of steps to reduce radon in the client's home.

A
Radon Mitigation Plan
for a Residential Home

Marie Edwards
Advanced Composition
Section 3

November 15, 1989

Radon Mitigation Plan

2

Radon—A Potential Health Threat

A naturally occurring by-product from the breakdown of certain rocks and minerals may be threatening the health of many Americans. Radon gas, found in soils containing uranium, granite, shale, phosphate, and pitchblende, seeps through the soil and into buildings through dirt floors, cracks in concrete floors and walls, floor drains, sumps, joints, and other small openings (Environmental Protection Agency, 1986). Many experts claim that this odorless, tasteless, and colorless gas is a major indoor pollution problem that increases the risk of lung cancer.

The author begins with a general overview of the problem.

The gas itself does not cause cancer; rather, its "progeny" cause the problem. The progeny are radioactive by-products that become trapped in the lungs of anyone who breathes air containing radon. As the progeny undergo further breakdown, they release small bursts of

She then explains how radon may cause the problem—increased chances of lung cancer.

Radon Mitigation Plan

3

energy that can damage lung tissue
and lead to cancer (Environmental
Protection Agency, 1986). Some scientists estimate that radon causes
5,000 to 20,000 lung cancer deaths
per year (Environmental Protection
Agency, 1986), while others estimate 10,000 to 30,000 deaths per
year (Lafavore, 1986).

> Note here the citation style and details, name, comma and date.

Although the Environmental
Protection Agency has recently expressed concern about radon in
schools and other buildings where
people spend long periods of time,
most radon research has focused on
the gas in residential dwellings.

> Here the author provides a historical background of the actions that have been taken that may lead to the problem.

During the energy crisis of the
1970s, many homeowners tried to
conserve energy by reducing the infiltration rate and exchange of
fresh air in their homes. Little
did they know that radon was seeping in through a basement or crawl
space and that caulking doorjambs
and weatherstripping windows was
trapping the harmful gas in their

> She now provides more specific details on the problem.

Radon Mitigation Plan

4

homes (Lafavore, 1986). Such homes
especially are vulnerable to radon
gas infiltration during cold
weather. During winter, when homeowners allow the lowest infiltration of outside air, radon gas
moves out of the colder, more pressurized soil into the warmer, less
pressurized areas of a house.

　　Despite all the research, no
one knows for certain how many
homes have a radon problem. Richard
Toohey of the Argonne National Laboratory in Illinois believes that 5
to 10 percent of all homes in the
U.S. may have unsafe radon levels.
Building construction, local geol-
ogy, climate, and occupant activity
all influence the amount of radon
in a home. For example, a home in
Pennsylvania had 1,000 times the
normal radon concentration, but the
home next door and only 100 feet
away was safe (Lafavore, 1986).
The contaminated home sat over a
small outcropping of low-grade

Note here the range
of evidence and infor-
mation presented.

Radon Mitigation Plan

5

uranium ore.

Some regions of the country do seem to have a higher incidence of radon contaminated homes. For example, uranium exists as a trace element in other types of rock, such as granite. But in the Northeast, granite contains about 10 to 50 parts per million, while it holds as much as 500 parts per million in parts of the West (Lafavore, 1986). The Environmental Protection Agency found that 39 percent of 900 Colorado homes surveyed had radon levels above federal safety guidelines (Woods, 1987).

Here the author begins to make the transition from a nationwide look at radon to a specific region.

Investigating the Possibility of Radon in a Colorado Home

Note that the head serves as a transition to the next topic — focusing on radon in Colorado.

Ed Carpenter, a Colorado resident, heard about the health risk from radon gas and read about its high incidence in Western states. As a result, he tested his home for radon. Carpenter and his family live in a 1500-square-foot,

Radon Mitigation Plan

6

tri-level house with three bedrooms
and two baths on the top floor; a
living room, family room, utility
room, kitchen and dining area on
the main floor; an 800-square-foot
garden-level basement; and 700-
square-feet of crawl space under
the main floor. In the crawl space,
Edwards covered the exposed soil
with 6-mil-thick black plastic
sheeting (a standard trash bag is
1—2 mil plastic). The well insu-
lated house, built in 1979, has
R-19 walls, R-60 ceilings, and
caulking around the foundation and
windows. Low utility bills suggest
that the insulation and caulking
are doing a good job of sealing the
home and reducing energy consumption. Carpenter heats the house
during the winter with a natural
gas, forced-air furnace, and cools
the house during the summer by
opening the windows and running an
exhaust fan. A sealed room with a
fresh air intake encloses the natu-
ral-gas-fired furnace.

Note the details that
the author provides
here to give a clear
understanding of the
home in question.

Radon Mitigation Plan

7

To begin his investigation,
Carpenter studied the soils and
foundation soils tests made in 1978
on his home's site, and he reviewed
the soil profile of a bore for the
irrigation well some 100 feet east
of the house. About 3 feet below
the surface begins a deep layer of
sand and fine gravel (Feighny,
1978; Sherrod, 1978). Also, large
water-bearing gravel exists from 36
to 56 feet down (Feighny, 1978).
When the house was built, the surface 3 feet of soil were excavated
for both the crawl space and garden-level basement. Because the
sand and gravel consist of granite,
they are good candidates for high
levels of radon (Environmental Protection Agency, 1986; LaFavore,
1986). Being porous, the gravel is
also likely to allow greater air
movement than would more compact
types of soil. Thus, the house may
be located on potentially radon-
producing material.

Edwards now pro-
vides background on
the Carpenter home
and the reasons for
suspecting a problem
here.

Radon Mitigation Plan

8

Therefore, Carpenter used charcoal grab samples to check for radon in his home. The grab samples are small metallic canisters about the diameter of a coffee cup and only about one-half inch high. Typically, they are placed in non-ventilated areas of the house during the winter for about three to seven days and then returned to a laboratory for evaluation. Carpenter obtained three canisters (from the University of Pittsburgh Radon Research Program for $15 each) and placed one on each level of his house.

After assessing each canister, the Pittsburgh research group reported that Carpenter's home contained radon at levels above the EPA safe exposure level of 4.0 pCi/L (picocuries per liter). The garden level had a 7.1 pCi/L reading, the main floor family room had 4.4 pCi/L reading, and an upstairs bedroom had 3.7 pCi/L reading

Edwards now details the radon testing methods used in the Carpenter home.

Edwards now reports the results of those tests.

Radon Mitigation Plan

9

(Cohen, 1987). Exact measurements
may be a little higher or lower because readings from charcoal grab
samples are accurate to only ± 25
percent. For radon levels between 4
and 20 pCi/L, the EPA suggests a
12-month monitoring to see if radon
levels change with the seasons.

Besides further monitoring,
Carpenter decided to find the
source of his home's radon problem.
From his literature review, he had
learned that the radioactive gas
could be seeping in through cracks
and joints in the basement walls or
floor, or around the edges of the
plastic in the crawl space, or being released from the concrete used
in walls, floors, and blocks (Environmental Protection Agency, 1986).
Therefore, Carpenter placed one
charcoal grab sample in the crawl
space and one under the plastic in
the crawl space. The crawl space
air tested at 4.4 pCi/L, while
readings under the plastic were

Note the details on testing and trying to identify the real radon source in the home.

Radon Mitigation Plan

10

150 pCi/L. Carpenter reasoned that
the radon was coming from the
soils.

A Proposed Mitigation Plan

Now Edwards pro-
poses a process of
trying one solution af-
ter another in a sys-
tematic way.

    The following mitigation
approaches the radon reduction
incrementally by suggesting that
Carpenter try the least expense
modifications first and then retest
for radon levels. If the radon
levels remain unacceptable,
Carpenter can then complete the
next level modification, and then
test again. He can repeat the
process until he eliminates the
radon or reduces its level to an
acceptable point. Being a moder-
ately skilled do-it-yourselfer,
Carpenter can do steps 1 through 4
himself. If the radon level remains unacceptable after step 4,
Carpenter can then hire a furnace
technician to install the air-to-
air exchange system as recommended
in step 5.

If the solution doesn't
work, Edwards sug-
gests trying the next
solution.

Radon Mitigation Plan

11

Step 1: Sealing the cracks

Brennan and Turner (1986) suggest that homeowners first find and
caulk cracks and holes in their
home's foundation and basement
floor. A quick survey of Carpenter's basement showed that six
tubes of polyurethane caulking (at
$5 per tube) and about four hours
of labor would be needed for the
task.

Step 2: Isolating the crawl space

As a second step, Carpenter
could weather strip around the door
between the crawl space and garden-
level basement and install a 6-mil
plastic barrier on the back side of
the 2x4 wall separating the crawl
space from the basement. These
steps would minimize the infiltration of radon-bearing air from the
crawl space into the basement. The
plastic, weather stripping, duct
tape, and staples would cost about
$50 and the task would take about
four hours to complete.

Now Edwards details
the proposed solu-
tions in increasing or-
der of cost.

Radon Mitigation Plan

12

Step 3: Pressurizing the crawl
            space
        In addition to these first two
steps, Carpenter could further
reduce radon levels by installing a
system to pressurize the crawl
space. The system consists of a
small fan and air distribution
piping system. Used during winter,
this technique draws fresh air
pressure into the crawl space,
thereby decreasing the infiltration
of radon-bearing air into the home.
The fan should be capable of making
.5 to 1.5 air exchanges per hour   Note the specific de-
                                        tails provided here.
and should increase the air pres-
sure sufficiently to create a positive pressure in the crawl space.
Such a fan should cost no more than
$150 (Environmental Protection
Agency, 1986), and the electricity
to run it year round may run $100.
Calculations of the crawl space
volume suggest a fan blowing 100
cubic feet a minute will produce
the recommended air exchanges (see

Radon Mitigation Plan

13

(Table 1). Edwards can reduce costs
by using a less expensive fan and
running the fan only during the
winter.

   The proposed piping system can
distribute the outside air evenly
throughout the crawl space (Figure
1), if Carpenter drills holes along
the pipes. To reduce the chances of
moisture from rain or snow reaching
the fan, Carpenter can install a U-
shaped pipe between the air intake
vent and the fan (Figure 2). He can
bend the U from thin, bendable, ac-
cordion, aluminum pipe, and attach
it to the fan. Finally, he should
cover the intake with screen to
keep rodents and insects out of the
distribution system and crawl
space. Because fans will wear out
and require periodic maintenance,
the design uses an electrical plug
for attaching the fan to a wall
plug or receptacle. Because the
system is in a crawl space, Carpenter should use a ground interrupted

Note here the reference to Figure 1. Also note that Figure 1 is at the back of the report and would be added if the research report were to be typeset.

Note the details Edwards provides as the proposed solutions become more complex.

Radon Mitigation Plan

14

fault plug (safety circuit breaker)
for the wall plug. Adding a ceiling
light near the fan will help light
the system for maintenance, and a
switch with a neon on-light will
show when the system is operating.
Other supplies include the pipe;
nails for the wire; a board, bolts,
and screens for making the fan
mount; and duct tape for sealing
any pipe joints. Standard heating
and cooling duct work, elbows,
adapters, and fittings connect the
duct work to the fan. The fan,
pipe, and other supplies will cost
between $100 and $200, depending
upon the source, and system installation will require an estimated 16
to 24 hours.

    During the fall, winter, and
early spring months, Carpenter
should close the vents designed to
ventilate the air space and turn on
the fan. The fan will bring more
fresh air into the crawl space;
that increases the air pressure on

Radon Mitigation Plan

15

the soil and minimizes radon movement into the house.

    Step 4: Installing sub-slab
          ventilation

    If the radon levels remain un-
acceptable, then Carpenter should
consider installing sub-slab ventilation sumps in the basement
floor. Both Brennan and Turner
(1986) and the Environmental Protection Agency (1986a) recommend
such a system that exhausts radon-
bearing air from the soil itself
(Figure 3). Brennan and Turner
(1986) recommend one fan per
300-500 square feet and at least
two ventilation sumps per basement.

    For this system to work, the
soil under the basement slab must
be porous and allow air movement.
If not, the entire basement slab
must be removed, and a piping and
gravel bed installed underneath the
slab. The sandy, gravelly subsoil
under Carpenter's basement should
allow enough air movement through

Radon Mitigation Plan

16

the sand and gravel without having
to remove the concrete floor.

    For each ventilation sump,
Carpenter must cut a 2 to 3-foot
diameter hole in the basement
floor, dig a hole 18 inches deep,
and install a standpipe, with holes
along its length, in the hole. Carpenter should then refill the hole
with crushed stone about 2 to 3
inches in diameter, cover it with
plastic, and pour new concrete
around the standpipe. To reduce vi-
brations from the fan, Carpenter
should consider bolting it to the
floor and installing flexible plastic tubing from the fan to the exhaust pipe system. An exhaust fan
and system of pipe would then move
the radon-laden air outside the
house.

    The cost for Carpenter to in-
stall sub-slab ventilation sumps
will run between $75 and $125 each,
depending on their location, the
cost of the fans, the length of

Radon Mitigation Plan

17

pipe required to exhaust the stale
air, and rental charges for a ham-
mer drill to cut the holes in the
concrete floor. Each sump will require 12 to 20 hours to install.
  Step 5: Installing an air-to-air
                exchanger
     If, after testing the results
of Step 4, Carpenter finds that the
radon levels within the house remain unacceptable, he should investigate installing an air-to-air
exchanger. Air-to-air exchangers
bring fresh air into the house and
exhaust stale air, while transfer-
ring the heat from the stale air to
the incoming fresh air. Contractors
usually connect the whole house
systems to the cold air return system of forced air furnaces. Installing such systems is beyond the
expertise of most do-it-yourselfers. If Carpenter considers
air-to-air exchangers, he should
contact a furnace contractor to install his system. Depending upon

Radon Mitigation Plan

18

the brand, size, required duct
work, and labor, a completely installed system will cost between
$1000 and $2000.

Conclusion

By following the sequence of
mitigation steps and retesting his
home, Carpenter should be able to
minimize the radon for the least
cost. Since the radon levels in
Carpenter's house are not considered dangerously high, he might,
after weighing the available information, perform the steps sequentially over two or more heating
seasons. That will enable him to
test carefully for radon levels after each mitigation step.

Note here how the au-
thor suggests that the
design proposed will
solve the radon
problem.

Radon Mitigation Plan

19

References

Brennan, T., & Turner, B. (1986).
Defeating radon. Solar Age,
11(3), 33-37.

Cohen, B. (1988). Test reports.
Pittsburgh: The Radon Project.

Cohen, B. (1987). Test reports.
Pittsburgh: The Radon Project.

Environmental Protection Agency.
(1989). Radon reduction
methods: A homeowner's guide
(3rd ed.). Office of Research
and Development (Publication
RD-681). Washington, DC: Environmental Protection Agency.

Environmental Protection Agency.
(1986a). Radon reduction techniques for detached houses.
Office of Research and Development (EPA/625/5-86/019).
Washington, DC: Environmental
Protection Agency.

Radon Mitigation Plan

20

Environmental Protection Agency.
     (1986b). A citizen's guide to
     radon: what it is and what to
     do about it. Office of Air and
     Radiation (EPA OPA-86-004).
     Washington, DC: Environmental
     Protection Agency.
Feighny, J. (1978). Well completion
     and pump installation report.
     Permit 23640-F. Denver: Colo-
     rado Division of Water
     Resources.
LaFavore, M. (1986). The radon re-
     port. New Shelter, 7(1),
     29-35.
Sherrod, N., & Smith, C. (1978).
     Report of a soils and founda-
     tion investigation for Ed Car-
     penter. Fort Collins, CO:
     Empire Laboratories.
Woods, M. (December 21, 1987). New
     device removes radon from air.
     Rocky Mountain News, p. 4.

Radon Mitigation Plan

21

Table 1. Projected air exchanges for crawl space.[1]

Approximate Air Exchanges per Hour	Size Fan Required (Cubic Feet Per Minute)
1.25	75
1.75	100
2.50	150

[1]Based on calculations of the air volume of the 784-square-foot crawl space with a 4.5-foot height. The suggested projections are based on the equation:

Volume × Number of Air Exchanges per Hour/60 =
   Volume of air moved in cubic feet per minute

Radon Mitigation Plan

22

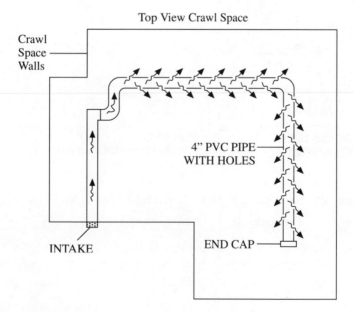

Top View Crawl Space

Crawl Space Walls

4" PVC PIPE WITH HOLES

INTAKE

END CAP

Figure 1. The design of the air distribution pipe system for the crawl space

Radon Mitigation Plan

23

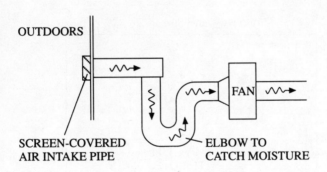

OUTDOORS

FAN

SCREEN-COVERED
AIR INTAKE PIPE

ELBOW TO
CATCH MOISTURE

Figure 2. Design of the flexible duct work between the fan and air intake vent

Radon Mitigation Plan

24

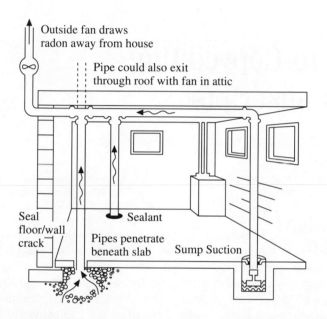

Figure 3. A cross-sectional view of the sub-slab ventilation system
Source: EPA. (1987). <u>Radon reduction methods: a homeowner's guide</u> (2nd ed.). (Publication OPA-87-010.) p. 10. Washington, DC: Environmental Protection Agency.

APPENDIX A

A Guide to Copyediting Draft Manuscripts

Copyediting symbols — marks on the draft manuscript — provide a shorthand for identifying the needed corrections. By using standard copyediting symbols, you can make changes more quickly than by having to rewrite in longhand throughout a manuscript. Further, by using standard copyediting symbols, you can have a typist or word processing operator make the final corrections.

When you copyedit, use a brightly colored pencil so you can easily see the desired changes. If you have composed your draft research report on a word processing unit, recall the file and make the needed changes. By making changes in a bright color, you do not need to read the entire manuscript word for word, and you are less likely to miss them.

Symbol	Meaning
(twenty-five)	Use numbers or abbreviate
project end. We began	Begin a new paragraph

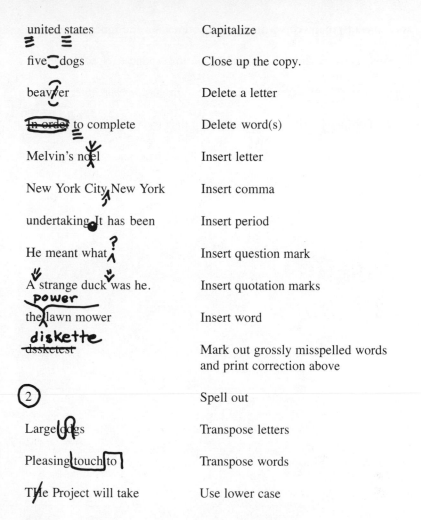

united states	Capitalize
five⁀dogs	Close up the copy.
beav͜er	Delete a letter
~~In order~~ to complete	Delete word(s)
Melvin's no͜el	Insert letter
New York City⌄New York	Insert comma
undertaking⦁It has been	Insert period
He meant what⌄?	Insert question mark
˅A strange duck˅ was he.	Insert quotation marks
the⌃lawn mower (power)	Insert word
~~dssketest~~ diskette	Mark out grossly misspelled words and print correction above
②	Spell out
Large⦵dⷦoⷢgs	Transpose letters
Pleasing⌐touch⌐to⌐	Transpose words
T/he Project will take	Use lower case

Using Copyediting Symbols — An Example

Expressive writing represents free flowing-writing where in you capture

your thinking about a specified issue witho�ut being concerned about

style, mechanics⌄spelling⌄and gramm⟋er. journal writing has emerged as

a common assignment in ~~courses, such as~~ art, geography, music, mathe-

matics, philosophy, physics, and sociology⌄professsors who give journal
(courses⊙)

asssignments you ask to write in your journal several times a week or

perhaps daily. Some professors ask you to respond to specific Ques-

tions, others ~~merely~~ ask you to think about discussions and other related

topics. For journ*a*l writing you do not stop to correct any errors. Instead, get ~~you're~~

~~more interested in getting the~~ *your* ideas out of your head and onto the paper.

APPENDIX B

Selected Style Guides

Achtert, W. S., and J. Gibaldi. 1985. *MLA Style Manual*. New York: Modern Language Association.

American Chemical Society. 1978. *Handbook for Authors of Papers in American Chemical Society publications*. Washington, D.C.: American Chemical Society.

American Psychological Association. 1983. *Publication Manual of the American Psychological Association*. 3rd ed. Washington, D.C.: American Psychological Association.

Associated Press. 1987. *The Associated Press Stylebook and Libel Manual*. Reading: Addison-Wesley.

CBE Style Committee. 1983. *CBE Style Manual: A Guide for Authors, Editors, and Publishers in the Biological Sciences*. Bethesda: Council of Biology Editors.

Gibaldi, J., and W. S. Achtert. 1988. *MLA Handbook*. New York: Modern Language Association.

Government Printing Office. 1984. *U.S. Government Printing Office Style Manual*. Washington, D.C.: Government Printing Office.

Howell, J. B. 1983. *Style Manuals of the English-Speaking World: A Guide*. Phoenix: Orynx Press.

Merriam-Webster, Inc. 1985. *Webster's Standard American Style Manual*. Springfield: Merriam-Webster.

Steenrod, N. E., J. L. Dobb, L. Carlitz, F. A. Ficken, and G. Piranian. 1984. *A Manual for Authors of Mathematical Papers*. Providence: American Mathematical Society.

University of Chicago Press. 1982. *The Chicago Manual of Style*. 13th ed. Chicago: University of Chicago Press.

HANDBOOKS AND GUIDES TO WRITING

Berstein, T. M. 1976. *Watch Your Language*. New York: Atheneum.

——. 1978. *The Careful Writer*. New York: Atheneum.

Brusaw, C. T., G. J. Alred, and W. E. Oliu. 1987. *Handbook of Technical Writing*. New York: St. Martin's Press.

——. 1987. *The Business Writer's Handbook*. New York: St. Martin's Press.

van Leunen, Mary-Claire. 1985. *A Handbook for Scholars*. New York: Knopf.

Williams, J. M. 1990. *Style: Ten Lessons in Clarity and Grace*. Chicago: University of Chicago Press.

APPENDIX C

A Guide to Selected Writing Resources

As you search for additional resources for your personal library, you may find the following list helpful.

GRAMMAR HANDBOOKS

Crews, F., and S. Schor. 1989. *The Borzoi Handbook for Writers*. New York: Knopf.

Hacker, D. 1988. *Rules for Writers*. 2nd ed. New York: St. Martin's Press.

Herman, W. 1986. *The Portable English Handbook*. Fort Worth: Holt, Rinehart and Winston.

Hodges, J. C., et al. 1990. *Harbrace College Handbook*. 11th ed. San Diego: Harcourt Brace Jovanovich.

Strunk, Jr., W., and E. B. White. 1979. *The Elements of Style*. New York: MacMillan.

DICTIONARIES

Gove, P.B. (ed.) 1986. *Webster's Third New International Dictionary of the English Language, Unabridged*. Springfield: Merriam-Webster.

Houghton Mifflin. 1989. *The American Heritage Dictionary of the English Language*. Boston: Houghton Mifflin.

Neufeldt, V., and D. B. Guralnik (eds.). 1988. *Webster's New World Dictionary of American English*. 3d college ed. New York: Webster's New World.

Stein, J., ed. 1984. *The Random House College Dictionary*. New York: Random House.

——, ed. 1987. *The Random House Dictionary of the English Language*. New York: Random House.

References

Achtert, W. S., and J. Gibaldi. 1985. *The MLA Style Manual*. New York: Modern Language Association.

Adams, J. 1976. *Conceptual Blockbusting*. San Francisco: San Francisco Book Company.

Alliance of Information Referral Systems. 1975. *Directory of Information and Referral Services*. Phoenix: Alliance of Information Referral Systems.

American Psychological Association. 1991. *Psychological Abstracts*. Washington, D.C.: American Psychological Association.

———. 1991. *PsycLIT*. Washington, D.C.: American Psychological Association.

———. 1983. *Publication Manual of the American Psychological Association*. 3d ed. Washington, D.C.: American Psychological Association.

Anderson, P. 1985. What survey research tells us about writing at work. In *Writing in Nonacademic Settings*, edited by L. Odell and D. Goswami. New York: Guilford Press.

Associated Press. 1988. Pastor mighty mad at Mighty Mouse. *Rocky Mountain News*. 10 June, 1988, 4.

Babbie, E. 1982. *Social Research for Consumers*. Belmont, Calif.: Wadsworth.

Barbour, A. G., C. R. Nichols, and T. Fukushima. 1980. An outbreak of giardiasis in a group of campers. *American Journal of Tropical Medical Hygiene* 25:384–89.

Bethke, F. J. 1983. Measuring the usability of software manuals. *Technical Communication* 30(2):13–16.

Black, R. E., A. C. Dykes, S. P. Sinclair, and J. G. Wells. 1987. Giardiasis in day centers: Evidence of person-to-person transmission. *Pediatrics* 60:486-91.

Bowker, R. R. 1983. *American Men & Women of Science*. New York: Bowker.

———. 1988. *The Literary Market Place*. New York: Bowker.

———. 1990. *Who's Who in American Art*. New York: Bowker.

Broadhead, G. J., and R. C. Freed. 1986. *The Variables of Composition: Process and Product in a Business Setting*. Published for the Conference on College Composition and Communication. Carbondale: Southern Illinois Press.

Bruner, J. S. 1986. *Actual Minds, Possible Worlds*. Cambridge: Harvard University Press.

Business Press. 1990. *Who's Who in Banking*. New York: Business Press.

Campbell, D. T., and J. C. Stanley. 1963. *Experimental and Quasi-Experimental Designs for Research*. Chicago: Rand McNally.

Caudra Associates. 1990. *Directory of Online Databases*. Santa Monica, Calif.: Caudra Associates.

Chaffee, S. 1975. The interview as a reporting tool. In *Gathering and Writing News: Selected Readings*, edited by R. L. Moore, R. R. Cole, D. L. Shaw, and L. E. Mullins. Washington, D.C.: College Press.

CBE Style Manual Committee. 1983. *CBE Style Manual: A Guide for Authors, Editors, and Publishers in the Biological Sciences*. 5th ed. Bethesda: Council of Biology Editors.

Cook, K., Jr., and W. Stoligitis. 1989. Profile 88—Survey of STC membership. *Technical Communication* 36(1): 39–42.

Cook, T. D., and D. T. Campbell. 1979. *Quasi-Experimentation: Design & Analysis Issues in Field Settings*. Boston: Houghton Mifflin.

Cooper, M., and M. Holzman. 1983. Talking about protocols. *College Composition and Communication* 34(3):284–93.

Cooperrider, A. 1986. Habitat evaluation systems. In *Inventory and Monitoring of Wildlife Habitat*, edited by A. Y. Cooperrider, R. J. Boyd, and H. R. Stuart. Denver: U.S. Department of the Interior, Bureau of Land Management.

Cornell University. 1986. *Library of Congress Classification System, Information Guide No. 5*. Ithaca: Cornell University Libraries.

Crews, D., and S. Schor. 1985. *The Borzoi Handbook for Writers*. New York: Knopf.

Darr, C. Personal communication, 31 May, 1989.

Davis, D. E. 1963. Estimating the numbers of game populations. In *Wildlife Investigation Techniques*. 2nd ed., edited by H. S. Mosby, and O. H. Hewitt. Blacksburg, Va.: The Wildlife Society.

Dick, D. 1967. The effect of meteorological conditions on the whistling of bobwhite quail in northeastern Kansas. Master's thesis, Kansas State University, Manhattan.

Dow Jones. 1990. *The Wall Street Journal Index*. New York: Dow Jones.

Dreschel, R. 1990. Telephone interview, 24 October.

Drum, A. 1986. Responding to plagiarism. *College Composition and Communication* 37(2):217–23.

Dun & Bradstreet. 1990. *Millon Dollar Directory*. New York: Dun & Bradstreet.

Environmental Protection Agency. 1987. *Radon Reduction Methods: A Home-owner's Guide*. Publication OPA-87-010. Washington, D.C.: Environmental Protection Agency.

ERIC Clearinghouse on Reading and Communication Skills. 1986. *How to Search ERIC*. Urbana, Ill.: ERIC Clearinghouse on Reading and Communication Skills.

Faigley, L. 1985. Nonacademic writing: The social perspective. In *Writing in Non-academic Settings*, edited by L. Odell, and D. Goswami. New York: Guilford Press.

Fassnacht, G. 1982. *Theory and Practice of Observing Behavior*. New York: Academic Press.

Felker, D., F. Pickering, V. R. Charrow, V. M. Holland, and J. Redish. 1982. *Guidelines for Document Designers*. Washington, D.C.: Document Design Center, American Institutes for Research.

Fields, A. 1982. Getting started: Pattern notes and perspectives. In *The Technology of Text: Principles for Structuring, Designing and Displaying Text*, edited by D. H. Jonassen. Englewood Cliffs, N.J.: Educational Technology Publications.

Fineman, M. 1982. *The Inquisitive Eye*. New York: Oxford University Press.

Flower, L., and J. Hayes. 1981. A cognitive process theory of writing. *College Composition and Communication* 32:365–87.

Francois, W. E. 1982/1990. *Mass Media Law*. Ames: Iowa State University Press.

Gale Research. 1990. *Biography Master Index*. Detroit: Gale Research.

———. 1990. *Business Organizations and Agencies Directory*. Detroit: Gale Research.

———. 1988. *Directory of Directories*. Detroit: Gale Research.

———. 1990. *Encyclopedia of Associations*. Detroit: Gale Research.

———. 1989. *Gale Directory of Publications*. Detroit: Gale Research.

———. 1989. *Trade Names Dictionary*. Detroit: Gale Research.

Gibaldi, J., and W. S. Achtert. 1988. *MLA Handbook for Writers of Research Papers*. 3d ed. New York: Modern Language Association.

Gilbert, A. H. 1977. *Vermont Hunters: Characteristics, Attitudes, and Levels of Participation*. Miscellaneous Publication 92, Agricultural Experiment Station. Burlington: University of Vermont.

Gombrich, E. H. 1972. The visual image. In *Communication*, edited by Scientific American editors. San Francisco: Freeman.

Graham, Jr., C. D. 1957. A glossary for research reports. *Metals Progress* 71:75.

Hayes, J., and L. Flower 1986. Writing Research and the Writer. *American Psychologist* 41(10):1106–13.

Heberlien, T. A. 1974. Methodological strategies for evaluating the effect on water resources on the social well being and the quality of life. In *The Social Well Being and Quality of Life Dimensions in Water Resources Planning and Development*, edited by W. E. Andrews, R. T. Burdge, H. R. Capener, W. K. Warner, and K. T. Wilksinson. Conference Proceedings. Logan: Utah State University.

Hill, M., and W. Cochran. 1977. *Into Print*. Los Altos, Calif.: William Kaufman.

Hodges, J., et al. 1990. *Harbrace College Handbook*. 11th ed. San Diego: Harcourt Brace Jovanovich.

Information Access Company. *InfoTrac*. Foster City, Calif.

Intermed Communications. *Nursing 91*. Jenkintown, Pa.

International Press. 1990. *Who's Who in Canada*. Toronto: International Press.

Kahn, F. H., and B. R. Visscher. 1975. Water Disinfection in the Wilderness. *Western Journal of Medicine* 122:450–53.

Kansas State University. 1986. *Book Arrangement*. Manhattan, Kans.: Farrell Library, Kansas State University.

Katz, W. 1979. *Your Library*. New York: Holt, Rinehart & Winston.

Kinneavy, J. 1980. *A Theory of Discourse*. New York: Norton.

Klein Publications. *Guide to American Directories*. Coral Springs, Fla.: B. Klein Publications.

Kraus, M., E. Clifton, H. Fineman, and J. McCormick. 1987. Biden's belly flop. *Newsweek* (28 Sept.): 23–24.

Lewis Historical Publishing. 1978. *Who's Who in Engineering*. New York: Lewis Historical Publishing.

Library of Congress. *Library of Congress Subject Headings*. Washington, D.C.: Library of Congress.

Locke, L. F., W. W. Spirduso, and S. J. Silverman. 1987. *Proposals That Work*. Newbury Park, Calif.: Sage.

Marquis, A. N. 1990. *Who's Who in America*. Chicago: Marquis.

Maryland, State of. 1989. *Directory of Maryland Manufacturers*. Annapolis: State of Maryland.

Massachusetts Medical Society. 1991. *The New England Journal of Medicine*. Boston: Massachusetts Medical Society.

Merriam-Webster. 1985. *Webster's Standard American Style Manual*. Springfield, Mass.: Merriam-Webster.

Mosby, H. S. 1963. Record keeping by means of field notes and by photography. In *Wildlife Investigational Techniques*. 2d ed., edited by H. S. Mosby, and O. H. Hewitt. Washington, D.C.: The Wildlife Society.

Nachimias, D., and C. Nachimias. 1987. *Research Methods in the Social Sciences*. New York: St. Martin's Press.

National Register Publications. 1990. *Directory of Corporate Affiliations of Major Corporations*. Skokie, Ill.: National Register Publications.

National Wildlife Federation. 1991. *Conservation Directory*. Washington, D.C.: National Wildlife Federation.

Norusis, M. J. 1987. *The SPSS GUIDE to Data Analysis for SPSS*. Chicago: SPSS.

Oberon Resources. 1990. *WPCitation*. Columbus, Ohio: Oberon Resources.

Odell, L. 1985. Beyond the text: Relations between writings and social context. In *Writing in Nonacademic Settings*. Edited by L. Odell, and D. Goswami. New York: Guilford Press.

Osborn, A. 1963. *Applied Imagination*. New York: Charles Scribner's Sons, Creative Education Foundation.

Pergamon Press. 1991. *Health Physics*. Elmsford, N.Y.: Pergamon Press.

Phelon, Sheldon, and Marsar. 1989. *Sheldon's Retail Directory of the United States and Canada*. New York: Phelon, Sheldon & Marsar.

Polk's World Bank Directory: North American Edition. 1991. Nashville: Polk.

Powers, R., L. E. Sarbaugh, H. Culbertson, and T. Flores. 1961. Comprehension of graphs. Bulletin 31. Madison, Wis.: Dept. of Agricultural Journalism.

Rodale Press. *Prevention*. Emmaus, Pa.: Rodale Press.

Roscia, J. 1988. Interview, 18 March.

Roundy, N., and D. Mair. 1982. The composing process of technical writers: A preliminary study. *Journal of Advanced Composition* 3(1–2):89–101.

Sage. 1990. *Communication Abstracts*. Beverley Hills, Calif.: Sage.

SAS Institute. 1988. *SAS Introductory Guide for Personal Computers*, Release 6.03. Cary, N.C.: SAS Institute.

Sheehy, E. P. 1982. *Guide to Reference Books*. Chicago: American Library Association.

Smith, M. K. 1989. The prescriptive versus heuristic approach in teaching technical communication. In *Technical Writing: Theory and Practice*. Edited by B. E. Fearing and W. K. Sparrow. New York: Modern Language Association.

Special Reports. 1989. *Who's Who in Ecology*. New York: Special Reports, Inc.

Standard & Poor's Corp. 1990. *Standard & Poor's Register of Corporations, Directors and Executives*. New York: Standard & Poor's Corp.

Steketee, R. W., S. Reid, T. Cheng, J. S. Stoebig, R. G. Harrington, and J. P. Davis. 1989. Recurrent outbreaks of giardiasis in a child care center, Wisconsin. *APJH* 79(4):485–89.

Stoligitis, W. 1991. *1990 Technical Communicator Salary Survey*. Arlington, Va.: Society for Technical Communication.

Russell Sage. 1990. *The Foundation Directory*. New York.: Russell Sage Foundation.

The New York Times Company. 1991. *The New York Times Index*. New York: The New York Times Company.

Time. 1988. Copyrights cakes, candles not included. *Time* 132(18):59.

Trazyna, T. N. 1986. Research outside the library. *College Composition and Communication* 37(2):217–23.

University of Chicago Press. 1982. *The Chicago Manual of Style*. 13th ed. Chicago: University of Chicago Press.

University Microfilm. Newspaper Abstracts ONDISC. Ann Arbor, Mich.: University Microfilms.

Van Buren, Abigail. 1989. Dear Abby. Choice Section, *Coloradoan* (21 August):3.

Van Buren, R., and M. F. Beuhler. 1980. *The Levels of Edit*. Pasadena, Calif.: Jet Propulsion Laboratory.

Wallis, P. M. 1989. The beaver's revenge. *Water Pollution Control* 127(5):22–23.

Webb, E. J., D. T. Campbell, R. D. Schwartz, and L. Sechrest. 1973. *Unobtrusive Measure Non-reactive Research in the Social Sciences*. Chicago, Ill.: Rand McNally.

Wilson, H. W. 1991. *Reader's Guide to Periodical Literature*. New York: H.W. Wilson.

——. 1991. *Social Science Index*. New York: H.W. Wilson.

Wimmer, R. D., and J. R. Dominick. 1987. *Mass Media Research*. Belmont, Calif.: Wadsworth.

Zimmerman, D. E. 1986. Written communication. In *Inventory and Monitoring of Wildlife Habitat*. Edited by A. Y. Cooperrider, R. J. Boyd, and H. R. Stuart. Denver: U.S. Department of the Interior, Bureau of Land Management.

Zimmerman, D. E., and D. Clark. 1987. *The Random House Guide to Technical and Scientific Communication*. New York: Random House.

Zimmerman, D. E. J. Peterson, and M. Muraski. Forthcoming. Explorations of the roles of technical communicators. *Technical Communication*.

Zimmerman, D. E., and M. Tharp. 1990. Learning desktop publishing systems: An empirical assessment of student attitudes, reactions, and experiences. Technical report for IBM. Fort Collins: Department of Technical Journalism, Colorado State University.

COPYRIGHTS AND ACKNOWLEDGMENTS

The authors would like to thank the following for permission to reprint the materials listed.

Dale E. Burkhead   For "The Use of Radioactive Isotopes for Marking Aquatic Furbearers in Capture/Recapture Population Estimates."

Mary D. Caris   For "Proposal for a Formal Report."

Marie Edwards   For "September Progress Report: A System for Reducing Radon in a Tri-Level Home" and "A Radon Mitigation Plan for a Colorado Residential Home." Reprinted by permission of the author.

Iowa State University Press   For excerpts from *Mass Media Law and Regulation*. Reprinted by permission from *Mass Media Law and Regulation*, 5th ed., by W. E. Francois. © 1990 by Iowa State University Press, Ames 50010.

McGraw-Hill, Inc.   For excerpts from *The Random House Guide to Technical and Scientific Communication*, by Donald E. Zimmerman and David G. Clark. Copyright 1987. Reprinted by permission of McGraw-Hill, Inc.

Modern Language Association of America   For excerpts from the *MLA Handbook* by J. Gibaldi and W. S. Achtert. Copyright 1980. Reprinted by permission of Modern Language Association of America.

Musser B. Moore   For "The Relationship of Students' Learning Style Types to Their Approaches to Writing."

National Council of Teachers of English   For Figure 1 from "A Cognitive Process Theory of Writing" by Linda Flowers and John R. Hayes in *College Composition and Communication*, December 1981. Copyright 1981 by the National Council of Teachers of English. For Table 1 from "Research Outside the Library: Learning a Field" by Thomas N. Tryzna in *College Composition and Communication*, May 1986. Copyright 1986 by the National Council of Teachers of English. For excerpts from "The Variables of Composition: Process and Product in a Business Setting" by Glenn J. Brodhead and Richard C. Freed, CCCC, 1986. Copyright 1986 by the National Council of Teachers of English. Reprinted with permission.

Oberon Resources   For WP Citation Manual, 1990. Reprinted by permission of Oberon Resources.

Alex F. Osborn   For *Applied Imagination*, 1953. Reprinted with permission from the copyright holder, Creative Education Foundation, Buffalo, NY.

Greg Shouse   For "Acid Rain: The Silent Crisis in America."

Susan McOllough Zimmer   For "Tensile Strengths . . ."

Joan M. Zito   For "Editing and Revising Strategies of Five Professional Writers Who Compose on Computers."

INDEX